DATE DUE			

BLUE-COLLAR
WOMEN

BLUE-COLLAR
WOMEN

Pioneers on the Male Frontier

Mary Lindenstein Walshok

Anchor Press/Doubleday
GARDEN CITY, NEW YORK
1981

Library of Congress Cataloging in Publication Data

Walshok, Mary Lindenstein.
Blue-collar women.

1. Women—Employment—United States. 2. Labor and
laboring classes—United States. I. Title.
HD6095.W19   331.4′8   AACR2
ISBN: 0-385-17845-X
LIBRARY OF CONGRESS CATALOG CARD NUMBER 81-43069

Contents

ACKNOWLEDGMENTS

It is incredible to me that this work has involved over seven years of my life, but through those years I have been able to rely on critical aids, resources, and friends.

The idea for the research grew out of my involvement with a women's storefront Project Repair, which had been established in the early 1970s to train women to be handywomen. They asked me to study the progress of their students, and put me in touch with Dick Wakefield at the Center for Work and Mental Health at the National Institute of Mental Health for possible funding. Dick and I corresponded and talked by phone extensively, and he transformed a faceless bureaucracy into a personal and concerned resource. He helped me develop my ideas about the broader potential of the research, he had knowledgeable social scientists review drafts of my ideas before I submitted my proposal, he helped me through a very critical site visit, and he solicited supportive references for me (at the time a young woman with no publications and no faculty status at the University of California). It is important to thank a man like Dick, and his boss Eliot Liebow, for the attitudes they have and the efforts they make for "unknowns" with good ideas and a willingness to work. Having never been a part of the "old boy" social science network, I probably would have never gotten the funding to do the research and eventually write this book without advocates such as Dick and Eliot.

Being at a great university like the University of California has been another important factor in the execution of this research. Even though I am not a faculty member, the full resources of the university have been available to me. Joe Gusfield in the Department of Sociology helped me get an office to house this project for nearly four years. Graduate students in sociology worked on the project and provided critical feedback, original ideas, and long hours helping track down respondents, conduct interviews, and transcribe and edit lengthy interviews. Judy McIlwee, whose dissertation was based on this research, was especially conscientious. Virginia Lang, Alexandria Todd, Pam Wilson and Jo Schwartz are also to be thanked.

University colleagues were also important sources of ideas, criticism, and personal support. In the early stages of conceptualization, Donald Carns at the University of Nevada spent a lot of time with me sorting out research priorities. Marc Schuckit of the University of California at San Diego Department of Psychiatry, Jacqueline Wiseman of UCSD's Sociology Department, and Warner Blumberg, an urban sociologist at San Diego State University, gave generously of their time and shared their wisdom as experienced researchers. Ultimately, what kept me going for the two years of conceptualization, funding, and design, three years of field research, and two years of data analysis and manuscript writing was the wonderful, ever so bright, and ever so loving women friends and colleagues I have. As I am a full-time administrator, my time for research and writing was always squeezed in at intervals when I could escape from the office, on countless evenings and weekends, and on practically every vacation day I have had for the last five years. Cathy Todd, my colleague, administrative aide, and friend at University Extension for the last eight years, has helped me succeed in this effort in ways I can't even begin to describe. Other women academics from Women's Studies at San Diego State and from a variety of departments at UCSD have talked with me about my work, have read and criticized writing I have done over the years, and have always treated me as a peer involved in a project that has validity and importance. This was terribly important to me because my commitment to research and writing, although appreciated by my peers in continuing education, is by no means expected or rewarded. The continued support of women friends on the faculty helped me keep at it.

I also want to thank Anchor Press/Doubleday for "finding" me. I had started writing my book when Angela Iadavaia Cox tracked me down after having read about my research in *McCall's* magazine. Her energy and enthusiasm got me to New York and in touch with Loretta Barrett at Doubleday. Loretta Barrett, an experienced and sympathetic editor and publisher, has helped my book realize much fuller potential than it could have had without her help.

Finally, two special friends must be thanked because they have done more than just respond when I have reached out for help or advice. They have been continuous resources intellectually and personally and never doubted the integrity or the significance of this work. I'm grateful to them for believing in me and my projects: Kristen Luker, a thoughtful, humane, and respected sociologist at UCSD, helped me search for the "important" issues; Joyce Fleming, an intelligent psychologist and savvy journalist, helped me accept my desire to communicate with the "general public" and not just academics. Thank you all.

Preface

As with most intellectual preoccupations, my interest in work and its significance in the lives of women derives not simply from academic concerns, but from personal biography—a personal biography peopled with women who have always been in the invisible female labor force, women whose experiences have been a source alternatively of pain and of pride for me throughout my life. Thus in an important sense this book and the research it describes represent a quest for a fuller understanding of myself and my own background.

Unusual for my generation, but typical of the generation before me, I am the daughter of immigrant parents. My childhood was not one of profound economic struggle and ghetto living, but rather one of ups and downs and long hard hours in a family restaurant where I was frequently expected to work after school and on weekends and holidays. There was time to do well in school and develop childhood friendships, but the fluctuations in the family business were always the most important factor in our lives. As a growing child, I often resented the long hours my parents spent in their restaurant and was deeply embarrassed by my mother's white uniform and her long hours in the pantry. Most of my friends had mothers who were homemakers—golf-playing affluent housewives who dressed well, entertained often, and presided over what seemed to me ideal family households. Although Mother read good books and took us to symphony concerts when she could, hers was not a life of cultivating herself or her children. Rather, she was devoted to

making a success of the family business so that her children
could be happy, go to college, and not suffer the sacrifices of
her own fatherless, depression-era childhood in Sweden.

Yet it would be a mistake to describe the work she did and
her feelings about it as simply an extension of her mothering
role. There was another dimension to my mother's work which
I sensed as a young girl and which I have come to understand
as an adult. She *enjoyed* her work. She did not feel embarrassed by who she was and what she did, only pained by the
embarrassment I sometimes felt as an upwardly mobile American teenager. Although she found her work frequently tiresome, she never disliked it or contemplated giving it up. In fact,
Mother did and still does take enormous pride in the tasty and
decorative preparation of food and in her ability to keep food
costs down by planning varied menus, using every item of food,
and avoiding waste. She takes pride in her management skills;
in her ability to teach and work with assistants, dishwashers,
and fry cooks; in her relationships with food and equipment
suppliers; in the praise and small bonuses she receives in her
work; in the occasional workshops she attends to upgrade her
knowledge of nutrition and institutional food services.

For a long time I thought my mother was crazy. After the
failure of the family business she was forced to take jobs in
food service areas where women made the minimum wage. She
continued for years to be energetic and enthusiastic about her
work, despite long hours on her feet in steaming kitchens with
ninety-degree temperatures and a yearly income of less than ten
thousand dollars. She never stopped worrying and talking about
her work as though it were as interesting and important as a
neurosurgeon's. Even in retirement she has remained active in
various food service organizations and enjoys nothing more
than menu planning for large groups of people.

I began to suspect there might be something universal about
my mother's experience of paid employment as I began to lec-
ture to various women's groups around California in my role as
a sociologist and Director of Continuing Education for Women
at a major university. In that capacity, in addition to encounter-

ing women students, faculty wives, American Association of
University Women chapters, and other middle-class women's
groups gripped by the women's movement, I began to develop
ties with federally employed women, business and professional
women's clubs, Soroptimists, and Toastmistresses. Through
them I began to encounter women working in jobs as varied as
hairdressing and equipment maintenance. I also encountered
city and county government program staff interested in helping
women train for and find meaningful work. I found myself increasingly involved in personal relationships and community
activities with women who were not of the university or the
women's movement but cosmetologists and salespeople, book-
keepers and bank tellers, clerical workers and operatives. A
significant number of them talked very much like my mother.

One of my community involvements at that time was with a
school devoted to training women to become handywomen and
to qualify for apprenticeships in the trades and crafts. At that
time (1972) women represented only 138 of the 38,709 registered apprentices in the state of California, and the majority of
these women were apprenticing in fields like bookbinding. Because of my involvement with this program I became familiar
with most of the job development programs and employment
sites in which the first waves of women in California were being
trained in skilled blue-collar jobs. With funds from the Center
for Work and Mental Health of the National Institute of Mental Health, I was able to assemble a research staff and over the
next four years talk with a large number of women up and
down the state who were pioneering in these occupational roles.

This book is about these women. It is the culmination both
of my own history and of over five years of personal relationships, agency contacts, and in-depth interviews with women
working in skilled and semiskilled jobs. The anomalies that
have characterized my own experience and the experiences of
many of the women you will meet in this book require a reex-
amination of many conventional perspectives. Before we too
hastily accept generalizations about the "female experience" or
the "quality of work in America," we must attempt to reach a

more balanced and deeper understanding of the multifaceted experiences of women at work. The experiences of the women in this book will provide insights into how to expand, refine, and make more relevant our ideas and theories about women and work, as well as about work in general in a postindustrial society. This book raises many general questions about both women and work, and it is my hope that it does so with a style and sensitivity that make sense to working women like my mother, as well as to the social and policy science communities.

Introduction

Until very recently, women who had a primary and lifelong commitment to paid employment were still atypical in our society. They were essentially marginal to a culture in which the essence of the female role was domestic and maternal. With the incredible changes in the participation of women in the labor force during the last twenty-five years, however, and our changed national consciousness as a result of the women's movement, the employed woman with a lifelong commitment to her job is seen less and less as an oddity. But this is true only so long as the woman pursues a career within occupational sectors considered acceptable and proper for her. Women who have an interest in a nontraditional field such as physics, engineering, aeronautics, or welding are still social oddities and continue to be marginal and regarded with skepticism. There is much to discourage women from pursuing employment in such male-dominated fields in the first place, and as they enter them they find themselves for the most part unwanted and often actively excluded from full participation. Thus it is still true today that a woman who enters a field outside the boundaries of "woman's work" has to be somewhat of a risk taker, an independent person who can go it alone if necessary and fight the often negative tide of family, public, and co-worker opinion. To succeed, she must have strong reasons for making such a move, and either compelling needs or a great deal of confidence to back up her decision.

This is a book about such women. It is about their experiences breaking into traditionally male blue-collar jobs such as welding, carpentry, mechanics, and machining. It is about the family and childhood contexts that provide them with important base-line experiences and capabilities, which in turn give them the potential to take risks and pursue nontraditional interests. It is about personal events and experiences in young adulthood that open up or close off life-style and employment options. It is about the character of general economic and employment opportunities and particular experiences at work that facilitate or inhibit nontraditional choices. It is a description of how the right mix of individual needs and interests and of structured opportunities to pursue new options enables some women to succeed as pioneers in male-dominated job fields.

Women pioneering in skilled blue-collar jobs are, regrettably, overlooked as a group of women and as a group of blue-collar workers. Studies of women workers have focused primarily on middle-class and professional women or those in traditional fields such as nursing. Most studies of blue-collar workers have emphasized the concerns and attitudes of males. This is beginning to change, and with that change has come a broader understanding of the character of women's employment needs, interests, and experience. As more and more descriptive data on the scope of women's work in the paid labor force are generated, it is increasingly clear that, beyond the traditionally studied occupations such as nursing and social work and the much discussed entry of women into such professional fields as higher education, law, medicine, and management,[1] there is a need for a better understanding of the occupational positions in which the vast majority of women work. Most women work in the paid labor force as waitresses and cosmetologists, secretaries and bank tellers, small-parts assemblers and manufacturing operatives, not as nurses, teachers, and social workers.[2] It is also becoming clear that important spheres of nontraditional or changing work roles for women are skilled and semiskilled blue-collar jobs.[3] However, these continue to be neglected in serious discussions of nontraditional career roles, while fields employing much smaller numbers of women—

for example, science, engineering, medicine, and law—have been given a great deal of attention. This is paradoxical in that census data show that it is in jobs such as carpentry and small-appliance repair, auto mechanics and plumbing, electronics and office machine services that the greatest rates of change seem to be occurring.[4]

It is somewhat paradoxical that, at the same time as increased attention is given to the alienating and unsatisfying character of the work experiences of large numbers of male workers, there are substantial indications that for most working women today paid employment is a rewarding experience. Regardless of the type of job, be it factory, secretarial, or managerial, women appear to be finding high levels of satisfaction in their employment.[5] This apparent anomaly is worthy of investigation. It is important to understand whether or not the motivations to seek employment and the actual experience of paid employment are qualitatively different for women than they are for men. If they are, it is important to understand why this is the case and what implications for the future these differences might have, not only for men and women workers, but for employers and supervisors. It is also important to understand what sorts of needs, perceptions, and opportunities enable women to seek out nontraditional occupational roles, particularly in those male-dominated work spheres which are often perceived as "dangerous," "dirty," "physically taxing," and "mundane."

This book is an effort to zero in on just such issues. Drawing on over three years of detailed research on the experiences of women working in nontraditional blue-collar jobs in three metropolitan areas in California, I will introduce you to women welders, carpenters, mechanics, forklift operators, and cable splicers, as well as women working in dozens of other skilled blue-collar jobs previously closed to them. The women here represent surprising anomalies in the face of popular notions about the character of blue-collar work and in particular the female experience of that work. Rather than being tangential, work is central to these women's identities; rather than lacking ambition and concern about pay, skilled women workers appear to be highly motivated; rather than seeking comfortable sociable work environments, the women workers you will meet appear to value physicality and solitary tasks; rather than wanting direction and supervision, these women want autonomy and control of the work process; rather than experiencing boredom and unhappiness in the workplace, these women see blue-collar employment as a satisfying alternative to domestic and clerical roles. Such anomalies demand discussion, analysis, interpretation, and ultimately understanding within a larger framework. My goal is not only to give you a picture of the variability and richness of women's work lives, but to challenge some of the conventional wisdom about work in general and its significance in the lives of women in particular.

There are a number of areas of conventional wisdom to which the experiences of nontraditional blue-collar working women are relevant. The first has to do with identifying the critical elements in the development of vocational interests, including the character of early childhood influences, school and counseling experiences, and the significance of planning and on-the-job experiences for skilled and semiskilled workers. Although there is a rich social science literature on these topics, it has a decidedly middle-class and male bias. It is also static; that is, it tends to focus on the vocational aspirations of high school and college students, with little attention being given to the dynamic processes of actual job searches, decision-making, and on-the-job training experiences. As a result, there is a gap in our knowledge, especially since most research also fails to include good samples of working-class women. It is important to understand to what extent young women expect to be involved in the paid labor force as adults and the factors that influence these expectations. It is important to assess the extent to which vocational interests develop early and are relatively fixed, and the extent to which they change and elaborate as the individual matures into young adulthood and mid-life. It is important to understand the events and processes that influence both vocational preferences and vocational decision-making.

A second area of conventional wisdom to which the experience of nontraditional blue-collar women is relevant is the significance of paid employment in the lives of these women. Little attention has been given to this issue, although the significance of pay to blue-collar men has received extensive treatment, both theoretically and empirically, in the literature dealing with work attitudes, job satisfaction, and alienation. The absence of women workers and of occupations in which women represent the majority from this literature poses some important questions.

There is much to suggest that what women workers seek in their work parallels in general terms what men seek in their work. Both men and women seek feelings of competence, of making a contribution, of being necessary, of being productive, and of being in control of their time and energy. What appears to differentiate the work experience and the meaning of paid employment for men and for women is differing economic opportunities and societal expectations.[6] Women's social and economic roles have always been characterized by lower levels of control, satisfaction, and power than men's roles, and the urbanization and industrialization of the twentieth century have left traditional female social and economic roles with even less power, autonomy, and satisfaction. While in no way discounting the primary significance of the economy's need for women workers, or the need women and families have for the money they make, one can still argue that paid employment has come to represent for large numbers of women an important end in itself. It is increasingly the locus of personal feelings of competence, challenge, and confidence that at earlier points in history were found in domestic and family roles and in relationships tied to family and neighborhood networks. With the decline in the economic and social centrality of the homemaking role and the routinization and trivialization of many central homemaking tasks, it is not surprising that women seek meaningful work outside the home.

Seemingly similar work experiences may also be evaluated and understood differently by women than by men because of the distinct perspectives women bring to particular jobs. Many jobs that over generations of male workers have come to be seen as routine, tiresome, and alienating, such as those in the blue-collar work world, may for new generations of female workers be challenging, rewarding, and interesting. A paid job, particularly a skilled job with the challenges of new and varied skills, gives women independence and varied relationships and may provide gratifications extending far beyond the work role alone. This is not to suggest that women and men value different qualities in their work or seek different rewards from their work, but rather that their judgments of how good or bad a job is are made not in a vacuum but with reference to their previous work experiences.

Unless we understand the perspectives women bring to the evaluation of their employment experiences, we may make incorrect assumptions about what it is they value in their employment and how they see their work combining with other roles. For example, the importance of money to women could be overemphasized. Men, in particular, often assume that the satisfactions women derive from lower-paying, more routine jobs are simply a function of their being less interested in the intrinsic character of their work and more interested in extrinsic consequences such as money and the easy integration of work and family roles. However, it is just as plausible that women are looking for the same intrinsic rewards—stimulation, variety, challenge, and so on—that men want. Women may, in fact, value their *apparently* routine jobs for these very things because, in comparison to domestic work, they *are* stimulating, varied, and challenging! Only by dissecting job content from the point of view of the woman worker can we develop a more generic understanding of the qualities of paid employment that women value, and of what we need to preserve and strive for in the future.

Research that emphasizes the point of view and experiences of women thus enables us to address a number of important issues about which there are conflicting, often hotly debated opinions. To what extent does the family continue to represent the primary identity of women working in blue-collar jobs? To what extent does paid employment represent a source of independence and power to women working in blue-collar jobs? To what extent do the skills and tasks required of a person in various skilled jobs satisfy needs and interests not to be found in domestic roles? To what extent do the relationships at work provide satisfactions unavailable to women elsewhere? To what extent do the historical, social, and economic positions of women have an impact on the ways in which they perceive and evaluate blue-collar employment options and experiences? To what extent is the female experience of blue-collar employment qualitatively different from the male experience of it? These and similar questions merit discussion and investigation for both theoretical and social policy reasons. We know next to nothing about women's experience of paid employment, and we must learn more if we are to have a truly comprehensive sociology of work and of sex roles.

A third area of conventional wisdom to which the experience of these women is relevant is the identification of the factors that differentiate persons making traditional role choices from those making nontraditional ones—i.e., understanding who the "pioneers" are in any society. There are always people who make choices or behave in ways that differ marginally or significantly from prevailing expectations. There are always people who take risks or explore new territory. The male nurse and the female auto mechanic are examples of people making vocational role choices that don't fit most people's ideas of what men and women do. Such persons often provide insight into the taken-for-granted world from which they differ. They may also signal the beginnings of some important social change or reveal dysfunctional aspects of the existing system. For these reasons, the study of marginal or nontraditional role choices is sociologically interesting.

There has been only minimal attention given to persons making nontraditional or unexpected career choices. There are indications, however, that increasing numbers of men and women are crossing occupational boundaries into fields characteristically dominated by the other sex. There is also increasing evidence that mid-life and later-life career shifts are taking place, with older men and women entering school and new jobs alongside students and workers twenty-five years their junior. What are the factors contributing to the development of such nontraditional interests? Who become the pioneers and why? In what ways is the work experience of the pioneer in a nontraditional job different from that of the traditional employee? What is the character of the personal and structural contexts that influence the degree of success a person has pioneering in a previously closed field? The experience of women moving into nontraditional blue-collar occupations should provide some insight into these and related questions.

Finally, an issue of deep concern throughout the population is that of the changing role of the family and the shifting ways of integrating work, community, and family roles. With the separation of home and workplace that fully emerged during the Industrial Revolution, family relationships and family functions changed as well. Now, with the transformation of our society into a postindustrial, technological society in which geographical mobility and paid employment in adult life represent the typical experience of most adult women, will there be further changes in how people integrate work and family roles? There have been many studies that touch on how families begin to resolve the functional and emotional problems introduced by both adults working full time, but the bulk of these studies focus, at present, on families in which both partners are well-educated, affluent professionals.[7]

The vast majority of working women, however, are not well-educated, well-paid professionals, but rather women working for wages, often as single heads of households, with more children and fewer conveniences to draw on than more affluent women. What does the paid employment of this group of women mean to the family, child care, and child rearing? What do these women see as the costs and benefits of their employment to their children, their husbands, themselves? What quality of life at home and at work are women in skilled and semiskilled occupations finding?

All of us are living with and experiencing the kinds of events and changes to which these questions relate. For this reason, I have tried to write a book that moves meaningfully and easily between interesting descriptive data on the one hand and questions of more general social interest on the other. The experiences of the women we interviewed should come alive for you, but it is also important that you see their experiences in larger perspective.

By focusing on the success issue—who makes it in a nontraditional blue-collar job, and why—I have tried to give the reader something more than just interesting personal accounts of work experience. I have tried to use success as a "hook" for zeroing in on the more general questions just discussed: how vocational choices are made; how people experience and what they feel about the work they do; what it is like to be a pioneer; and how complicated role commitments—work, family, and community—are managed in a blue-collar context.

The book has three parts. The first, "Risk Takers," examines the family and young-adulthood experiences of women in nontraditional jobs in an effort to reveal some of the roots of their essaying employment in a nontraditional job. Part Two, "Working in a Blue-collar Job," focuses on the on-the-job experiences of women—learning the job, developing relationships on the job, and factors that help women succeed in nontraditional jobs. Part Three, "Spin-offs," discusses the impact of nontraditional work on other roles, such as those in the family, and the implications of the experiences of these women for policies related to the recruitment, training, and retention of women in nontraditional skilled occupations. In order to protect the anonymity of the women we interviewed, I have given each a pseudonym. I have also disguised the names of employers and of cities. All other information contained in this book is exactly what was reported to us.

PART ONE

RISK TAKERS

I

Blue-collar Pioneers

WHAT ARE NONTRADITIONAL BLUE-COLLAR JOBS?

I found what I really liked when I was working in the shop was that my body felt better, I was getting exercise, and I need exercise really bad because I'm so out of shape, and that was really important to me, that my job wasn't a sit-down job, I liked that. It got hard at times, you know, where your body was pooped out, but then it feels good because you felt like you had exercised so you had more energy in the long run. And doing something with your hands was kind of cool, because you could see what you were doing. Actually see the results—when you fixed a car it ran—the immediate satisfaction, and that's something I never have had in a job. In a factory you don't see where it's going or anything, so that's cool, plus you know that you did it. It's like solving a puzzle—when you get the answer—yeah!

This statement was made by a woman in her early twenties who is an auto mechanic—an unlikely person, in an unlikely job, to be making such a positive statement. In fact, our commonsense assumptions about women and work would lead us to assume that few women would feel this way about work, let alone blue-collar work, which in its routinized and degraded contemporary state seems unlikely to provide many rewards for any worker. Despite the women's movement and the extensive treatment of women's changing roles in the mass media, despite the disillusionment with formal education and the resurgence of interest in working with one's hands, in being outdoors, and in being physically fit, we are surprised when anyone, much less a woman, articulates such feelings about manual labor. Nonetheless, there is a wide range of blue-collar jobs traditionally the exclusive domain of men in which large numbers of women have recently developed an interest.

These "nontraditional blue-collar jobs" include a variety of manual and technical jobs that are more or less physically taxing. These are jobs for which some agreed-upon skill level and formalized training are necessary and which, because of the skill and training involved, command a high hourly wage (anywhere from $5 to $25 an hour) or an annual salary in excess of $10,000 a year. Men's traditional domination of such jobs has in large part occurred because of deep-rooted cultural assumptions about women's lack of mechanical aptitude and physical strength. Also, the many years of training required for such jobs, the environments in which they have traditionally been performed, and the long working hours they frequently require have not made them particularly attractive to women, especially in periods when employment was defined differently by women and for women than it is today. Even when women wanted such jobs and had the mechanical competency and physical prowess to do them, it has been extremely difficult for them to penetrate the skilled blue-collar world. This is because of the closed character of many skilled trade unions and because of deeply felt concerns and stereotypes among many employers and supervisors about the inability of a woman to do a "man's" job for a "man's" pay.

In a recently published guide for women interested in getting into skilled trades, Muriel Lederer points out that such jobs represent a fantastic opportunity for women because of the pay and benefits and because of the increasing demand for workers in many of these fields. Her book describes a cross section of skilled job opportunities in the construction occupations; in industrial production and related occupations; in mechanics, repair, and maintenance; in transportation; and in scientific and technical fields such as computers. In addition to providing information on the more familiar skilled trades opportunities in carpentry, plumbing, welding, or auto mechanics, she provides a "best bets" list of skilled jobs for the eighties that gives a sense of the types of employment we are discussing as "non-traditional" for women. They include:[1]

Drafter
Dental lab technician
Forestry technician
Surveyor
Animal technician
Agricultural technician
Chemical technician
Drug technician
Electronic-engineering
  technician
Nuclear technician
Construction electrician
Carpenter
Painter and paperhanger
Plumber and pipe fitter
Air-conditioning, heating,
  and refrigeration mechanic
Office-machine servicer
Computer-service technician

Dispensing optician and
  optical technician
Instrument repairperson
TV and radio repairperson
Motorcycle mechanic
Pest controller
Police officer
Landscaper
Lithographer
Photographic lab worker
Waste-water treatment plant
  operator
Welder
Electric sign repairperson
Electrical technician
Food-processing technician
Metallurgical engineering
  technician
Appliance repairperson

Women entering fields such as these are interesting in and of themselves, and they also represent a significant portion of the little-understood but greatly increasing female labor force. As was pointed out in the Introduction, research into this category of working woman has not kept pace with research into more highly visible fields such as science, medicine, and law. Yet the problems and recent gains of women in blue-collar fields are as significant as and often more dramatic than the problems and gains in many of the male-dominated professions. Lederer points out that in the middle seventies women represented, overall, about 18 percent of 29 million blue-collar jobs in this country.

The 1975 U. S. Bureau of the Census *Handbook on Women Workers* points out:

Perhaps the most dramatic shift that occurred between 1960 and 1970 was the large influx of women into the skilled trades. In 1970 almost half a million women (495,000) were working in the skilled occupations (craft and kindred worker group), up from 277,000 in 1960. The rate of increase (nearly 80 percent) was twice that for women in all occupations. It was 8 times the rate of increase for men in the skilled trades.

Employment increased in almost all the skilled trades—in construction, mechanics and repair, and supervisory blue collar occupations. In fact the increase for women exceeded the rate of growth for men. For example, the employment of women carpenters increased by nearly 8,000 (from about 3,300 to about 11,000), compared with a growth of less than 6,000 among male carpenters. Other skilled trades registering significant gains in employment of women were: electricians from 2,500 to 8,700 (0.7 to 1.8 percent); plumbers from about 1,000 to 4,000 (0.3 to 1.1 percent); auto mechanics from about 2,300 to about 11,000 (0.4 to 1.4 percent); painters from about 6,400 to 13,000 (1.9 to 4.1 percent); tool and die makers from about 1,100 to 4,200 (0.6 to 2.1 percent); and machinists from about 6,700 to 11,800 (1.3 to 3.1 percent).

Women still represent a small percentage of these employment categories, but their rate of increase is impressive. The Census reported that women made significant employment gains in some predominantly male professions as well.

. . . Employment of women lawyers grew from less than 5,000 to more than 12,000 between 1960 and 1970 and women nearly doubled their proportion of all employed lawyers (2.4 to 4.7 percent). Similar gains in employment were made in the medical professions. The number of women physicians increased from about 16,000 to nearly 26,000, and the proportion of doctors who were women rose from 7 to 9 percent. The number of women dentists increased from about 1,900 to more than 3,100 (from 2.3 to 3.4 percent of all dentists).[2]

These gains in the professions are not any greater than those just cited in blue-collar and working-class occupations, and in fact the absolute number of blue-collar gains and opportunities are substantially greater. Nonetheless, the attention in the sociological and general literature on occupations continues to emphasize the needs and problems facing women in the professions.

PORTRAITS OF WOMEN MOVING INTO SKILLED BLUE-COLLAR JOBS

Pioneering blue-collar working women cannot be reduced to a single prototype. Because the vast majority of working women have been limited to fewer than a dozen occupations, many conventional notions about what kinds of people get interested in what kinds of work are not relevant. When options that for decades have been closed begin to open up, a rather dazzling array of types of people from highly varied backgrounds emerge as the pioneers. Our research underscores the extent to which this is the case.

Women in nontraditional blue-collar jobs emerge from diverse contexts, arrive at their jobs motivated by a variety of concerns and needs, make their choices at different stages in the life cycle, and define the place of work in their lives quite differently. They are not, it turns out, a mirror image of the Archie Bunker stereotype. They are not the flaky but endearing personalities represented by the popular television series, "Laverne and Shirley." They are not essentially masculine or gay women resolving fundamental gender identity problems through manual labor. They are a complicated, articulate, and interesting group of women with a breadth and depth of experience and insight far beyond what commonsense stereotypes suggest. But then, they are pioneers. Their pioneering spirit and tenacity can be understood only through an examination of how family roots, personal history, unforeseen crises, and lucky and unlucky accidents and opportunities contribute to the development of a secure adult identity, particularly one rooted in a strong commitment to paid employment.

One woman succeeding in nontraditional blue-collar work as of our third year of interviews is Ardath Hoover. A Margaux Hemingway type, six feet tall, with enormous blue eyes and thick blond hair, Ardath was loud, expressive, and at ease with her large, attractive body. Her energy was slightly overwhelming, and her sensuality was unmistakable. Ardath works for a public utility company. When first interviewed, she was working in the gas meter repair shop, testing meters for leaks and soldering over the leaks. By her second and third interviews she was doing varied outside work and her title was Reserve Gas Serviceman. She described her job this way:

Well, lately I've been in three different categories; I've worked—been working in the streets, wearing a hard hat, digging holes, working with a couple of guys on a big truck—lots of stuff. Tearing up the streets. But recently I got transferred back to what I was trained for in the service department, which was actually running around making calls to, ah, customers and checking out their gas appliances, going into their homes. That's what I was trained for, but being a helper and a very low seniority position, I'm riding with the two-man crew 'cause they're experienced servicemen, and we're setting gas meters, so we don't deal with the public as much. There are two of us, and we're driving a truck full of plumbing fittings. I'm a gas plumber right now. That's what I've been doing this week. Last week, I was out on the heavy work. Yeah, tearing up the street, looking for gas leaks . . . and fixing them.

Ardath grew up in California and Colorado. She was raised by her mother and her grandmother, and because her mother was a divorced working woman, Ardath described herself as having assumed a great deal of responsibility at an early age. By age eleven she was shopping, cooking, and cleaning the house for her mother and younger brother and sister. She got into a lot of trouble during her teens, was "busted" for drugs, "slept around a lot," and eventually was such a problem for her mother that at age sixteen she was sent away to live with her grandmother in Colorado for a year. She returned to California at seventeen and immediately began living with her boyfriend in her mother's house, with her mother's approval because "he kept me in line." At nineteen she married her boyfriend and also finally graduated from high school.

Ardath reported liking swimming and math when she was in school and said she always wanted to be an astronaut when she was a kid. She is an avid science fiction reader and is "really into extraterrestrial contact." After a number of years working Renaissance Faires with her husband up and down the state and occasional work as a postal carrier, Ardath decided she wanted to get into a more stable job that was "technical," since she had always been interested in math and science. She also liked the idea of an indoor-outdoor job, so she went to work for the utility company.

When first interviewed, Ardath was highly frustrated because she was working in a dark, damp shop testing meters and not getting much training. By her second interview she was delighted with her work because she was outdoors a great deal, was doing varied jobs, and had developed a number of friendships with her male co-workers. Ardath likes men a lot and indicated in both her first- and second-year interviews that she liked working with men and being "pretty, soft, something there, to relieve the otherwise dreary environment." By her second year she was having a "delicious affair" with one of her co-workers, a lineman, and had moved to the country with her husband and daughter. With the long commute and the two relationships, her life was a bit fragmented, but she appeared, for the moment, joyous.

Ardath believes that men and women are basically different and that more women aren't in nontraditional jobs because they don't develop the "smarts" or "logic" needed for technical work. She believes that women need to learn how to think better and men need to learn how to cry more. She sees herself as special and exceptional, as a "flower in a field of wheat."

Another woman who was extremely successful in a nontraditional job over the three years we were in contact is an engineering draftsperson doing schematic drawings for electronic
equipment. She has a civil service classification at a naval facility in Southern California. In her early fifties when we first met
her, Molly O'Hara had what could only be described as an
idyllic childhood and an extremely conventional early married
life as a homemaker wife to a career military husband, raising
three lovely children. All this changed at age thirty-seven when
Molly and her husband were divorced and she was left to face
life alone with three children aged eleven, twelve, and sixteen.
Before the divorce, Molly had never expected or desired anything but the security and happiness of a conventional family
life-style.

Born on the East Coast, one of three daughters of a successful division manager for a laundry, Molly recalled an extremely
happy childhood with her mother at home, lots of school activities and friendships with neighborhood children, and long family vacations. Although not rich, her family was virtually un-
touched by the depression and she remembers never wanting
for anything as a child despite the difficult circumstances most
of their neighbors were living through. Her parents' roles in the
family were very traditional, and she remembers her father as
the "boss." Her father did not allow his daughters to work until
they had graduated from high school, even in the middle of the
depression. She described herself as a tomboy, a common
theme in many of the interviews, and she was voted the most
athletic girl in her high school. She graduated from high school
with honors, but because World War II had started she immediately went to work rather than to college. Since she had taken
typing and shorthand in high school, she took a series of secretarial jobs. At the end of the war she married and became a
housewife for eighteen years, primarily in California.

By the time we encountered Molly, she had been working at
the naval facility for thirteen years in clerical positions and had
just moved into an apprenticeship. She described her employment picture this way:

I was trained in, as I say in clerical, I took shorthand and typing in high school 'n' now naturally went into the clerical field when I started to work for the government, an-ah, I had hoped to get a job as a budget analyst with the Navy. I . . . they were having some job opportunities an' I thought, well, that probably would be my field even though I'm terrible in math, I like figures [laugh], an-ah, when this opportunity came up to be a draftsman, it was just something out of the clear blue, didn't plan on it, have any idea, or didn't know anything like that was available. My son is an architect, I worked, an' so I had some idea of blueprints and I worked in the industrial planning division where blueprints went across my desk all the time that the fellas made 'n' I had to send out type of thing, but as far as doing any of it, never entered my mind. . . .

Molly was in many ways unusual among the women interviewed, although possibly not that unusual in the larger universe of women pioneering in new fields. By the time she had begun her apprenticeship, her children were grown and no longer at home. Her incentives to seek nontraditional work were in part economic, but challenge and mobility were equally important to her. In addition, Molly's age and family circumstances left her free for a wide range of activities, including travel with other women friends and voluntary associations, such as the Toastmistresses and Business and Professional Women's Association. She is also active in the local Engineering Technicians Association and the Presbyterian Church.

As the only woman draftsperson in a very large facility, Molly continues to put up with her share of kidding and practical jokes. She constantly refers to herself as the mother superior or mother hen of her twelve-person work group, and she has accommodated to the special attention she gets by falling back on her age. She is supervised by a man who is younger than her architect son, but he treats her fairly.

Overall, Molly is extremely happy with her job, her coworkers, and the accomplishments she has made in her middle forties and early fifties. She looks forward to retirement so that she can travel and do more volunteer work. She is a candid and self-disclosing person who also reported her increased interest

in women's issues and women's rights in recent years. She concluded her third conversation with us with an animated "Defend
womanhood!"

Working at the same facility as Molly O'Hara is a twenty-five-
year-old single mother who is an example of "just falling into"
a nontraditional job as an electronics mechanic, radar, because
she really needed the money. Born and raised in Southern California, Maggie Patterson is one of two daughters of a shoe
salesman father and a mother who was a housewife. Maggie described herself as a tomboy while growing up, active in sports
and extracurricular activities, and a good student. She had done
baby-sitting and had summer jobs but mentioned that she spent
a lot of time playing basketball and football with the neighborhood boys all through her childhood. Maggie has a deep interest in biology, particularly marine biology, but never pursued
it academically because she became pregnant by a serviceman
at age seventeen and decided to get married and have the baby.
Divorced at eighteen, she, with the baby, moved in with her parents. Within six months it was clear that the arrangement was
not going to work, so on the advice of a friend she took a data
processing course at a community college. By the time she was
nineteen her data processing course and high school bookkeeping and typing classes had helped her land a job as a
keypunch operator at the naval facility for $2.10 an hour. She
worked long hours in an all-female job where the turnover was
quite high. After three years she was earning $3.25 an hour.
Supporting herself and her child, paying her aunt to baby-sit,
bored and discouraged with the work, she responded immediately when a recruiter came through her office saying that they
were looking for women apprentices in the blue-collar trades.
The four-year training program, the chance to attend community college on company time, and the opportunity to more
than double her hourly wage were all factors that made her
apply even though she knew absolutely nothing about skilled
trades. Maggie described her experience this way:

So I went into the interview and he asked me what I wanted to do, and I said, "What do you mean, I thought you were going to tell me." I thought this was some kind of aptitude test, you know. And I figured there was electronics or machinist type things. I didn't know. Under electronics there's fifteen different titles and you had to pick one and I went, "God, I don't even know what these are," and I recognized one that was electronics mechanics, radar, which my girl friend's husband was in, so I said okay, put me down for that, I didn't know what it was, but he put me down for it. He said that there was another girl who was in the class ahead of me and she was an aircraft instrument mechanic, which meant doing little tiny precise things—in a dust-free room—so I said okay even though I didn't know that's what it was at the time, I said okay. So he put me down. You had to put down three things and then from the group of people they chose they went through, and if your first choice nobody else was hired, then you could have that, and that kind of thing. So I got the radar and that started at—in fact I took a cut to start the program—I think it started at $3.14 and every year you got a regular increase for your apprentice steps. And then on top of that we got a cost of living raise. So anyway, three and a half years later I'm now making $5.96, which is not too bad.

Maggie described herself in the first year as having a lot of problems with electronics, particularly in comparison with the men. She had no interest or background in such things as drafting or repairing radios which could be related to the kind of work she is now doing. She had uneasy relationships with her co-workers and described many of the men as hostile and difficult. Her first interview was very low-key and at times depressing as she described how hard she worked, how little time she had for herself and her child, and how uncertain she was about remaining in her job once she finished the apprenticeship. She talked at length about her continuing desire to be a marine biologist and how she spent almost all of her free time at Sea World with her young son.

When we talked to Maggie a year and a half later she seemed a different person. She was by then a journeyman and the acting foreman in her area, doing less bench work and more paper and scheduling work. She had been making $7.03 an hour, and

in the six weeks she had been acting foreman she was earning
$9.06 an hour. She was working in a different shop than before
and was much more satisfied with her co-workers and supervisors. She was still ambivalent about electronics, but by this
point was positive about the naval facility as a place to work
and about remaining in a nontraditional technical area. Good
pay and security were really important to her as a single
mother, and she cited these as primary reasons for keeping at
and succeeding at a nontraditional trade. She'd also begun to
pull away from the marine biology dream and reported not
having been to Sea World in months. At the second interview
Maggie was living with a man, a fellow journeyman at the naval
facility. She reported that they shared equally in all the household responsibilities and that having him around made things
significantly easier for her than when she had been alone. Her
aunt was still taking care of her son after school. Maggie cred-
ited the new man in her life with helping her get out of the
shell she had been in for years, both at work and at home. She
was doing more things, playing on a softball team, seeing more
people. By our third contact, Maggie was in her same job but
looking around for management opportunities at the facility in
technical areas similar to her trade.

Jan Spencer is a highly successful mechanic working with a
rapid-transit company. Jan grew up in a rural nonfarm community in the Midwest. She had two sisters and one brother, all
younger than she. Her father was a skilled tradesman, a tool
and die maker, and her mother would periodically get jobs such
as waitressing in order to get away from the house and the kids.
Jan described a childhood in which her father's income was low
enough and unstable enough that they were always worrying
about the gas and electricity being turned off. She guessed that
at the most he made what would, in today's currency, amount
to about $8,000 a year. Her mother was nervous and uncom-
fortable with her children, and the house was always unclean
and chaotic. In fact, on a couple of occasions the welfare department complained about the lack of cleanliness and unsani-

tary conditions of their house. "Clothes piled in corners, dog shit on the floor, no telephone: a real pigpen" is how Jan described her home. It was in some ways difficult to talk with Jan about her past, because she had tried to block out the first sixteen years of her life, which were lonely and unhappy. She described her parents as "never having any idea what I was doing, and they didn't much care." Their attitude was, "You do for yourself." If she wanted anything, she earned her own money.

Jan began getting odd jobs at age ten and by age fifteen was working nearly forty hours a week as a waitress in the afternoons and evenings after high school. Her school, in a working-class area, was on two shifts, so she got out by noon. She didn't have friends because "the house was the pits" and she didn't want to bring them home, but she also stayed pretty much to herself because she discovered she was gay at age twelve and was "terrified someone would find out about it." While growing up, she spent some time playing baseball and soccer with neighbors and a lot of time by herself, "in the garage building things, using tools. . . . I liked reading a lot."

Jan didn't like high school much. She described people as what she disliked most about high school and band as what she liked most. She "liked band the most because it was a structured way of being in a group. I knew what to expect and what was expected of me." By high school Jan knew she wanted to go into the Army, because she felt that the Army was "realistically the only way to get out of that goddamned town." She also liked the prospect of a structured social environment, the idea of being with other women, and, most important, the opportunity to get an education in a trade—mechanics. Jan got little counseling in school and got C's in most of her classes. She never even considered college prep classes or going to college because she knew she could never find the money and her grades weren't good enough for a scholarship. Jan has on numerous occasions been informed she has an IQ of 152.

Jan got some of the vocational training she was looking for in the Army. She also got into a lot of trouble because of a romance with another woman. To avoid a court-martial and to cover up her involvement with the woman, Jan decided to "try the other route" and got married. With the GI Bill, she could now afford to go to school, and she started out in a community-college medical technology program and tried to live a conventional life as a married woman in school. She speaks fondly of her former husband and of his family, but she also realized that marriage with a man wasn't what she really wanted—nor was a college degree. ". . . Anything you get with a college degree will have you pushing papers, and I didn't want to do that. With the divorce I realized I had to do what *I* wanted to do, so I switched from college to trade school."

The next six years of Jan's life included two years of trade school, which in the beginning was "just horrendous; where I'm sure guys wanted to beat me up in the parking lot," to the end of trade school, where "people had a lot of respect for me, and on the basis of the work I had done there, they decided they were going to recruit women themselves."

During and after trade school Jan worked in gas stations and eventually moved to Northern California, working in a couple of major car dealerships as an apprentice mechanic, despite her two years of trade school training. She was recruited by a major metropolitan transportation system as a junior mechanic, which was her occupation when first interviewed. She is now a senior mechanic and the team chief of a group of male mechanics who do repair work and preventative maintenance work on rapid-transit vehicles. Jan has a great deal of respect for her fellow workers and is irritated by the abrasiveness and political rhetoric of some of the other women—particularly "politicos who are very intolerant of working-class men," whom she encounters at work. She occasionally bowls and drinks beer with some of her co-workers, and she has also been invited home with some of their families for dinner. She is making over $20,000 a year and has just bought a house. Her love life is complicated, and she wishes she had a "wife" who could cook and help with all the daily problems of keeping her house and her life together.

Jan is obviously competent at her trade. She likes her work and where she is working. She has been a tremendous success from the days when she was the only woman in a trade school of 1,300 to today, when she is a team chief and senior mechanic for a major rapid-transit company. Her love of her trade came through in all of our encounters with her. She has developed a diversity of interests and skills as a function of her interest in mechanics and working with men in blue-collar jobs. The following comments highlight Jan's sense of what and how she learned about blue-collar skills over the years.

Well, the skills and abilities are technical, and women aren't trained; they're not trained to get them. They're not encouraged to go after them, and I mean it's obvious that they don't have them; they just don't have. They don't go into the armed forces—I mean, half the guys on a crew learn their skills in the Navy.

You know, I went into the Army. I learned my electrical there. There aren't a lot of women veterans, however, and the ones that are around generally weren't in technical fields because—now, anyway—because they just in the last couple of years started putting women in technical fields. And there aren't that many women who go in in the first place. That accounts for a large portion of people. Then there's also the fact that men just tinker around with these things . . . they talk to each other about things. I mean, I've learned things from men; if it hadn't been a situation where I was working with men all the time and doing the technical things, and having them talk to me. Just think about other stuff—you know, about diesel engines. I never worked on diesel engines, but I know a lot about them from talking to guys back and forth, you know. About six months ago, they took me out and I learned to drive Mack wreckers, three-quarter-ton trucks, road diesels, and tractor trailers, and I went down and took a test—I have every license that California offers right now. And that's because I'm in a male job, because they—you know, I'm around them all the time, and I express an interest. They said okay, you . . . I mean, how is a woman who is in college or, ah, or being a secretary ever going to run across an opportunity to even discuss those kinds of things with men. I had to, like, aside from actually going out and driving a truck—I had to like bullshit with them for hours to find out how to change lanes, what a downshift is, how to downshift, what an over-rev was. You know, before I could even entrust myself to go out on that—on a road with that truck, and you know, like what cops look out for and so on.

Jan is a success. She is getting information and is exposed to opportunities. She is certain that her success is due to her skills, but she also kept emphasizing the importance of understanding and respecting the needs and competencies of the blue-collar men with whom she works. At the conclusion of her second interview, when asked what her ideal or fantasy life would be, she responded, "I would like to live in the country and do bench work, which is take small components and repair them. That would be what I would like to do. Someday I will do that, I hope."

In sharp contrast to Jan is Ann Baker, another woman interviewed in Northern California, who was working for the same metropolitan transit company but who ultimately was unsuccessful in her job. Ann's feelings about her job and her co-workers were almost antithetical to Jan's. Her social background and her educational and work experiences were radically different as well. On the surface they seemed very much alike: late-twenties gay women living in an "open city"; political and feminist in their understanding of society; and working as some of the first women employed as mechanics in a major rapid-transit system. The similarities stopped there, however.

Ann was quite definite about not really liking to work. What was important to her was doing what she "likes to do" when she "feels like it" and playing music in an all-female band. She indicated that if she could make money at her music, she might do that, but the abiding impression of Ann is of a woman still finding herself, for whom exploring life was still more important than stable, paid employment. Even her music had never been seriously pursued as a vocation. The only child of an upper-middle-class Wasp family in the Midwest, Ann's conversation was laced with metaphors and preoccupations familiar to anyone who has taught affluent undergraduate students. Describing her parents as well off, deeply religious, and conventional in their life-style, Ann recalled a childhood characterized by a great deal of flexibility. She got good grades and was active in band and music in high school. She determined her own hours when dating, was given her own car on her sixteenth birthday, and attended a private church-related college. She had fantasies as a child about going on the stage and described herself as frequently being lonely. She belonged to a sorority and had her first serious affair with a woman in her sophomore year. As she got more disenchanted with college, her grades got worse, and with her parents' support she left college to do some traveling.

Ann had intermittent odd jobs working in retail sales, as a correspondent for a book publishing company, and as a baker's assistant. The first job she had for any length of time was as a counselor and teacher in a drug rehabilitation center in a major midwestern city where she worked for over two and a half years with a group of old school friends who had helped set up the program. At age twenty-five, Ann and two friends decided to hit the road in a van and traveled around the country from Iowa, to Denver, to Albuquerque, doing odd jobs and seeing the sights. They ended up in Northern California, and Ann decided by then that she "really wanted to get into electricity." She had always been curious about electricity; playing music had piqued her interest in amplification, and she wanted a skill "with power." She signed up for a training program at a community college skills center, was easily the best in her class, and within five months landed a job as an electronic technician with a major metropolitan transit authority. She indicated that affirmative action helped her get the job, for which she felt she was "fully capable though not yet entirely qualified."

By her second interview Ann had just quit her job. She had been working the graveyard shift for many months, was isolated, and was getting very little training. She had been passed over for training and advancement opportunities. Other women were not having her same problems; in fact, they were doing well, she reported. She also emphasized that they were "straight" and "really into their cars and paychecks and things like that." She emphasized that she really enjoyed electronics but that she couldn't take working for "the bureaucracy" and having to cope with those ignorant slobs (blue-collar men). She had to get out. When I asked her what her ideal job would be, she replied, "Playing beautiful music for lesbians."

In our interviews Ann shared a number of contradictory feelings. On the one hand she was conscious that her middle-class background had freed her from a lot of the pressures that kids with working-class parents face, but on the other hand she really disliked the values of her working-class co-workers and talked about feeling isolated from their world.

I mean, I existed in two worlds. I spoke a totally different language . . . was around people I would never otherwise associate with . . . around equipment I never saw anywhere else, doing something I would never do anywhere else, and when I would get home, I would leave all that behind. There's lots of things that interest me, and three hours a day is enough for technical stuff.

Ann also described her work as terribly lonely.

It's lonely; I mean, when I *do things,* I like to . . . well, I like to do things by myself, but there's a lot of times when I at least like to show off. I mean, there was nobody there to see me who I cared about, you know . . . ah . . . here I am sitting in this little room, all surrounded by screens, and working on this radio—I felt—I felt like a surgeon a lot of time. I felt real lonely. It was not a job I could share anywhere else, I mean, the language is different and everything.

Ann's comments about her experience of her job and her feelings toward her co-workers were in sharp contrast to those of Jan, the successful mechanic. While Jan "palled around" with her co-workers to some extent, respected their abilities, and felt a great deal of pride in herself for impressing them with her abilities, Ann felt isolated and downright superior to the men and women she was encountering in the blue-collar world. She was also highly critical of Jan, whom she described as "hiding her lesbianism and playing up to the men." Jan in turn described Ann as a middle-class radical who had "no sensitivity to where these working-class guys were coming from" and who "could always write home to Daddy for money." Jan also had a compelling and long-lived interest in mechanics. She spent much of her free time "tinkering at a bench," while Ann felt divided between her work world and her personal life, not only socially but intellectually.

Katie Jenkins, a successful welder in a service shop who by our third-year contact was looking forward to teaching welding in a vocational school, is an only child who grew up in Queens, New York. Her parents divorced when she was ten. Her father committed suicide not long after the divorce and Katie recalled how deeply shaken both she and her mother were by the entire sequence of events. Her father had been a journeyman electrician and her mother went to work as a bank teller in order to support the two of them. Katie remembers her mother sometimes taking a second job, such as cashiering at a movie theater, in order to earn extra money, and she remembers her mother's working as a positive thing while she was growing up. Katie's upbringing was fairly traditional, but she recalls having behavioral problems early in high school and she thought of herself as "a bit of an eccentric" in her last years of high school—"wearing dark clothes, being interested in reading and drama, not socializing much with other kids." She developed an interest in art, eventually going to art school for two years. Her childhood fantasies, however, centered on adventurous outdoor activities, such as being a jockey, racing cars, or being a photographer for *National Geographic*. Katie held a number of odd jobs upon graduating from high school and through her two-year college program, and was discouraged by the fact that even after finishing a college program she couldn't get work she really liked. She stated it this way:

When my two years of college were done I was cleaning houses full time and I felt in the same place when I got out of college as I did when I got out of high school—there was a blank space, and I had to fill it up. I didn't know how I was going to do it, so I went to a

career counselor. She was a feminist, it was mostly for white-collar
women who were middle-aged and they needed some kind of skill
or to develop something because of economic reasons. I went to her
and she, through her counseling, she suggested that I try looking
for work in blue-collar traditional male jobs. This was in New York
and I was just finishing up school and I thought by going to college
I would find something that I liked and I would fall into it and everything would clear up nicely, but that didn't happen. . . . I
thought, Oh shit, I'm getting desperate, I gotta think of something,
so I thought I would let someone take over who would be to my
benefit, which it was, so I was headed in the right direction there.
At that point I decided I wanted to go into woodworking or make
furniture, custom-make furniture.

Instead of woodworking, Katie eventually got into a welding
course on the West Coast, after moving from New York, and
found that she really liked the skill as well as the opportunities
and money. At the time of her first interview Katie had been
working in a service shop for a few months and articulated a
keen sense of responsibility as one of the first women working
in this area. She was extremely concerned that she succeed, to
pave the way for other women.

I'm pretty content. I want to change my work situation—I'm trying
to work on that with relation to my job now. Getting more women
into the field would make it better for people like me. I feel like, in
this place, the Joan of Arc, you know. Here I am setting the example, every time if I have to be absent for a doctor's appointment or
getting my gas turned on, I feel, Oh my God, they're going to think
this happens to every woman. I'm missing work, so how does it
look for me and how does it look for everybody else that's trying to
get a job? I always think how does this look—I'm representing all
the future women that are going to be in. . . .

She reported her job as being satisfying and increasing her
self-confidence, and she also revealed that she felt it had contributed to her appreciation of all her mother had accomplished. Katie shared that sentiment in this way:

Wait, could you ask me that other question again. I think I could
talk about my mother there. She's kinda looking at this from a dis-

tance—kinda thoughtfully stroking her chin, saying—wow, that's how she turned out. She told me one time that it was a shame she finally understood the fact that I didn't want to have a nice car or a nice boyfriend or nice clothes or a good job. Now she realizes that is what I wanted all along—financial stability. Growing up, that was really ingrained in me. Make sure you can earn money. It really became—when my mother was taking care of me and the house and had two jobs. She was doing everything I am doing except that she had a kid and another job besides the one she had. She was a clerk in a movie theater and also a bank teller. I decided to hell with this—if I'm going to have to do this, I'm only going to have one job.

During our second- and third-year contacts with Katie, she was still enthusiastic about her trade but continued to express reservations about the work context and the prospects for women. She described having experienced a fair amount of harassment, such as finding pornographic photos in her locker, but she did not seem angered or deterred by it. Her comments constantly returned to how much she enjoyed the process of welding and the good pay she was making. She stated quite matter-of-factly that there was no such thing as an ideal job or work situation and that despite the problems with her work environment she was really lucky to have a job she liked as much as welding. Katie lives alone, but is involved a lot with women's issues and female friendships. She reported that she was increasingly interested in friends who felt a sense of responsibility toward their jobs because of the centrality her work as a welder had in her life. She feels satisfied with the choices she has made thus far and feels she's accomplished a great deal.

Another highly responsible female worker is an apprentice we interviewed in Southern California who after years in traditional female jobs signed up at age forty as an apprentice electronics mechanic. Born and raised in the rural South, May Rogers was one of three children. Her father was an older man when she was born and was retired from skilled trades to work their small farm most of the time she was growing up. She had many responsibilities and spent a lot of time with her father milking cows, chopping wood, and learning to do bookkeeping as early as age ten. She thinks working with her father this way gave her a lot of confidence other women never had a chance to develop. May married a year after high school and had three children by age twenty-three. She was a housewife until there was a major strike at the local chemical plant where her husband worked and they began to need money. She went to work at the minimum wage as an inspector for a local lingerie manufacturer. At twenty-three she and her husband divorced because he was "fooling around" and everyone in their small southern town knew it. She described the decision to leave him as brave and unusual, given traditional southern values at that time. When asked what made her do it, May responded:

I just felt it was a better advantage to me and my kids. Because I didn't figure we were going to get anywhere where we were. And if we were going to make it, I was going to have to make good. So I just got out.

May passed a civil service exam and, relying on the secretarial and clerical skills she had developed in high school and some clerical work experience in the principal's office, got an entry-level clerical job at the local air force base. For the next dozen years May held clerical positions at military sites. She remarried an air force officer, lived in France with her three children, and continued to work. She moved to Texas, divorced her second husband, and continued to work. She remarried a third time, moved to California, and continued to work in clerical positions at military installations. Her level of responsibility and earnings improved somewhat over the years, but her work for the most part was boring and unrewarding. Despite the fact that her kids were no longer home or in need of her support, she wanted something that would give her a sense of challenge and accomplishment. When civilian apprenticeships opened up at the military installation where she worked, she applied, and was very satisfied with the change when first interviewed.

May has experienced very little harassment or resistance on

the job, which she thinks is due in part to her excellent prior reputation as a clerical worker at the installation. She also noted how important it is always to take the extra step to keep busy or help out your co-workers. She pointed out that the one woman in the job before her would read or do cross-word puzzles once she had finished an assignment, which had left a bad attitude toward women. Her present husband's also being a tradesman at the installation gives her a great deal of moral support and insight into her new job that she might not otherwise get. May is beginning to feel financially well off and vocationally successful after seventeen uninterrupted years in the paid work force. She takes pride in her children and lets her husband help around the house only because it's necessary be-cause of their work schedules. She would prefer to take care of all the household matters herself.

In sharp contrast to May is a young Asian-American woman from a middle-class family who, after getting a degree in Chi-nese studies at the University of California, spending two years studying in Hong Kong, and holding a series of clerical jobs, became a successful engine lathe operator in a steel mill. San-dra Wong grew up in Southern California, one of two children. Her father was an inspector in industry and her mother did bookkeeping until she became an invalid. Sandra spent most of her summers in Arizona with relatives and felt she had a lot of independence as a growing child. Her parents shared equally in housework and cooking, and since her mother has been an in-valid her father has taken care of everything. Sandra reported no knowledge of or interest in anything related to industry, me-chanics, or electronics as a child. She played with dolls, pur-sued individual sports such as tennis, was popular in high school, and earned good grades. Active in student government and pursuing a conventional college career at a major univer-sity, Sandra described her childhood and young adulthood as happy and uncomplicated. Sandra's problem was her inability to get a job that she liked and felt challenged by and that paid what she wanted to earn. The following comments, made early

in her first interview, summarize the employment dilemma
faced by many college-educated women even today.

I wanted to learn some more and they weren't training me, I'd go
up and talk to the personnel supervisor and say why don't you let
me have this job? Why don't you train me and do this, and I got
very upset because she—well, they hired me, they had reservations
because I had so much education, but you have no alternative when
you can't find a job, you have to take what you can get and especially if you aren't in a situation where you have some financial
flexibility. Like I mean when you get out of school you've got debts
to pay and loans to pay and you've just got to take what you can
get—typing anything. It turns out typing is the best thing I ever did
and I did that in high school and it turns out that's how I got a job.
Everything else was superfluous. I mean it didn't make any
difference whether I took it or not—it was that typing class, and so
they gave me this job because they had to hire people and they
trained me as the head secretary of the tax division 'cause the
woman I was replacing was gonna have a baby. When she got back
I had to go to another position—right? So I was demoted to clerk.

Unable to break out of typing jobs after three years, Sandra
made one unsuccessful stab at a nontraditional job on the advice of a friend. Sandra then went to a career opportunities and
counseling center for women in her city. They got her into the
machine trades training program she had been in for about
eight months at the time we first interviewed her. Sandra wasn't
enthusiastic about her job or the workplace in her first year.
Everything was new for her and she received very little directed
training. She was just expected to learn things as she went
along, and no one took the time to demonstrate many fundamental operations, so her productivity was low. After many discussions with supervisory personnel she began to get more help
and feel more competent running the machine. She had already
begun to see machining as a long-term career activity because of
her knowledge of the high demand for such skills and the high
pay. Despite her concerns about the quality of her training,
Sandra's impressions were that for the most part men liked having women in the shops. She described a number of her co-

workers as helpful and reported eating lunch with her co-workers and occasionally going out with them for beers after work. Sandra had problems with lifting and endurance and also had an allergic reaction to the oil she was required to use on her machine.

By the second-year interview, Sandra's job was less physically taxing because she had been working as the gofer in the tool crib—giving out tools and supplies to the machinists in the shop as well as monitoring, ordering, and maintaining supplies. She was not working the machine but still had her classification and salary. She was feeling much more positive about the work and the workplace, emphasizing again how much money she was making. At this time she was romantically involved with a fellow tradesman and feeling more a part of the industrial community generally. Her respect for the work of machinists had also increased as the following comment reveals.

People who become machinists, a lot of them, I think, have a tendency to be loners. They . . . they're actually very creative people. But they like, you know, to do things on their own. And do it their way and have it a certain way and . . . it comes from that craft mentality of, like, making a part from beginning to end but what has happened is that they only now do a certain operation in the job so instead of it—robbed them of the . . . satisfaction that they could take out of doing their work. And so, a lot of people just do it, what they have to do, and get out and some people still work very hard.

At the third-year follow-up, Sandra was in her same job in a higher classification and making around $14,000 a year. She commented that she was going to night school to improve her skills because there was no guarantee of her job at the steel mill. She had clearly decided to remain in a skilled trade, however.

Some of the women we interviewed were interested in developing a skill in order to be free-lance handypersons or start their own businesses. One carpenter we interviewed was primarily interested in free-lance cabinet and furniture making; another was interested in doing small home repairs. We interviewed a plumber trying to make it on her own, working out of her own truck, and a small-appliance repairperson who had also learned auto upholstery in an attempt to have skills she could hire out directly to individual consumers rather than having to work for a big company. Overall, such women were not as successful as women tied into continuous on-the-job training or apprenticeship programs. Jane Kurtz is a good example of this kind of woman moving into nontraditional skills.

Jane grew up in Minnesota, in what she described as a close, cooperative family with three children. Her father was an engineer and her mother a housewife. With her father's help, Jane was an entrepreneur at a very early age. He helped her purchase and maintain two coin-operated automatic washers, which she put in apartment buildings for tenants to do their laundry. Within a few years she owned 400 washers, which she sold in order to open one laundromat. As a teenager, she also sold refreshments at a movie theater and did odd jobs. When she went away to college she sold the laundromat to her brothers. Thus from age fifteen to eighteen Jane had been earning her own money, and she reported having as much as $300 a month pocket money when she was a teenager. In addition to being an entrepreneur, Jane described herself as athletic and outdoorsy in high school. She didn't date at all in high school but was active in extracurricular activities. Jane went to college because her parents encouraged her to and she expected to become a nurse. She confessed, however, that as early as age thirteen she knew she wasn't like other girls. She always had and wanted more freedom.

She was always interested in skilled occupations like barbering or machine repair because she liked working with her hands and seeing "products," but her parents would respond with, "No way are you going to do that. You're going to college." She lasted in college for a year and a half. When she left, she got caught in the secretarial-clerical track, working for an ad agency, the civil service, and the military. She did bookkeeping and receptionist work and managed a supply room. She needed money, and these were jobs she could get with a high school typing background. At age twenty-seven, after eight uninterrupted years of employment, Jane decided she had to get out from behind a desk and went to a community college for vocational counseling. She looked over its catalog of course offerings and, recalling her successful washing-machine business of twelve years earlier, enrolled in a course in appliance repair. She loved the class and the work. Jane's problem has been in finding employment. She made some efforts to work for large department stores and appliance service centers, but couldn't get hired, primarily, she believes, because she's a woman and the private sector is still slow to hire women. Having worked independently as a youngster, she decided to try to make it as a free-lancer and spends time finding used but repairable appliances, which she then repairs and sells at swap meets. She also took a class in auto upholstery and has been doing some independent contracting in that specialty. Her lack of employment experience and limited formal training have made it difficult for her to get jobs in auto upholstery. Rather than accepting traditional employment, Jane is still trying to make it on her own, but so far her repair and upholstery work haven't paid back the up-front investment she had to make in tools and equipment. Her husband is a skilled tradesman who helps her a great deal, although he is ambivalent about her desire to succeed as a nontraditional handyperson because he sees all the heartache and hard work she has had so far. They have a very egalitarian marriage, sharing all the household jobs. For medical reasons they do not plan to have children.

Every independent handyperson we talked to expressed frustrations similar to Jane's, both because of the problem women face gaining acceptance in such roles and because, as one woman put it, "working for yourself just ain't all it's cracked up to be."

Among the total of eighty-seven women breaking into nontraditional jobs whom we interviewed there were many with other types of backgrounds, employment experiences, and out-

comes after three years. A number of women talked about
using their skilled trade as a step into management or more-
white-collar technical areas, such as electronics. Some women
who had been doing well in their first two years had returned
by the third year to more traditional work in bookkeeping, running a day care center, or sales. Some of the women, although
still in nontraditional fields, were uncertain how long they
would remain. Nonetheless, the portraits just presented are
fairly typical of the types of pioneering women we interviewed.

By way of contrast, I would like to share just two portraits of
women in traditional jobs who are not meant to be prototypes
of women working in the traditional female labor force. Their
life experiences and values contrast markedly with the women
you have just met, and highlight the unusual qualities of the
pioneering group of skilled women workers.

Clare Fraser is a successful cosmetologist whose first-year interview was filled with references to childhood preoccupations
that are stereotypically "female." She talked a great deal about
being concerned about her weight and her appearance. For example, when asked (as all the women interviewed were) about
what she liked least about high school, she made the following
statement:

I don't know . . . I guess—well, I liked PE, but the only thing I
didn't like about PE was that I got my hair all messed up, and now
I'm a fanatic about my hair; I can't stand to have it messed up.
Now, that's stupid, but that's the way I am, and I love PE, but
when we came in, my hair was usually messed up, and that is the
way it had to be the rest of the day. I wasn't smart enough then to
think about taking hair spray or something like that.

A later question asked of everyone was how important personal appearance was in high school. Clare made the following
comment:

I've always worried about my long nose—always. That bothered me
very much, up until I think it was seventh grade. I didn't think any-

thing about it, because no one had ever said anything about it, and one of my girl friends teased me one time. I can remember only one time being teased, and from then on, it bothered. In fact, here lately I was thinking about having my nose fixed and my husband —he doesn't really want me to, but a friend of mine had her nose fixed—of course I couldn't say this to her—but she looks worse now than before she had it fixed. I don't like her new nose, so I don't know if I'll ever do it. Probably not.

This contrasted sharply with the responses of "Not very" or "Not at all" given by most of women.

Clare also spoke of the women she admired as a young adult and her aspirations for the future in what we think of as conventional "feminine" terms, as the following two statements dramatically demonstrate:

I was always interested in office work, and I saw a very lovely girl one time in an office. Her hair was perfect, and her clothes were perfect. She had very long nails for typing a typewriter, but she did it and that's what I wanted to do. I dreamed about that a lot.

My sister-in-law had an important influence on me, too. My brother was seventeen and she was fifteen when they got married, and I was three. After she had her baby, she was quite fat, and her house was quite dirty, and I saw her grow into this beautiful, well-kept woman with a spotless house all these years. I saw her get out of this sloppiness and go into—she is quite a pretty thing and very understanding person. So whenever my mom wasn't available and I needed someone, I felt that she was my sister. I thought it would be neat to be like her someday: married and settled and happy and pretty and nice house and you know. . . .

Such statements by Clare have to be understood in context. On the surface they suggest a rather simple-minded sense of life. In fact, Clare's childhood was complicated and unhappy and her current life as a wife, mother, and cosmetologist is not without depth or complexity. Clare grew up in a small town in Southern California. Her father was a violent alcoholic, a welder whose drinking resulted in arguments, fighting, and a very insecure economic base for the family. Clare remembers being embarrassed by her secondhand clothes and toys, and she was conscious that had it not been for her mother's work as a power sewing machine operator, there wouldn't have been food on the table regularly. Her father's drinking problem became a terrible source of anxiety for her in her teens, and she was so sick and nervous that her mother finally decided to leave her father. When Clare was fourteen, she, her brother, and her mother were on their own. By the time she was fifteen her mother had remarried.

Upon graduating from high school, Clare trained to operate a keypunch. Meanwhile, with her mother's help, she got her first job—as a seamstress in a shirt factory. Then she got a filing job with another company while waiting for a keypunch job to open up. She met her husband, married, and moved to his hometown, a small town not far from her own. She still couldn't find a keypunch job, so, with the help of her mother, she went back to sewing in a shirt factory. Her husband was an apprentice plumber at the time. Later she worked as a bank teller for a few months, but pregnancy removed her from the paid labor force for nine years.

Her decision to go back to work was based on the fact that although she wanted more than two children, she was unable to have more, and her children were now old enough for her to be able to be away from the house part-time. She and her husband felt they could use the extra money. The most important reason for this need was the seasonal nature of her husband's work. Since he worked in construction, they always had to live with two to three months of unemployment a year. Clare stated it this way:

So with plumbers and construction there is always a layoff sometime during the year. Whether it's raining or what—there is always a layoff. We have been married almost thirteen years, and there's only one year that he worked completely through the whole year in that thirteen years. This is why I wanted to go to work. I told him if there was something I could do that wouldn't affect the kids too badly, and we were going to put all my money in savings, and then when he is laid off we'll have that to fall back on. It seems like we just get over a layoff and get caught up, and it's time for the next one and we can't get any money in the bank.

Clare enjoys her work immensely and takes great pride in her skill as a beautician. She also enjoys the "extras" her money has been able to buy them, as this comment about getting a color television demonstrates:

I think being and having the life I did as a child makes me appreciate things. In fact, now—at the point we are at, we are getting goodies like a color TV, and we usually have a new vehicle to drive and things like this. When we got our color TV, I was all excited, as anybody would be to get something new, and get it all set up and started watching it and I started crying. My husband says, "Why are you crying?" and I said, "I feel guilty having something so nice, because I guess my mom never had it."

Clare and her husband and children are deeply religious, deeply committed to one another, and essentially oblivious to the life-style changes that are going on around them. Clare is now working part-time in her mother-in-law's beauty salon and feels extremely proud of her perseverance and success in cosmetology school and the increased comforts her family is able to enjoy because of her employment. She relies on an extended-kin network for help with her family needs and for her social life. She thinks her husband is "fantastic," even though she takes care of everything at home. Clare sees her life as a constant "adventure," as these closing comments in her second-year interview reveal.

I recently wrote a girl friend a letter and I said, "Well, I'm off on another adventure." I'm always doing something. I . . . ah, well, I put myself through IBM school and I got a job and I worked at that for a while, and then I was trained to be a teller in a bank and I did that for a while. And, ah, then I worked in that dress shop, which was just a very fun job because it was here in town and I knew everybody that came in, you know, and . . . um, then what did I do? I always wanted to learn how to swim, so when I, in between working, . . . at the dress shop, when I quit that and was off for a couple of years, I, ah, went through the backyard swim program and learned how to swim, became an instructor for swimming, and even took senior lifesaving and the whole bit, so, ah, I was very pleased I learned how to swim; my children were too, and now I've finished training and I'm working as a cosmetologist.

A number of the cosmetologists we interviewed were less stereotypically feminine than Clare; all, however, tended to have more uniformly working-class backgrounds, fewer opportunities to develop autonomy at an early age, and a far greater preoccupation with appearance and acceptance than the majority of the pioneers we studied.

Another woman unlike many of pioneering women is María Hernández. María was in a training program for launderers and pressers when we first interviewed her. Like many of the working poor, she holds jobs on and off and is frequently on welfare. She has been through a number of government-sponsored training programs but has never developed a secure enough sense of herself or of a skill to get into a permanent employment situation. Although not typical of most of the women in our sample, she is in many ways typical of a large and significant category of women in the semiskilled blue-collar labor force.

María was born in Mexico and came to the United States at a young age in 1943, living in a border town, Mexicali, for most of her childhood. She was the eldest of eight children. When her father died, she immediately went to work at the age of fourteen to help support the family. Because of this and her poor grades (due to her poor English), María dropped out of high school at fifteen. She helped her mother raise the kids and worked primarily in the fields and canneries. Even when her father was alive the family would go north every summer to pick fruit. María gave all of her money to her family. She did not describe her childhood as unhappy or as poor, particularly when her father was still alive. When asked what she expected in her adult life, she said she always expected to have a family and kids. In fact, one of the reasons she dropped out of high school was that she "took the attitude, you don't have to have a diploma to have a baby."

María has had a variety of jobs earning as little as $35 a week and as much as $85 a week. She's worked most frequently in her adult years as a seamstress and stitcher in a men's suit factory. She has done other kinds of factory work, has been a hospital aide (and considered going into nursing), a waitress, cook's helper, punch press operator, and electronics assembler. In all these years María has never held a job for more than a few months at a time because of injuries, layoffs, or transportation problems. At one point she was training to be a presser and quite excited by that, but she confessed that she wasn't very good or fast at it, according to her instructor. Later she was back at the suit factory sewing after a brief period of unemployment, and by our third-year interview she was unemployed and living on welfare. María stated that her ideal income would be $3.00 per hour.

María and her family have been on and off welfare most of their lives. Divorced from her erratically employed husband and supporting four children, María on the one hand says that she needs and wants a secure job, but on the other continually expresses values indicating her feelings that men should work hard and be responsible for their families and women should be able to stay at home and care properly for their children. She has been in nearly half a dozen government training programs over the years and spends a lot of time going to school and working in an effort to develop a skill and get a good job. María seems to fail at whatever she's tried, however. Her kids skip school a lot and get into trouble with the police more than she would like. She's often threatened that her phone and electricity will be shut off, and her groceries and gasoline expenses are more than she can afford. Unlike her family of origin, the children do not seem to be contributing to the family livelihood. What emerges from the interviews with María is a picture of family and economic disorganization. All of these problems lead María to see the good life in very conventional terms.

The good life for me would be—and this has nothing to do with women's—to find me a better man and stay home and enjoy myself for a while with my family. Don't you feel—I mean, if you're away from your family all the time, you feel they're growing up so fast in front of your eyes and you have not really enjoyed your family. You—like going to sleep or feeding them at night and then waking up in the morning and saying, "Hey, kids, get up and go to school," and you don't share your life with them, you know; you feel like you're cheating yourself. When they were babies you enjoyed them 'cause you were with them, but as they are growing up, that's their main—you know: growing up is when they need you, I think. As teenagers, you know, I know I just feel like I like to be sometimes, spend some time with them 'cause I tell 'em, "You know, you kids are forever telling me I got good kids, but once in a while, when I come home, then I get problems and the principals get in touch with me. They want to see me in school—that's a very uncomfortable feeling. I'm out there trying to, you know, do things for you kids, and it seems like you don't appreciate. That's when 'Momma's not home,' you know; 'we don't have to go to school.'" So I feel real strongly that sometimes I think a woman should spend more time at home, you know, and then it would be—like men would be: more—you know, they would hold a steady job; like my old man, you know; he works off and on and off and on, and if he was to hold a steady job, you know, like, ah, a woman could spend more time at home and would enjoy life more. It's career women, you know; I think maybe those women are different, you know; they enjoy working. They're more independent, and they enjoy what they're doing—you know, it's a career person—'cause I don't know anything about careers. I started in nursing, and it didn't work out. I'd just like to stay home some.

María is not typical of most of the women we interviewed, but she is representative of a type of woman we encountered in the first year, most of whom we were unable to locate or contact in the second and third years. Such women were characterized by exceptionally low educational attainment (usually only one or two years of high school), frequent participation in government training programs, and erratic employment histories. They are unlikely prospects for heavily demanding skilled jobs, and yet many employers, including the government in the rush to fill affirmative action quotas, often hire anyone needing a job into a slot that ultimately does the individual and the employer a disservice. María has been such a casualty on more than one occasion.

COMMON THEMES IN THE LIVES OF NONTRADITIONAL WORKING WOMEN

As you can see from these brief introductory portraits, women who are pioneering in nontraditional blue-collar employment have a wide variety of experiences and abilities. In all, 87 of the original 117 women we interviewed fell into the category of "nontraditional" blue-collar worker. Thirty women were in traditional jobs such as cosmetology or small-parts assembly. Nine of the 117 interviews were only partially usable, so frequently totals reported vary.

The table below summarizes the types of nontraditional jobs in which the 87 blue-collar women worked.

Nontraditional Jobs
of the Blue-collar Women

TYPE	NUMBER
Technical workers	
Photographer	1
Engineering Technician	1
Engineering Draftsperson	1
Surveyor	1
Clerical workers	
Production Control	4
Shipping	1
Crafts workers	
Auto Upholsterer	2
Carpentry/Woodwork	2
Electronics	1
Machinist	9

Telephone Repair/Installation	1
Plumber/Pipe Fitter	3
Appliance Repair	5
Gas Service Repair	3
Office Machine Repair	1
Shipfitter	2
Painter	2

Mechanics

Auto/Motorcycle	10
Aircraft	4
Electronic	5
Railroad	1

Operatives

Welder	7
Press Operator	2
Metalworker	1

Transit equipment operators

Forklift Operator	2
Truck Driver	4

Laborers

Gardener/Landscape	5
Maintenance Worker	1
Truck Loader	1
Factory Helper	2

Service workers

Chef	2
GRAND TOTAL	87

The nontraditional women came from the three major metropolitan areas of California: San Diego, Los Angeles, and San Francisco. Seventy-five percent of the women were Caucasian, 72 percent were between the ages of twenty-two and thirty, and 19 percent were college graduates. Less than half of the women were currently married. In fact, 49 percent had never married. Twenty-eight percent of the women had children under eighteen at home. In many ways the blue-collar group we followed for three years was not typical of the general female labor force in that its members were younger, had fewer children, and were unexpectedly well educated for the type of work they did. In the first year we conducted open-ended tape-recorded interviews of approximately two and one-half hours. In the second year we were able to reinterview, in depth, 60 percent of the original group of nontraditional women, and we have reliable information on 75 percent of them. We reached 40 percent of the original group of 87 in our third-year telephone interviews. Out of these contacts intimate portraits of working women emerged.

Even though there is no prototypical woman entering and succeeding in nontraditional blue-collar employment, there are nonetheless some common themes and threads characterizing the experiences and concerns of the women we encountered. Most of the women felt they had to work in order to support themselves. They are single women, or single parents, or divorced or widowed, or wives of men in working-class jobs that are seasonal or lack security. The income these women generate is central, not tangential, to the economic livelihood of their households. The extent to which these women are willing or able to be experimental or selective about the kind of jobs they pursue varies, however. It is closely tied to attitudes and resources linked to social class background and current marital and financial status. Our research suggests that a number of sociological factors facilitate or inhibit initial risk-taking and ultimately success on the job. Family size and income, paternal and maternal employment, and the types of jobs and industries in which a woman has previously worked are among the many such factors that will be more fully discussed in subsequent chapters.

In addition to background experiences, opportunities, and resources, these pioneering women seem to share some temperamental and attitudinal similarities, particularly those women who continued to be successful in nontraditional employment over the three years. Many of these attitudes and dispositions emerge from childhood experiences and opportunities, but the accidents and opportunities of young and middle adulthood are also not to be minimized. A parental crisis such as illness, death, or alcoholism; an unwanted pregnancy, early marriage, or divorce; the discovery of alternate life-styles necessitated by a sexual preference such as lesbianism or stimulated by encounters with political or ideological movements such as trade unionism or the feminist movement: each in its way can touch and change an individual's life. Of the women interviewed for this book, a large number came from divorced, fatherless homes in which the mother was a primary breadwinner. For many, becoming a breadwinner at age nineteen or thirty-nine was a result of a husband's abandoning or divorcing them or dying. Women with comfortable and conventional family backgrounds and early childhoods have turned to roads less traveled by women because of personal crises, sexual preferences, or dawning political consciousness. For all the women we interviewed, the world is a problematic place in which to live and a place which they feel they must master themselves. Neither their fathers or husbands nor their family name or resources are sufficient for their sense of place and security. They have been forced to independent action, and one of the steps in the complicated process of making a place for themselves has been to take a chance on nontraditional blue-collar jobs.

Another common thread in the lives of nontraditional women is early childhood. Their interests, abilities, and aspirations differed from those of most girls. Being extremely athletic with a keen interest in sports; having opportunities to "tinker" and work with tools; taking an active interest in cars or boats; dating less than other girls; identifying themselves as tomboys; having dreams and fantasies about being an adventurer, a traveler, a pilot, or an outdoorswoman: these were common to most of the pioneers. Even though most of the women reported that they expected they would probably "end up in a woman's job" and get married and have children, their childhood preoccupations and activities were atypical.

This is not to suggest, however, that success is purely a function of individual risk-taking, vocational circumstances, or efforts. Contexts inhibit and/or facilitate successful pioneering. The women whose stories make up this book have interesting and varied educational experiences and work histories. All have benefited from the employment opportunities that have opened up as a result of the women's movement and efforts to promote equal employment opportunity. Their stories vary greatly in the extent of planning, counseling, and training preceding their entering nontraditional employment. Their on-the-job experiences, formal training, personal relationships, job security, and opportunities for advancement also vary significantly. They all, however, seem to have an ability to assess realistically the problems and opportunities facing them and have mastered strategies for taking control of their environments rather than letting their work environment overpower them. They have "work savvy." Almost all have had the good fortune of finding coworkers who have helped them learn the rules of the game and become competent at whatever skill they are attempting to master. At a quite basic level, they like what they're doing and whom they work with.

Contexts at home and in the community are both important. What emerges from the interviews with the women described in this book is an impression that for the most part relationships with family members and spouses are supportive and helpful—in large part because of the size and importance of the paycheck to the family. Some of the women we interviewed are superwomen doing everything at home, working full time, and going to school. It is clear, however, that over time the demands of skilled blue-collar working life give rise to a lot of help at home on the part of blue-collar males, despite their "macho" stereotype. Concepts of child care and hopes for children also seem to be considered less compromised than one might initially expect. The pioneers we encountered seem, for the most part, to consider their solutions to these problems satisfactory.

A final thread linking many pioneers is their level of self-consciousness and articulateness. The education of the women we interviewed varied from never finishing high school to post-graduate study, but we were consistently impressed with the general intelligence and conceptual clarity with which our respondents related to us. Very early in the research process any middle-class tendencies to minimize competencies or trivialize experiences of less-educated working-class women were completely laid to rest. Very few of the women we interviewed had lived simple, uncomplicated lives. Most had complex and interesting work histories. The candor of these psychologically complex and reflective women has made it possible for us to understand a little better the process of starting and succeeding in nontraditional areas.

In later chapters we will delve into the ways in which employment settings, training programs, and job security affect success in nontraditional jobs. It is clear, however, from this first look—and will become clearer in the next few chapters—that the pioneers in any field are a special group of independent, risk-taking individuals with unusual energy, tenacity, and focus. This is not to say that one must be a superwoman to be a skilled blue-collar worker. It does suggest that it helps to be highly independent if you're in the first wave of outsiders trying to penetrate and succeed in a new field. The women we studied in the mid-seventies were forced to be entering wedges, and most of them had the personal resources to succeed.

II

Working Roots: Family Background and Childhood

This chapter is about the family backgrounds and childhood experiences of women pursuing nontraditional jobs. Women who have the interests and abilities that enable them to make these pioneering occupational choices emerge from certain family and childhood contexts. Such contexts cannot in and of themselves create adult pioneers, but they can give rise to an individual with the *potential* for risk-taking and pioneering efforts. Whether or not that potential is ever realized is a result of opportunities and personal events later in their lives. Clearly this potential cannot be realized if specific opportunities do not exist, but it is equally true that specific opportunities cannot be taken advantage of unless people with potential interests and abilities move on them. Thus it is important initially to take a look at factors that give rise to this kind of potential in individual women.

What the experiences of the women we met indicate is that the capacity for risk-taking and ultimately succeeding as a pioneer is not something that just happens because a new opportunity opens up. Rather, it emerges from a number of earlier experiences that contribute to the development of nontraditional interests and capacities and, as important, give someone prior experience with risk-taking. In simple terms, risk takers are made, not born. Because of the very different patterns of male and female socialization in our society, the experiences that "make" girls who have a capacity for independent behavior and risk-taking may be qualitatively different from those forming boys. With regard to independent action and risk-taking, it is probably fair to say that in the family and in society such capacities are strongly valued and reinforced in developing male children whereas they are discouraged in developing female children.

From infancy on, in a hundred subtle and not so subtle ways, parents and society, by providing experiences and opportunities, reinforce qualities in boys related to developing independence, competency, and risk-taking as adults. This typical pattern of male socialization is paralleled by a distinct pattern of female socialization in which personal qualities are rewarded and experiences offered that reinforce cooperative, noncompetitive, nurturing, and accommodating capacities. Thus, if a girl is to grow into an adult with the capacity for independence and risk-taking, there must be something that is "pattern-breaking," something that deviates from the usual expectations and experiences most growing girls have. There must be something that requires a girl to face expectations and experiences going beyond the typical range of female expectations and experiences. This enables her not only to expand her own behavioral repertoire, but also to begin seeing that what may be true for most girls is not necessarily true for her. This ability to see alternatives to taken-for-granted norms about appropriate female behavior and the practice at using capacities and behaviors not typical for girls are significant first steps in the development of the capacity to be a risk taker.

When one examines the family backgrounds and childhood experiences of women pioneering in nontraditional blue-collar jobs, one finds, with but one or two exceptions, family contexts that "broke pattern" with what one would normally expect to be the typical expectations and experiences of growing girls in their families. These expectations and experiences fall into three general categories, which will provide the basis for our discussion in this chapter: (1) independence building experiences within the family nexus; (2) strong mothers and positive female role models; (3) access to nontraditional occupational knowledge and skills.

THE FAMILY NEXUS: INDEPENDENCE-BUILDING EXPERIENCES

Just as there is no prototypical "blue-collar pioneer," there is no prototypical family context from which such a pioneer emerges. The women we interviewed came both from intact families and from families broken by divorce or abandonment. They had mothers who worked and mothers who were housewives. They had fathers who were tradesmen and fathers who were professionals. Some were only children and some had as many as ten brothers and sisters. Some came from farms and small towns and some came from cities and suburbs. Some were well off and some were exceedingly poor. Nonetheless, there were some recurrent themes in the family histories of the pioneer women that gave rise to atypical or "pattern breaking" experiences for many of them.

The most common theme in their life histories was having grown up in a family context that intentionally or unintentionally gave rise to early experiences of being on their own and a growing sense of personal autonomy, responsibility, and independence. Independence is not typically valued in young girls, as a great deal of research has documented. In fact, most families actively discourage girls from being independent or competitive. The fact that so many of our women either made direct reference to independence as an element of their early family experience or reported events or opportunities that gave rise to independence at an early age was something that united them despite important differences in other family characteristics.

It is important to underscore the significance of this quality and define more precisely what is intended by the term *inde-*

pendence. Early and continuing research on adults who are high achievers reveals that they experienced a great deal of freedom, responsibility, and independence as children and young adults. Additionally, research suggests that high performance expectations, as well as parental tolerance for aggressiveness and even sexuality in young children, seems to be a concomitant of adult achievement. Boys are typically given much more license in these spheres than are girls. A context allowing freedom and experimentation—climbing trees; traveling distances from home; being trusted with valuable things; being given a great deal of physical freedom in dress, play, and even fighting—gives rise to a heightened capacity for independent action, exploratory behavior, and, ultimately, achievement. The child who is protected, who is cut off from task-oriented responsibilities, who is told to cross her legs and behave like a nice little girl, who is prevented from "reaching" physically or spiritually, is going to develop less independence. Riding horses, driving tractors, playing team sports with boys, working on the job with one's parents, and earning one's own money at an early age all foster independence in ways that traditional notions of appropriate girls' play and family responsibilities do not. Most of the women we interviewed were required by parental values or circumstances to develop independence at an early age. The sources of this learning varied—in one instance, a money-conscious father putting his kids to work so they would learn the value of a dollar; in another, a divorced mother working two jobs to support her children, expecting her daughter to assume all the homemaking responsibilities and care for younger children; in another, a large, poor family expecting the girl to work in order to contribute her earnings. Common to all these cases is a growing consciousness that a woman has to take care of herself if she wants things and, in many cases, if she just wants to survive.

One example of having to develop independence at an early age because of difficult family circumstances is Polly Nichols. Polly was the youngest of five children whose mother divorced when she was four. Polly's mother was an extremely strong woman who, after the divorce, finished her education and became a probation officer. She had to have some of her children live with friends at times because of the difficulties she had caring for them while working, and one of the older daughters had serious behavioral problems. Polly remembers sharing almost full responsibility for household management with her brother and sisters at an early age, but she also recalled having a great deal more personal freedom than other kids her age.

While we were growing up, my mother sort of took on a working-man's role, she went to work, came home and sacked out, and we worked to clean the house, make dinner. We were a collective housewife. This was more than usual because she has a bad leg and has a tendency to want to be catered to anyway. She used to make us bring her cup of coffee, and I mean if we were downstairs doing our homework and she was upstairs watching television in her room she would call us downstairs to come upstairs and change the channel, or make her a cup of coffee. There were times she'd call like every fifteen minutes. We had Saturday chores and stuff like this.

The three of us kids really took on the role of a housewife, we cooked, cleaned the house. We did grocery shopping, laundry, and stuff like that.

Polly went on to say that she was on her own a lot.

I always felt incredibly independent. I only had one parent . . . in some ways I didn't have any parents, it was like—it was clear to me that I had much more freedom and liberty than other kids did. If I wasn't going to be home until five I didn't have to call. I could go over to one of my friends and not call and none of my friends had that liberty. And I earned my own money. I got an allowance. But I had to do a lot of work pertaining to housework and if we didn't do that work we got our allowance docked. That was always the threat.

Polly got only average grades and recalled liking science a great deal. She was a loner who spent most of her free time by herself, playing with things like her chemistry set. Polly was overweight and not very popular in high school, and when asked about her memories of her family life she described them as unhappy; she had to be on her own too much as a child. Upon graduating from high school she found herself totally self-sufficient financially. Having no doubts about her lifelong need for work and good pay, Polly was training as an electronics technician in a major research laboratory when we first interviewed her.

Ynez Large was working in landscaping and maintenance when we interviewed her. Although she had grown up in a household where both parents worked and made good incomes, her stepfather didn't feel he should be responsible for her or her brother and sister. Her mother worked full time as a nurse and also encouraged the children to work in order to have their own money.

Dishes was mine. We cleaned because Mother worked. We helped out with the housework. You see, when she married my stepfather there was this big hullabaloo. He's supposed to have told her the first two months they were married that he wasn't going to support another guy's kids, and that's why she continued to work after she married him. But that's neither here nor there and I'm not really interested in it, you know, but that's why she said she worked after she married him. I don't care, we grew up anyway, no matter who supported us. . . .

When I was nine I had a paper route. We all had paper routes, when we wanted them. I think my sister was about eleven and then I got in on the act. I carried papers for the Rocky Mountain *Post* and I carried papers for the small town weekly—and I got bit twice by dogs. And I fell off the monkey bars and broke my arm, and that's why I gave up my route. But then when I was fourteen, my mother sent me off to a summer resort and I lived up there the entire summer and I thought, wow—my own boss. I was a dishwasher . . . what else. I had a lot of experience at home, so why not turn it into money.

Ynez described herself as an average student in high school, but there are indications that she was more independent than most girls. She had numerous jobs throughout high school and used much of her savings to help her brother's efforts as an amateur competitive athlete. She left home before finishing high school and became totally independent at about age seventeen.

I did good until my senior year and about this time my mother and stepfather had divorced and I was kind of at loose ends and didn't really know what was happening. It really bothered me for a long time that they got divorced. It really upset me, you know. I expected them to get a divorce, but it did bother me now that I think back on it, it really shook me up. And I kind of just flew off the handle and quit school and ran off. And ah. . . . I was seventeen —I always think of being sixteen because it was right before my seventeenth birthday, but when I actually left I was only seventeen when I left. And my mother—I wrote to her a week later and told her I was in California, and I've never gone back.

Ardath Hoover, the gas company repairperson, was typical of many of the successful nontraditional women we met. She had to assume a lot of household responsibility at a very early age and also had an unusually open and emotionally demanding relationship with her mother.

My mother was divorced and her first husband, my father, left when I was a baby. I never knew him, but it doesn't matter. My sister was very alienated. My brother was always loved and coddled by my mother. I was the favorite. I was my mother's companion, I'm the favorite of my grandmother and was of my uncle. I grew up in a very loving atmosphere, but my mother is very emotional. If she had a hard time, she'd take it out on me.

From age eleven to sixteen, I was mother to the family and she was father, going to school and working. She worked at various sundry jobs, temporary work. Clerical type of work. She really wanted to be a psychiatric social worker. We didn't have much money, but I never really thought about it. There's that old saying that you're only poor in your head, and I don't think we felt that way. I was given lots to do. For an example, when I was about eleven, I was given an amount of money that I was to take out and spend for food. I was in charge of the kitchen, the cooking, the shopping—sort of overseeing the house. My sister was in charge of the living room, my brother was in charge of absolutely nothing. Everything for Mother was her work and going to school.

An unusually large number of the women we interviewed had some sort of early family experience requiring that they grow up a little sooner than their peers—that they take a larger share of financial or emotional responsibility in the family. For a number of the women, especially some of those from more "middle-class" and "better-educated" family backgrounds, independence was usually required because of a financial or personal crisis such as parental divorce or alcoholism. Sandy Harold is a successful auto mechanic who never thought of herself as anything but upper-middle-class while growing up and who, while at a university, identified with many of the issues middle-class youth were concerned with in the sixties. Nonetheless, the discrepancy between her father's pretenses and actual financial status, and his growing problem with alcoholism while she was growing up, instilled in her a sense that she was different than most other girls and that she would ultimately have to take care of herself. She described her family life in this way:

There was a lot of financial strain; I come from a real . . . lily-white upper-middle-class eastern suburb and . . . we lived there because my father was on that kind of a trip. Like he grew up in a moneyed family and went to Exeter and Harvard and had this idea of . . . the address and the house that you had to live in although he never made the bucks to back it up. He had to have this to show, right? . . . and . . . we all suffered as a result, trying to live up to this image. I think together my parents never made more than $10,000, and although that was more money then than it is now, it wasn't a lot. I don't know how they paid the taxes on the house or anything, 'cause it was a really nice house in a real old neighborhood, the big lawns 'n' stuff, and we were then wearin' Salvation Army clothes, a '61 Ford with all the Lincolns 'n' Mercedes, y'know, an' the doctors an' the lawyers, and my father was, I guess, basically a traveling salesman and my mother went to work as soon as we realized what a disaster . . . I guess when my brother started kindergarten, so I would have been eleven or twelve or something like that. We always did all our own housework, our laundry, our cooking. the dishes. My mother was a pretty much of a lousy housewife, I think she doesn't live up to those kinds a standards

. . . and both my parents were always in night school because they really believed in school as an improving on the job type situation, and so there wasn't a whole lot of, we didn't spend time together as a family. But we faked it a lot. . . . Uh, my father was an alcoholic. I don't know how long it was very serious, I was only aware of it when I was in high school. . . . I don't know how long it had been going on really bad or if that's when it started, y'know, really gettin' bad or whatever. He was out of work for three years and I didn't even know it, that's how little people really talked about things. It was more just the feeling, the atmosphere . . . nobody yelled . . . nobody got mad at each other in the house, nobody screamed or yelled, it was all very subdued and undercurrent right. Lotsa tension.

Sandy went on to describe her father:

My father was a salesman, a field representative for some chemical company that made up lacquers and sealers and paint and stuff like that, I guess they made a lot of things, that's all I remember. It was a pretty big firm at one point, I guess . . . covering a lot of the northeast part of the country. He had the New York area an' then the whole New England area but . . . it . . . went out of business, essentially. He . . . knew that was coming and stuff, so he started going back to school, but I didn't know it had happened until afterwards. . . . I guess from the time I was eleven till I was thirteen or something he wasn't working at all . . . and . . . that was about the same time my mother started working. During that time he became a teacher, a high school teacher, that was what he had been studying to do, an' he was real into it, he was really good, he taught, um, Spanish and French in high school. I remember he got his first teaching job when I was a sophomore in high school. He had to go all the way to New Hampshire 'cause he didn't have his Massachusetts license yet. He grossed that year forty-eight hundred dollars . . . which . . . I mean . . . I mean, I make more than that now, an' I sure don't have to support a family of six. It didn't go very far . . . during those times I know my grandmother, his mother, gave him money, and my mother was working, so it was pretty tight. For example . . . my sister and I made all our clothes in high school in an effort to keep up with all the matched skirt and sweater sets that everyone had. Our friends always went away to summer camp in the summer, went skiing in the winter, and to

Florida, and to the White Mountains in the summer. Shit, you know, we always had lots of friends, that wasn't the problem, there were some poorer people, people definitely poorer than us in the town, but socially, the people I hung out with were . . . all a whole lot better off, especially in the neighborhood right around us.

Sandy recalled her father's death as the most significant event in her life, not because of the crises it precipitated but because it *freed* the family, including Sandy, for the first time.

My father died . . . definitely did, that released us all to come to California. We had talked about it before that and it was always just a sort of a dream, but once . . . he was dead, there was . . . I mean, he was the big link to Boston, 'cause that's where his family was. My mother grew up in Ohio, and she wasn't particularly attached to New England winters. That released us . . . all to be able to make real plans.

In sharp contrast to the social and economic milieu in which Sandy grew up is the rural South and Midwest from which a number of the nontraditional women came. Edith Sayers, an extremely successful apprentice in the civilian military, is from such a background. She described her childhood thus:

I was born in Springfield, Ohio, and I lived there until I was two, then we moved to a very small town in Ohio and most of it, to me, seemed like everyone in this small town was my relative. And that's mainly where I grew up. My mother and father have been separated since I was two years old, and I lived with my mother's mother—my grandmother—and it seemed like all her brothers and sisters had sent their kids to their mother—I figure there were about twenty-six to thirty kids living with our grandmother, and as far as my personal family, there's three brothers and myself and I'm the youngest. We were poor—very poor—as to even today, I know outhouses are ruled out, but you know, some places they still have them, like my mother still has one. My dad worked at a steelcasting company, and as far as his income, I really don't know, because I was never really with him that much.
My mother had to work as a housekeeper, and in those days income was very low.

Sometimes I lived with my father, sometimes with my grand-parents, sometimes with my mother. It was a situation where I was rotated back and forth, but not really living with either one of my parents, so I was really fouled up.

I always had food to eat and things like that, but I wanted us to have a nice house like everyone else. I mean, 'cause there was—when I finally did live with my mother, it was a three-room house—one bedroom, a kitchen, and a living room—and we slept on the floor or wherever we could find a place to sleep.

Edith was not at all active in high school, had only a few close friends, and spent most of her time away from school working. When asked how important it was for her to be popular in high school, she responded this way:

To be honest, not at all. Because when I was working my way through high school, because like I said—we were very poor—and my mother was working like a slave, making eight dollars a day—you know; and when I turned sixteen I was determined to get a job, so I got a job in a restaurant washing dishes and I worked my way up to cooking on the grill, so that was—for me to support myself and buy my clothes and food, buy my books, so I really didn't get that involved with a lot of people. Go to school and work, that was it.

Edith's experiences are not that dissimilar from those of Jan Spencer, the successful mechanic introduced in the previous chapter. Having no hopes of going to college, Edith enlisted in the Air Force and, after her tour of duty, began the apprenticeship she was in when we met her. She was determined to be successful, particularly financially, and saw herself as rising above her family roots, even though she expressed affection for her mother and periodically visits Ohio.

Some of the women interviewed grew up in families where they were expected to work not only for their own needs, such as clothes and books, but in order to make a financial contribution to the family. Dolores Blanca is one such example. Her parents divorced when she was eight and her mother worked to support Dolores, her brother, and her sister. She described her background this way:

I was the oldest of three children. There were always people in my house. I had an aunt and occasionally up to three cousins and there was a steady flow of relatives coming in and out throughout my growing years. We were not very well off. Very poor. My father was at one time a foreman in construction. I don't know what his income was at that time, but he became an alcoholic, so he just started doing odd jobs, moving all over the place and not ever having a steady income or anything. My mother was a cook for a Mexican restaurant for a lot of years, and then she became a window cleaner in construction and she was making $5.00 an hour way back when, when minimum wages were $1.35 an hour. She did okay, but it was seasonal. We were about the poorest people in our neighborhood. All the time there were things I wanted but couldn't afford. I always wanted to have clothes and, you know, be able to participate in all the social events, but I couldn't because I couldn't afford it.

Dolores went on to describe the kinds of responsibilities she had while growing up.

We had a—to work around the house, clean the windows, clean our rooms, do the dishes, and occasionally out in the garden and the lawn. And there was washing and ironing, you know, all the household chores, and I think I got a greater part of them because I was older. And my brother and sister, they had their chores to do, my mother wasn't as demanding because they were younger. When I was twelve years I started baby-sitting. By the time I was about fourteen there was a laundromat next door and I used to go over there and help them fold clothes and they'd pay me for that also. So I'd bring the money home. But it wasn't mine. I'd have to give it to my mother. It was money for the family.

I did pretty good in school. I had straight A's all the way up to the ninth grade and then I went downhill—all the way down; I quit school in the tenth grade—no, it was in my junior year. We had financial difficulties, plus we moved from Chula Vista to San Diego. It was a rough school, and I didn't want to go.

By the time we met Dolores she was in training as an engineering technician doing precision work calibrating such things as thermometers, weights, and measures in an upward-mobility program through the civil service.

The women just described developed a sense of independence and responsibility because of the requirements of family circumstances. Many left home as early as possible and became self-sufficient in reaction to the burden of their family responsibilities. We also interviewed a number of women with more positive family experiences who developed a sense of personal independence because their parents deliberately gave them opportunities to be self-determining and responsible. Jane Kurtz, a small-appliance repairperson interviewed in Southern California is a good example of this kind of childhood. Her father was a successful engineer in the Midwest and her mother a homemaker, but they nonetheless encouraged her to make her own money and to follow her entrepreneurial interests.

I usually did the cooking or the baking and I usually worked a lot outside. In the summertime we'd take care of the land and go fishing, we lived on a lake, we'd go fishing and bring back fish, and as a kid, we used to sell fish to the fishermen and make some coin money. In the winter time, we'd build icehouses and rent the icehouses to the fishermen to make coin money. So we always had a few coins in our pocket. Then as we grew up, we had go-carts that we needed gasoline for, so instead of hitting up our parents all the time, we'd work out things that we could bring in more money on. We used to catch turtles and sell them to restaurants, different things. We used to trap minks and sell the skins; just whatever we needed, if we needed money, we'd go work for it. I felt really independent.

I think I did because my folks, when we'd sit down to the dinner table, would say, where'd you get the money for that? and I'd say, Oh, I did this and this and this and I got enough money and I saved it up and went out and bought it, and then they'd say, But we told you you couldn't have that, and I'd say, Well, I thought that was a part of life, if you wanted something you went out and worked for it, and they'd turn around and look at each other and not know what to say, so finally rather than seeing me groping and out earning money trying to get the things I wanted, my dad started me in the

direction of a small business of my own. I call it a junior laundromat because he went and bought me a couple of washers at Sears on
credit, and I remember the hassle, because I was fifteen years old
and I wanted it in my name and I was a minor and they wouldn't
put in my name, and I asked them if they'd put it in my name
with my dad as co-signer and they said they still wouldn't do it.
They wanted to put it in his name in the first place but I'd
be stuck with the payments, and I didn't like that arrangement
at all. But that's how I got started. And from a couple of machines in an apartment—and then I got another apartment and put
a couple more in there—by the time I ended up I had over four
hundred machines scattered all throughout the Twin Cities. They
were in the basements of apartment houses and they would have
coin-operated things on them. I'd take care of them. I made quite a
profit for a kid, too; I had about $300 a month in coin money,
which I thought was quite a bit when I was fifteen years old. Then I
turned around and sold them all and got one laundromat that was
located close to us, and then from that, I sold that to my brothers
and went to college and they got their coin money off of that, so it
started all of us. We didn't have to ask our parents when we wanted
something or for lunch money, gasoline, or whatever—we were
rather fortunate in that way, when we were old enough to drive we
had a car available that we could drive and go places, and it gave
our folks time off because they didn't have to take us to the show or
the football game or the dance or whatever.

May Rogers, the apprentice electronics mechanic, is another
example of a woman from a happy family background who
recalled many opportunities to be self-sufficient and take responsibility:

Let me tell you about one experience I had—I had an older brother
and an older sister, I was the baby of my parents' children. I was
always getting practically everything I asked for within reason, and
one day I asked my father for something—my brother and sister
had put me up to asking for something—and he said, because they
figured I would get it because I was the baby, and he said, "You
know, it really hurts me when you ask me for things that I honestly
cannot give you." And I thought, "It really does," so I decided
from that day on, unless I really needed something I didn't ask because I knew how hard he worked for what little we had. I've al-

ways liked the outdoors, the work outdoors and stuff, and after my dad retired, I did a lot of the work out in the fields and with the cattle and stuff with my dad, so I felt real close to him. My family was strictly country. We were happy—my mother was, sometimes I felt she nagged a lot with my dad, I didn't know how he stood it, he was a very patient man. I don't remember him in my life saying anything against anyone—you know, derogatory remarks in any way, you know, and he put up with a lot. And he was awful patient with us and her. But I thought, compared to some friends of mine, I felt that we had a really satisfactory home life, it was comfortable and we like each other.

May went on to describe the kinds of responsibilities she had while growing up.

Again, the South—we were raised, my mother didn't believe and still does not believe that boys are to do things in the home, so my brother was given the jobs of mowing the yard and things like this, so he milked the cows until I got old enough, then I had to milk the cows, but we got up early, my sister's duties and mine kind of rotated until she decided she couldn't milk the cows anymore. But it was get up early and help with breakfast, and do all the milking and clean—make the beds, and I don't mean like we do today, it was take each person's off separately, turn the mattress, beat it, and 'bout that time Mother would walk in and say, "You didn't make it, you spreaded it," and it'd all come off and you'd do it all over again. So my sister would do the making of the beds and stuff one day while I helped in the kitchen. I wondered when I was a kid what my mother did all day because I felt everything was done, but I can remember her calling me back—we walked to school—and she would call me when I was a half a mile from home and go back and hang up my pajamas or something. She was kind of fanatic about the house, she expected it to be clean and you didn't touch the beds after you got up—sit on them or lay on them, and you didn't lay on the couch, you sat, ladylike, on the couch. But she's relaxed a little now, the years have passed.

Mother was sick a lot, she'd had so much surgery up until I was finished high school—she seemed like every couple of years, she was in the hospital for surgery, so we had to learn to cook and I can remember making biscuits and I had to stand on a chair to do it. And washing dishes, or these old comfort stoves, you know. I

earned—most of my clothes—well, I bought a sewing machine off
of money I made selling milk and butter because my father let me
keep the money because I milked the cows, even though he paid for
the feed and everything, I could keep the money. So I bought a
sewing machine and I also got paid for the A's and B's that I made,
so I got a piano that way. Then from my uncle—he had a lot of
cage layer hens, so my father got three to four hundred to supple-
ment the income, and so my cousin would swap the sacks of the
chicken feed back and forth, and that was the clothes I wore
through high school and college and I could, of course, I never had
to iron clothes or anything like that, my mother was very good at
that, so she would starch those skirts so they would practically
stand out by themselves. When I got up in my teens I was close to
my dad. He started me out—this was after he retired, and he
started enlarging the cattle, and he leased more land, he gave me
these—I had to keep up the bookkeeping kind of things and taxes
and things like this, and he gave me a lot of responsibility to do,
and I learned a lot from him. And I was aware then that this was a
possibility—you never know when you're going to have to go to
work and have to take care of yourself. And I think this experience
is what gave me a lot of courage that I had—a little more
confidence that I had in myself.

It is clear from these examples that many of the women
pioneering in nontraditional jobs had already begun to learn at
an early age how to take care of themselves, how to take responsibility for others, and in a number of instances learned out
of necessity that "you better know how to take care of yourself
because you can't count on anyone else to do it." That may
seem like a rather hard lesson or bitter pill for a growing girl to
swallow, but with very few exceptions the women recalled their
childhoods in positive terms. This is perhaps because although
many of them recalled "hard times" during childhood, most of
them had a strong family context, whether it was the nuclear
family, an extended kin network, or the presence of a strong
and hardworking mother. They also had a sense of progress, of
things having gotten better. Virtually none of the nontraditional
women felt victimized, abandoned, or abused in their childhoods despite the presence of divorce and alcoholism in some

instances, or employment instability and poverty in other instances. Nonetheless there were some instances of this, especially among women we interviewed who were pursuing more traditional jobs.

HARD-LIVING FAMILY CONTEXTS

If one looks at only superficial characteristics, the family contexts of the traditional and nontraditional women we studied do not seem that different. Close to half of each group came from families with more than four children. The family incomes of the two groups were similar, with the exception of a slightly larger number of managerial and professional fathers in the nontraditional group. About 20 percent of each group grew up in female-headed households. However, nearly half of the traditional women had lived through a parental divorce, separation, or abandonment, with a number of them having been raised entirely by aunts or grandparents, two in foster homes, and two actually having married by age fourteen. This contrasted with a divorce or separation rate of about 25 percent among the parents of the nontraditional group, which in practically every case resulted in either a second marriage for the mother or a securely employed working mother. Even though many of the nontraditional women reported difficult periods in their childhoods or being poor, it was clear that most of them had a sense of stability and continuity with at least one parent. Many had a strong mother, and for most their father or stepfather was an accepted presence in the home. The experiences of the traditional women parallel closely those reported by researchers such as Lilian Rubin, Joseph Howell, and Jackie Wiseman, in which children grow up watching poor and working-class parents being victimized by uncertain economic circumstances and mothers who were often in oppressive relationships with men.[1] Children growing up in such contexts are less likely to be optimistic about their capacity to affect the environment positively or to take control of their own lives, and therefore they may be less likely to take risks. Such children also have fewer "cushions" in terms of family-based emotional or financial resources. Thus they may be reluctant to explore avenues with uncertain outcomes: better to pursue the more certain routes. Such women often remain dependent on men, even unstable men, and if they need a job and money, unskilled jobs or fields such as cosmetology or electronics assembly are more secure for a woman than plumbing or welding. Even if she makes less money and has less long-term security and benefits, at least she can take care of her short-term needs.

It is important at this juncture to meet some of the women who came from these genuinely "hard-living" backgrounds. The contrast between this type of childhood and the childhoods of the nontraditional women, particularly the successful ones, suggests that for a person to develop a positive, risk-taking capacity, opportunities for independence in childhood need to be surrounded by certain fundamental security-giving, positive experiences. Just to be set loose in childhood, to be battered about, can have very negative consequences. We interviewed a number of women in the first year who came from "hard-living" backgrounds. Most of them were in traditional jobs when we met them, and virtually all of them were unlocatable when we went back for second- and third-year interviews.

Karen Collier has lived a particularly troubled life, beginning with an early childhood of moving back and forth between her mother's and grandmother's houses, then being married off by her drunken mother at age fourteen, and having three unsuccessful marriages, a nervous breakdown, and very troubled children of her own. Karen had been working at her first nontraditional job, in a steel mill, for only a few weeks when we first met her. We quickly lost contact with her. Her troubled life suggested she would have difficulty lasting in the equal-opportunity slot she had. As best we can assess, she lasted only a few months. Karen was born and raised in California and lived in a number of small towns until she was fourteen, when her mother married her off. Karen described her growing up in the following ways:

I come from a very . . . neurotic kind of sick family, my mother was alcoholic. I don't think she was when she was younger, but by the time I was fourteen I knew she was and . . . my grandfather was, my stepfather was, my grandmother was not . . . she was very rigid . . . religious, oh, hypocritical religion . . . not really a Christian in that sense. My grandfather drank . . . he wasn't a continuous alcoholic, he was like more like, y'know, binges for him. I have one sister sixteen months younger than me and . . . let's see, I had an older sister, she was almost fifteen years older than I was, and there was two brothers in between there, one I've never seen and one who'd been in troubles . . . I guess he ran away from home when he was eleven. It's really a weird story. He was in and out of jails and mental institutions biggest part of his life. We were rather poor. Sometimes, sometimes my mother would buy a little café of some sort and we'd seem to have a better existence, but . . . we lived . . . I lived with no supervision after I was eight years old. Earlier I lived with my grandparents a lot. My mother married when I was about six years old, and then there was a period of about two years there where I was with my mother for a few months and . . . then . . . I don't exactly know why, maybe her financial situation, I moved back with my grandparents. Maybe she was unable to take care of us, she was working . . . my stepfather was working. I really don't know. . . . I know I spent the biggest part of my childhood thinking . . . you know, just waiting . . . to be with my mother, an' then . . . when I'd get with her, it was nothing—you know . . . there was no warmth, nothing. My father . . . I think I remember him up till the time I was about two years old, and . . . I think he just didn't, I know he farmed and I know he did mining and I don't know what else.

I think he got in trouble with the law and split and I haven't seen him since. My mother, she's done many, many things, she's worked in a circus riding on top of an elephant, she's been a nightclub entertainer, she was also a restaurant owner, a café . . . little café, um . . . she's been a secretary. . . .

I think she was a cocktail waitress at the time I moved back in with her.

Karen went on to describe how she moved around a lot when she went to live with her mother and stepfather, who were both alcoholics. She did poorly in school and was frequently truant, and because she physically matured at an early age, she was able to be around adults a lot and not be taken for a child. She reported that by age twelve she was dressing up in high heels and going to bars with her parents and had a lot of older men paying attention to her. She described her early marriage:

The man I married when I was fourteen . . . I met at my mother's restaurant. He and a friend were over from . . . Selma vacationing for a couple of weeks or picking oranges or something, I don't really remember now, but it wasn't really clear to me, why they were there. They hung around the restaurant a lot, and uh . . . he and my mother were drinking one night, there in the restaurant, and I think he probably wanted to . . . go to bed with me and he said something to her after he'd had many, many drinks, I oughtta marry your daughter, probably thinking she'd let me go out on a date with him. He didn't know, he hadn't even explored whether I would be allowed to go out, then she said something like, oh, I wish you would, then I could get a decent waitress, 'cause I was sorta fooling around in there, by one o'clock that morning I was married to him. In those days you could go and get a . . . justice of the peace up outa bed, an' he'd issue a license to you and you could get married. I didn't really have any feelings about it at all. My mother asked me on the way, you know, even in her drinking, she, she said are you sure this is what you wanna do, which was a question she never asked me in my life, and my only answer was, yeah—you know, I didn't know, and . . . the worst part of it was the next morning was . . . the poor man woke up and we were in a hotel room and he didn't remember . . . getting married, he was that drunk. . . . He didn't remember why I was . . . he didn't know why I was there. He was really kind of scared, I think. . . . Well, his reaction was that, I mean, he, he didn't say too much. He took me back to Selma with him and . . . it was a very strange scene. First place I think I lied to him. He thought I was older than I was . . . then he kept . . . expecting me to behave at the age I told him I was, an' I didn't want to. He had some . . . young relatives that'd play softball er something or other, and I wanted to play with them and I wanted to wear shorts and I wasn't allowed to wear shorts 'n',

y'know, it was really strange. Since I was so passive I . . . tended
to kind of—passive-aggressive is more accurate. . . . I would kinda
sabotage something . . . um . . . there was a lot of things I
resented but didn't have the guts to talk about or say anything
about, and . . . I really . . . was kind of trapped in the situation
too: even when I really wanted out, the only place to go was home
. . . which I did when I was pregnant with my . . . first child, and
I stayed there until the child was two months old, and then I . . .
reconciled with him, and separated again and went back and . . .
had another child and, by the time that child was one year old, I
wanted outa there. I was eighteen then, and that's kinda the age
when, when a girl is wanting some independence and wanting to
leave family or . . . mother and father, and this man was sort of,
y'know, he was a parent to me . . . he never treated me like an
equal, I was . . . a child . . . or the wife, which is kind of the way
some men treat you.

There was one . . . one point, I grew to love him very much, but
he also drank a lot and I was left alone a lot. He'd go with the boys
and drink, but I was always left behind. That was part of the reason
I left him, was the biggest reason, the only reason, 'cause he'd been
good to me, I would have done anything for him—but in the end,
that's why I left him, because I was so unhappy about being . . .
left alone, and all I could think of was a life of . . . havin' some
fun.

These comments reveal only a few details of Karon's early
life, but it is nonetheless clear that her early experiences and
relationships with her mother and stepfather differ significantly
from those of the successful pioneers.

Another dramatic contrast is Anita Locke, a successful cosmetologist who was retraining to be an instructor of cosmetology when we first interviewed her. Anita was in her middle forties, had been married five times, and with the exception
of her skills as a cosmetologist had had a very erratic adult life.
Her childhood was no less erratic.

When I was eight years old, my mother died, and I was farmed out
. . . the orphanages 'n' foster homes 'n' stuff. My father remarried,
he remarried when I was about nine years old, but I . . . didn't live

at home. I lived in foster homes 'n' convents 'n' orphanages. When I was twelve years old, I wasn't adopted but this foster family took me in and that's when I started working, when I was twelve years old. I can remember stripping cotton when I was five years old. My mother had tuberculosis, and she was in a sanitarium . . . when I was five, and so we were farmed out. Those days they farmed kids out, you know. My father lived in a big midwest city, which was a great distance from the small town where we lived, at that time and we seen him maybe once a month or somethin'. . . . I had a brother and sister and we were just farmed out to different people. But the last foster home before my mother died that I was in, I was there for three years, it was a farm an' it was someplace around Madison, I don't know where, and it was a farm and we were put to work. . . . I was put to work, strippin' tobacco in the fields an' we were there fer three years and then my mother died. Then my father took us to the big city . . . but I can't really remember too much about that part of my childhood other than . . . being . . . out in other foster homes, back to the orphanage, in foster homes, back to the orphanage. Now whether it was because my father didn't pay fer us or what, I really don't remember too much about that other than being moved around a lot to different homes and back to the orphanage. Then, when my father had remarried when I was twelve years old, I lived at home one period there when I worked in a curtain factory. It was a laundry where they had lace curtains, and because my hands were so small, and they had nails, and they had to be stretched on this frame an' we had to put the edges of the curtains on these nails, because I was little and had tiny hands, I could put these curtains, I could stretch those curtains on the frame. That was my first job that I ever got paid for, I can't even tell you how much I made—it was a few dollars a week, but I had to turn over to my stepmother and father, then. I lived with them only for a very short period. It wasn't even a year, just a matter of months. . . . Then I was taken in by a Jewish family, two Jewish families, one I didn't stay very long and I can't remember, and the second one I stayed with till I was sixteen and I married. The thing that sticks most in my mind is I can't ever remember a time when I wasn't hungry or cold and I can't ever remember a time when I felt loved. I used to . . . go to school and see other kids' parents come to school to pick them up, or the mother, and I can remember thinking, I wonder what it would be like to have 'em, and I'd pretend

. . . my mother's name was Barbara, I knew that, and uh . . . I'd pretend that Barbara Stanwyck was my mother 'n' Robert Taylor was my father or something. But I think that, mostly, I wondered what it would be like to be a part of a family . . . to have a parent and somebody that loved ya like the other kids' parents loved, but mostly, it's being hungry . . . I was never hungrier, never, never seemed warm, I've never had enough clothes to be warm.

The only pleasant childhood memories Anita shared with us were of the last foster family she lived with until going out into the world alone at age sixteen.

No, the last Jewish family I lived with was wonderful to me, they treated me like one of the family. I had my own room and my responsibility was taking care of a little boy that they had. They had maids to do the housework and stuff. The only time I had to do anything around the house is on holiday or when they had company, to help serve, like the dinners an' stuff. No, they treated me just like one a the family, they were wonderful people and, uh, I stayed with them . . . I was with them a coupla years. . . . I found the job in a newspaper or some way . . . more or less I was just a nursemaid for their little boy—little child, an' I loved him very much and I . . . they treated me just beautiful, she bought me clothes, you know, 'n' . . . er, gave me clothes. For the first time in my life I had nice clothes and I always had plenty to eat there . . . but, before that, so much of it is blacked out in my memory I don't know, I . . . can't really . . . like I say, all you remember is the bad things . . . there weren't any good things that I can remember.

Anita was an average student in high school and was quite popular. She was a cheerleader and belonged to clubs. She was very concerned about her personal appearance and developed an interest in becoming a beauty operator early in her teens.

This friend of this Jewish family that I lived with had a beauty shop and I would go there after school and on Saturday. I'd wash combs and brushes and take out rollers. I always wanted to be a beauty operator, and the only thing that I wanted was to get outa high school to go to beauty school, so I uh . . . I got married before I did that, an' then I couldn't afford to go to beauty school . . . until, uh . . . I went to work, you know, later on. . . . Let's see, but I always worked around, I always tried to get a beauty, a job . . . like I'd get a dollar a day for cleaning brushes, cleaning up the beauty shop, or something like that.

At the time we met Anita she felt her life was finally falling into place. Her children were grown and gone, she had been married to her fifth husband quite happily for over a year and she was working to satisfy one of her biggest, as yet unrealized, lifelong dreams: to own her own home.

A final example of "hard living" is a woman who, like María Hernández (described in the first chapter), came to the United States from Mexico in her preteens because her parents felt there would be more opportunities for her here. The only child of a Mexico City baker, Irene Montilla was sent to the United States at age nine to live with her aunt and uncle and their children. Her uncle was a warehouseman and her aunt a cleaning woman. They were not impoverished, but there were five children to feed and care for. Irene became a burden to her American family, so they married her off at age twelve.

It was kind of hard because first of all I had to come here and I didn't want to be away from my mother, you know, and my mother thought it was best for me to come right now. But things didn't turn out the way they planned—my mother, she wanted me to study English and be something, but it didn't turn out to be that way. I can't blame my mother for everything that happened—she tried her best, but see, I came to live with my aunt and all the promises they made and everything, they didn't keep. So then my aunt wanted to be me in this school where I could pay for my things and go to school, but they said I was too young to do that, you know. So my aunt had to arrange with this man in Tijuana to marry me. And they would fix papers for him, so he married me. So I was about eleven or twelve years old. And they couldn't do anything over here because she gone to Tijuana. It was a terrible experience when I married. My father had to sign for me, I was so young, to get divorced when I was fifteen. And I had three kids already. When I got divorced I didn't know where to go, so we moved in with my parents. I had a hard time because I wanted to go to school and I wanted to learn something, you know, and get ahead because I knew

I had the kids and even if you knew how to speak English and Spanish, it wasn't enough. You had to go to school, but I just didn't know where to turn to. My father liked this one guy, he was an older guy. I didn't like him that much, but I thought he would be a good father for the kids and my father liked him, so I married him. And it ended in another divorce. And I had two more kids, so that makes it very hard. So now I've been by myself for eight years.

At a time when most girls were still in high school and just dating, Irene, at age fifteen, was back home with her parents, with three small children of her own. By her twenties she had five children, no high school education, and a second divorce. She had spent the last eight years working on and off in essentially unskilled jobs.

When we interviewed her, she was training in electronics assembly, but she left that job for reasons we don't know. She has all the problems of illness, no transportation, and dependent children. In addition, even though three of her children are now in their late teens, they make no contribution to family maintenance and in fact are a source of problems for her. The older boy never finished high school, is on probation, and is actively discouraging his younger siblings from being "straight." Her other children still have "half a chance" of finishing school.

These three examples of "hard living" have one thing in common: parents or a parent who couldn't handle the relationship with their child and left her in a situation where she felt vulnerable and/or abandoned. What I have tried to suggest in the earlier discussion of the backgrounds of successful pioneers is that, even though they experienced "hard times," which forced them to see the world in complicated terms, something kept them from developing a sense of total vulnerability or helplessness in the face of circumstances over which they, as children, had no control. Most often, that something was a mother.

STRONG MOTHERS AND POSITIVE FEMALE ROLE MODELS

Even for women who had relatively uncomplicated childhoods, the presence of a strong mother was a recurrent theme. Close to half of the nontraditional respondents spontaneously made reference to the importance of their mother as a source of early family stability, as a source of encouragement and direction, and as an actual model for adult roles. Once again, the comments of the women themselves make the point best. For example, one woman who was in a skills development program while holding a job as a filer and polisher in a laboratory producing artificial heart valves described her mother in the context of talking about how much money her family had while she was growing up.

When we were growing up, I know that we had very little money because we lived mainly on bread, cereal, beans, potatoes. We lived in a tent, a condemned building. Mother was talking about one place we lived where a baby was eaten by the rats [when] a woman laid her baby down to go wash some clothes. When I was about five years old and we were in the South, we were living in an old house that had a steam pipe running up and Mother was fixing cinnamon toast and a rat about the size of a cat came up and ran off with a piece of it. So I can understand a lot of the situation of blacks and their attitudes because I've been there. I can understand when people say, well, they just don't care. That's an easy situation to be when you don't have the money to live like normal, civilized people. You get an attitude of not really caring, I guess. But my mother made very little, she worked two jobs, sometimes three, she had—we had to raise ourselves most of the time. Some of the time, before we started schools, we lived with a woman at a place, my sister and I, while Mother was working two or three jobs. It was very difficult for a woman who was as intelligent as my mother was, for most women who had husbands to understand or care because she didn't have a husband, they were afraid she would try to take theirs or something, while the husbands were always afraid because she always outdid everybody else, I mean, if there was a mechanic, she could outdo anything he could do. She was a very brilliant-type person, and I look at some of the places we lived and all, and even though we never had much, we had something that many people didn't have, we had a mother who really cared. I mean, I look for instance at my husband's mother, aristocratic Louisiana family, never showed any affection, warmth, friendliness, the companionship that my mother had with us. I always felt very fortunate in that. I know that sometimes she went without anything just to give us what she could, and that wasn't always a lot.

This sentiment was echoed again and again—"We may have been poor, but Mother really loved us and worked hard for us." A successful twenty-six-year-old welder stated it this way:

Well, this is sort of a personal experience, but my mother sort of took over when my father became ill, and became head of the family, and due to that she was very important and it brought us all very close together, 'cause those were hard times for our family. So she was very important in a very important emotional way. And she's a very strong woman. She was a secretary herself, and made it very clear that I should take shorthand and typing in high school. And since I didn't express an interest in anything in particular, I went along with that program. Oh, I took all those, and became a secretary. So she did have a lot of influence over that.

Hardworking mothers who were able to hold the family together financially were remembered by some of our respondents as hard-headed and domineering. Nonetheless, according to these women, their mothers had the strength and energy to keep everything from falling apart without a man in the house. Ardath Hoover, who in previously quoted passages talked about the loving environment of her family despite their many hard times, had a very close relationship with her mother and still does. She perceives her mother as willful and headstrong.

My mother is very intelligent and very headstrong woman. I come from a long line of loner women, no men, you know, obscure. She was very much in love with her brother, who committed suicide when I was fourteen, and all kinds of very strange male hang-ups. My grandfather is a woman chaser and that brought all kinds of weird trips on her. My mother is large. Right now she is a deputy labor commissioner in a major city. She's very headstrong. My mother has been pushing or trying to push me into these heavy state programs, apprenticeship programs. I went to the Women's Storefront because a friend of my mother's works in the apprenticeship areas for the state of California and he said to go see them.

Polly Nichols, the technician who grew up with four brothers and sisters, shared these observations about her strong mother:

I'm the youngest of five, four girls and one boy. As far as I can remember, my mother was divorced from my father when I was about four. I was really close with my brother and had a pretty close relationship with the sister next to me. Typically in our family, the females are very strong and the males aren't as strong. My father was not an emotionally strong person; he's also bisexual. And my brother is bisexual too, by the way. My mother is a very strong person, she's more domineering than she is strong actually. She's never had a long, successful relationship with a male and I think that's due to her need to be domineering. My mother had a hard time handling five children. Then my other older sister was in trouble all the time and in juvenile hall a lot, so the family situation was very unstable. Eventually, Mother became a probation officer and became successful and made more and more money. Life started getting better when I was about eight. She climbed up through the time I was twelve or thirteen. She was pretty much at the top by the time I was in high school.

Even women from families with more stable marriages or financial resources recalled strong mothers. A welder in Northern California stated:

I think I have always felt women could do almost anything. My mother is like the head of the household. My father is there and he worked every day, and did construction work, but she . . . you know, like the raising of us and the discipline—and he just, well, if he had something to say about something, well, there was no question asked, but ah, she always was a strong, you know, image and was, "you think you can do it, give it a try," you know, whatever, you know, there's nothing there that really a woman can't do. So I think that I got a lot from her, 'cause she's into everything.

An aircraft electrician whose mother has always worked described her feelings this way:

I feel like I could do most anything. Maybe it's been that my mother's always worked, but she's been in traditionally a woman's job except for the last year and she went into what is called a man's job. Ah—well, she's working in hearing aid dispenser and, ah, there were no women in it—for Sears. She works for Sears and they picked her up to do that. I don't know, I guess ever since I was little and had a paper route with my brother I figured I can do anything.

Jan Spencer, the chief mechanic, cited her father's technical skills as important to her development, but went on to talk about older nontraditional women in her community.

I always knew it was possible 'cause there were women around me who had done such things. You know, I was surrounded by, like, independent women when I was a youngster. There was a woman in my hometown who during World War II had been the president of the auto mechanics union—a friend of my folks—and um, other women in my family have been independent in different sorts of ways . . . in more traditional ways but very strong and, ah, just I've always had the impression that if you want something you go after it, you work and you get it, you know, you don't take no for an answer . . . you just do it till it's done and then you're largely responsible for your own reality—whatever it is. And that's what I wanted and so I went after it.

Sandy Harold, the auto mechanic whose well-educated father died of alcoholism in her early teens, described her relationship with her mother in a way that captures the essence of the relations a large number of the pioneers had with their mothers: one of independence backed by mutual trust and support.

Oh, I think I made decisions for myself as far as whatever choices were offered to me. My parents really made a point, especially my mother, once she really felt like she was in control after my father gave up hope or . . . whatever . . . she made a point of not making decisions for us, and . . . almost forcing us into places where we'd *have* to make decisions. They never influenced our choices of

friends or the clothes we wore or whatever we did with our time. I
went through a battle of wills with my mother about giving me a
curfew and I won and she never gave me a curfew and I never
stayed out late. We developed a sort of a trust that way, and that
was what she wanted. I always felt real good about it, and when I
made mistakes, she'd still stick by me. Like one time I stole her car
before I got my driver's license and was in a wreck. She kept it
from my father and we did all the insurance forms together and
stuff and that was . . . dynamite, then. She was right there. A couple of things like that, you know, where . . . even when I used my
own judgment and I fucked up . . . it was still me. I think that was
important.

She went on to share another observation about her mother.

I remember my grandmother saying to me once not to raise my
voice, it wasn't what young ladies did, right, or something like that.
But, ah, my mother screamed, she displayed her emotions, she
slapped us and we slapped her back and we screamed at each other
but that . . . was sort of few and far between. She was a really
strong woman, she was a big influence in my life. She was gonna
. . . when she was growing up she wanted to be a doctor herself
and she couldn't, the only medical school that . . . she could afford
to go to she couldn't get into because some doctor on the panel that
let people get in didn't like her . . . I dunno what it was. She made
it seem like it was grossly unfair. She couldn't get in, and she became a lab technician and she was really good and . . . she was
about to sign up to go to Czechoslovakia under the Marshal Plan
when she met my father and got married. She was twenty-seven
then and . . . I mean now . . . that's pretty, that was over the hill
during the war era, right. I guess she bowed under pressure from
my grandmother, her mother. I don't know how she stood it. I always admired that, that . . . kind of a determination to do something with herself . . . she talked about it a lot.

These comments suggest that some pioneer women had not
only strong mothers, but mothers whom they perceived as having their own needs for achievement, as well as the money they
earned. A machinist in her early fifties stated it this way:

I had a complete attitude of complete equality between men and
women. Part of the reason was because my mother and father

agreed that men and women were intellectually equal, which was pretty progressive for that day and for the circles that they were in. My mother stayed home, and my best girl friend, her mother worked and her father stayed home. I'm not sure exactly why that was, but anyway I grew up with the attitude that people chose what they wanted to do. What I thought when I was a kid was that I wanted to teach people that they could both work and both share the housework. Then I grew up and had a good many shocks, you know.

A successful plumber shared this observation with us:

My mother did encourage us to be independent. I think she always felt that she got burned in her growing up. She wanted to make sure—she always pushed us, like I want you to get a college education because I don't want you to support some guy through college and then when he finishes he leaves you for some college-educated girl. She had some friends that that happened to. She had a couple years of junior college and always felt somehow inferior to my father. It wasn't anything that he put on us, it was her trip. He had a master's degree in math. She would encourage us to make our own decisions from an early age.

References to mothers were recurrent throughout the various interviews, particularly with regard to their significance in the development of independence and self-confidence. The majority of the pioneer women grew up in families in which there was a strong female image. This may be an essential ingredient in the development of a strong self-image for an adult woman. These comments on female images are in no way meant to undercut the significance of fathers and adult males in the lives of pioneer women. Seventy-five percent of the pioneers we interviewed grew up in two-parent families and very few reported negative or problematic relationships with their fathers. What they do underscore, however, is that whether a man is present or not, a mother who contributes to family income (as over 60 percent of the pioneers' mothers did), who is not made vulnerable in the absence of a man or who is not overshadowed by the presence of a man in the household, has a strong impact on the *potential* for nontraditional choices and behavior in daughters.

ACCESS TO NONTRADITIONAL
OCCUPATIONAL KNOWLEDGE AND SKILLS

Fathers and adult males emerged as important to the development of pioneering capacities because of the access and encouragement they provided to the often "mysterious" masculine world. Mothers seem more important to character building for these women; fathers, uncles, grandfathers, and older brothers are especially important ingredients in the development of specific interests and preferences. Once again, the comments and observations of the nontraditional women themselves bear this out.

Jan Spencer, our chief mechanic, grew up with a father who was always fixing things.

My dad was always tearing up our house; he built the place from the ground up. For a while it was a duplex where we rented out the bottom to help make the payments, and then when we were more financially stable we turned the whole thing into one house. So we had a nice big place to live. All us girls had a room, and my brother had a room and my folks had a room. It had a big garage in the back. And my grandmother had a garage too, so after my grandpa died we used that one too. There was a lot going on as far as fixing cars and my dad was always tearing up things and buying something new for the place. I worked with him a lot.

Jan also remembered spending time playing with tools.

I spent a lot of time by myself. I liked to just get away by myself. Not that I had that much trouble with people and being around. But we were out in the country, and I spent a lot of time out in the garage building things and using tools. I liked reading—read a lot.

In her second-year interview she reiterated the importance of her father.

Well, I guess I've always been sort of technically oriented . . . showed a lot of interest in that area. My dad, of course, is a millwright and all-around mechanic, and quite a few times he encouraged me. He encourages me more now than he did then 'cause I don't think he wanted to push me over the edge into it—but now that I'm there, he doesn't mind helping me out.

Another woman, who by her third-year interview had moved out of diagnostic work in auto mechanics and then back into another technical field as a computer analyst, remembered having an early mechanical aptitude, which she shared with her brother and very likely developed because of her father's jukebox machine repair business.

When I was a little bitty kid I used to play with dolls, I had a little teddy bear. My brother and I used to always play house. Then I was always taking things apart and putting them back together. As I was growin' up—I think I had a great mechanical ability. I'd work on clocks . . . anything I'd find in my dad's shop. Part of my dad's work was fixing jukeboxes and I used to sit and watch him all the time. He had a shop out back, and anytime I could sneak into that shop and just play around in it, it was great. Then I got very interested in building radios and things like that—I wanted to be a ham operator but I never got my license. My brother got very interested and he got his license. But we made telegraph sets and I used to like to make model airplanes. I was always exact about everything I did, I noticed my brother was always sloppy, but I was more of a perfectionist.

Another woman, who was an auto mechanic for two years but decided to move back into a traditional job because of the long hours, reported her lifelong interest in mechanics as having been influenced by her brother and stepfather.

Well, my brother's a mechanic—so even though I really didn't learn too much from my brother, I was just always fascinated. He just wanted me out of the way, but I'd sort of hang around and watch, and then especially after my mother divorced my father and my stepfather started dating my mother—he did all the farm work around home. So there's always things with tractors and trucks and people showing things to me. I've never been, ya know, the typical

. . . I've always been a tomboy, so I just kind of fit in, and I like being dirty and stuff.

A woman who by our third-year contact was a very successful pipe fitter, active in her local union, identified her grandfather and her brother as important to her eventual development of an interest in skilled trades after more than ten years in clerical work.

My brother had very interesting toys—when he was five years old he was given a hatchet and there were thick swamp maples surrounding the house and the family thought it was sort of constructive . . . we had a hatchet and could go and cut down some of them and we thought it was swell. We played various wilderness games and we were always building things. My grandfather was a carpenter and he gave us a big supply of very big nails, so we would cut down these swamp maples and build structures.

In our second-year interview she elaborated on the significance of such early childhood experiences.

I think that you have to have had certain kinds of, you have to get into certain things, like you have to have some mathematical skills. It really is true, like if you can't add and subtract you get all goofed up doing this kind of job. But they're all the kind of skills that anybody with a high school or elementary school education could have. What women don't have is access to tools and knowledge of the names. So sometimes a woman coming on the job will maybe sound stupid when actually she's in the same place as a guy, but the guy maybe had a crescent wrench to fix his bicycle whereas a young girl would not have either been allowed or expected to fix her own bicycle. She'd be doing the dishes and hoping her brother would fix hers or something. I grew up on a farm and I realize now I did things that were nontypical, but at the time I was not aware of that because I lived in the country and knew very few other children. I spent most of my time with my brother and we spent a lot of time —like chopping down trees and building little log structures. My grandfather was a carpenter and he would draw designs of kites we could build and then we would go out and build them and fly them. There was a period in the middle where—like I guess it was—I was supposed to grow up, and so I was just supposed to be learning how to sew my hems on my skirts and to comb my hair right and all that kind of thing, and so I was. My brother had more mobility than I did because like he was given a three-speed bicycle when I had an old clunker with a heavy frame and I couldn't keep up with what he was doing, so I mostly kind of hung around the house and read and didn't do much of anything. This was while I was a teenager, you know, daydreamed, and then I had to do a lot of work on the farm and, uh, so there was a period in the middle there where like I stopped doing the stuff I did while I was a kid where I was a tomboy. I hadn't found anything else to do, and then when I started working I did basically the kind of jobs women could get but I would do maybe little things at night, like maybe refinish a table or something like that. I think I always admired my brother a lot and he always did very nice things with his hands and I always wanted to be able to do the things that he did and also like my grandfather, who's a carpenter. Always, it seemed like he not only made nice things but he enjoyed making them and had a good time, and I wanted to do some kind of work that was fun, and so I would do things after my job like maybe build something that there was a plan for in some magazine. But it took me a long while to find out that I could have a job where I got to do things like that.

Another woman, who was about to finish a four-year machinist apprenticeship, stated it this way:

Ever since I can remember, I've been mechanically inclined. I've always been fascinated by machinery.

You know, as far as people specifically, my grandfather used to do carpentry in the basement and I used to really enjoy watching him and I'd try to do things. That, plus some achievement tests that showed a high mechanical score and just my basic fascination with almost all kinds of machinery, that's mainly what led me to this finally.

One woman's childhood admiration for her brother and frequent play with him resulted in her deciding to pursue his vocation—welding—when she found herself divorced and in need of a well-paying job with a future.

In May I started looking around, you know, but I didn't really see anything I wanted to do, so I took this—I always wanted to be a welder because my brothers have always done that, you know, that's what they do. They work in construction and all that, and they weld. My older brother, who is thirty-one, has a garage and he has the welding equipment, so I go and do that for him once in a while. But I like to see the lights when you weld, and it's really interesting work. It's kind of dull sometimes doing the same thing over and over, but once you're out in the field, the shipyard, you're doing something different. I like that training.

My mom didn't really like it. She said, "Oh, what did I raise—a tomboy? You could be doing something like a secretary and all that and dress really nice," and I said, "I don't like doing that." Most of your money goes into clothes, you know, your earnings.

But she got used to the idea, because my brother, he's a welder for South Coast Steel and my other brother was a welder, too, but now he's a bricklayer—he gets better money. So she kind of—it runs in the family, you know, but at first when we were out working on my brother's truck she said, "Get out of there, get out from under that truck," and I said, "Mom, I'm helping them," and the boys said I was doing it good. They kind of thought that I would never learn, you know, and they said, "You don't mind getting dirty and all that," and I said, "No, it doesn't really bother me." And it really doesn't.

A small number of the nontraditional women in this study identified their fathers rather than their mothers as the primary source of their independence and capacity for trying nontraditional alternatives. In two such cases the fathers played the primary caretaker role because of difficult work schedules when both parents worked. In a third case, the father's role was the result of an alcoholic stepmother.

Penny Widmer is a UPS delivery truck driver who eventually wants to get into driving big rigs cross-country. She has a lifelong interest in nontraditional employment both because of her desire for a good income and because of the physical skills the job requires. Penny was a competitive athlete as a child and had an extremely close relationship with her father.

I was real close to my brother and I was real close to my father because of sports. He encouraged me in sports and I was a competitive speed skater, so we went to meets all the time and stuff. I was close to my mother, too, but she was a cocktail waitress and she worked nights and I went to school days, so we didn't see a lot of each other. Being a competitive athlete, nationally, cost my family money, so that's why my mother worked nights as a cocktail waitress. During the winter, which was the competitive season for skating, it cost us more money than we had. Then my mom would work lunches also. So her main responsibility to the family was financial. She didn't clean house. She didn't like it and wouldn't do it except once a year, basically. The house was mine and my brother's and my father's responsibility, meaning it didn't get done.

My father spent a lot of time with the kids, took us places. I was also in softball. He basically worked every day and then at night he'd come home and we'd go to a training session. During the weekend I'd play softball. That's what he did . . . that's how I remember him. He worked days and then when he'd come home we'd do something.

I actually believed I could be President. I don't know why. President of the U.S. My parents never encouraged me, but they never told me that I couldn't do something. They said I could be anything. My father is shocked that I'm in a nontraditional job or anything along those lines, he always encouraged me along those lines and then once I got it he wonders why I'm not a secretary or something. I would be if it paid more.

I think my father really swallowed the American dream. I think he really believes you can be anything you want if you work hard enough. If you want it you can get it—there's room enough for everybody. I grew up thinking I could be anything. I'd have to have been if I grew up thinking I could be President. I thought about being a fireman, pharmacist, doctor, and a nurse, so reality didn't hit me as to what I could really be until I got out of high school and was working.

Elaine Elmer, a production control trainee, also had a close relationship with her father even though, as a navy captain, he was frequently away from home. Her mother had died, and because her stepmother was an alcoholic (especially during her husband's long absences at sea), Elaine had a somewhat distant relationship with her. She described her feeling about her father this way:

I was really close to my dad. He would tell us about his days, about growing up and things he wanted to be when he was younger and

things that he started going after when he got into college, and he
always thought you should be your own person and, but he wasn't
really around enough to give it the strong support it needed, you
know, as far as goals and career goes and things like that. But I
think he really led a lot of us to better things even though he was
really strict and stuff like that.

Many of the women we encountered in the course of this
research considered male family members significant in the development of nontraditional interests, even though their support
was not consistent. For example, Jane Kurtz, who had the
successful washing-machine business while in high school,
identified her father as crucial to her development of nontraditional interests because of all the independence he gave his
children and the skills he taught. Nonetheless, like many of the
women we interviewed, Jane reported that her father had very
conventional expectations for her, and that that was one of the
reasons she spent so many years in clerical work before finally
deciding to pursue her primary interest, small-appliance repair.
She described the situation this way:

I must have been twelve or thirteen at that time, but I knew that I
didn't want to become a nurse, like my father had asked me to be,
and I knew at that time that it would never work out. I thought I
could get into something that I liked and still get his approval on it,
but I found that when parents pick out a field for their kids, which
I think is wrong, but most parents try to push their kids into something that they feel is better, when they push them into something
they have such strong motives and they are so thoroughly disappointed if their kids don't do it that, no matter what choice the kids
pick, the parents are going to be disappointed. I've always wanted
to go into a skilled occupation, but when I suggested it one night at
the dinner table—I told them I wanted to be a barber—I not only
got "NO" but I got about four other noes and one "No way are
you going to cut my hair," so I decided I better not go into that if
they feel that strong about it, so I didn't and this was when I was
quite young. At that time I got thrown at me "You're going to college," and I said all right and let it drop at that. I never got into it
and always thought it would be fun to do, and to this day I still

think it would be fun to do, but I would never be accepted at it, so I dropped it.

PARENTAL REACTIONS TO DAUGHTERS' NONTRADITIONAL JOBS

Even though close to half of the pioneer women described their parents as having a positive impact on their eventual nontraditional choices, virtually all of them were influenced by traditional sex role expectations. With the exception of a few (but not all) of the gay women, the respondents reported that their own realistic expectations as young adults were that they would grow up and get married and have kids. Over half of them also indicated that they assumed they would be employed as adults, but the occupations that they realistically expected to have were factory work, secretarial work, nursing, or teaching. Very few women realistically expected to enter a nontraditional occupation. Yet over half reported having fantasies and dreams about growing up to be in nontraditional roles, such as explorers, airplane pilots, and veterinarians. The point is that even though these pioneer women were given or required to assume high levels of responsibility in childhood, even though large numbers of them had access to and "tinkered" with tools and mechanical equipment, even though half of them had fathers who were successful technical or skilled tradesmen, both the parents and the women themselves expected very conventional adult roles—wife, mother, and employment in an acceptable woman's job.

That is the second critical point. The parents of the nontraditional women also continually had traditional hopes and expectations for their daughters. When asked about how their parents felt about their nontraditional employment, only a few of the pioneering women reported unequivocal parental support and enthusiasm or said, "My parents always hoped I'd grow up to be a plumber." Most reported a positive reaction from their parents because of their well-paid, steady employment but consid-

erable ambivalence about their daughters' working in nontraditional jobs. Even the daughters of tradesmen reported such
ambivalence.

A machinist trainee whose father was a welder and mother a
housewife stated:

My mom doesn't say too much about my job and my dad probably
thinks I won't make it. I don't talk to them that often. They know
that I'm going to school. And like my mom will say I hope you do
good in it and try, and like I said, my dad—he thinks he's a jack-
of-all-trades. He's a master of everything.

A woman plumber who later switched to bookkeeping had a
father who was skilled in machine maintenance. She described
his reaction to her efforts at being a plumber:

I don't really know how my parents feel about it exactly. I can
remember talking to my father over the phone and telling him I
wanted to be a plumber and he said, "Well, you don't hear about
too many women plumbers." They have mixed feelings—they want
me to be happy, but they worry. I think they're sort of worried
about me moneywise . . . they can't understand why I'd give up a
"good job" being a legal secretary. I think they sometimes get a little nervous about me being happy their way. But I'm happy my
way. I used to think, well, maybe I'm doing this to please him, or
maybe because I wanted to be a boy, or all kinds of psychological
things. But I don't feel that close to my father anymore. I feel
closer to my mother. . . .

The successful auto mechanic whose father died of alcoholism and whose mother worked as a secretary to a lab technician
stated it this way:

My mother's supportive but she . . . doesn't quite . . . I don't
think she'd let me work on her car. I mean, she doesn't quite take
me seriously yet. She doesn't quite believe me. She wants me to
have work, for sure, and she's never pressured me about getting
married or having kids, that's for sure. But in terms of the specific
work I do and that I do it . . . that's still kinda too close to home.
She can't deal with that yet.

A successful electronics apprentice, the daughter of a tool and die maker, described her parents' reactions:

Well, it's hard to say—I think they're probably happy to see me settle down, since up to this job I would be traveling a lot and have little nothing jobs like housekeeping. They're probably happy to see me settle down in a job that's promising and especially in a job that's secure. My mother might be happy to see me settle in a more traditional job, but they've never said anything against my job.

A woman who was working as a gardener, cutting wood and running heavy equipment, reported that her mother, a store clerk, was upset with her employment but that her father, who had owned and operated a lumberyard, was more sympathetic.

I've only . . . I haven't seen him since I got this job, I haven't seen him now for about a year and a half. On the phone when it first all came out and I was telling them about it, she was just kind of appalled. I kept, I had to keep saying this, I really enjoy it, this is what I want, before she would have any recognition. And he was just kind of impressed with the money, you, like, wow, that's really great you're making that much money. Also I think he can identify more with it in the lumberyard, he was doing physical work and he's in fairly good shape and she's never been real physical. I really think that he can just identify more with the fact that I like the independence of it, I like being outside, I like doing some physical thing, although I haven't talked to him closely about it.

A machinist from a middle-class managerial background who worked in a steel mill reported her parents' reactions:

I think they have mixed feelings. I think they are astounded at the amount of money I'm making. They think I could make that much teaching or doing a much easier job. My father worked in the shop and I think he's—they really don't question me. My mother would like to see me work elsewhere. She thinks it's a fad where I'll probably work there awhile and then quit. She hopes that I would find an easier job eventually. Maybe, she doesn't care about the money, but it's easier on my health or whatever.

I think I see myself working there quite a while. At least until I learn a trade.

A forklift operator who is the daughter of a retired railroad man described her mother's ambivalence:

She doesn't like it at all. She doesn't like anything that I've done. She's the type of mother who wanted her daughter to be a nurse or a lawyer—something very high. She's embarrassed to say I'm a forklift operator. She's embarrassed to say I work in a warehouse or anything like that. She always wanted me to work. She always wanted me to go to school, too, and be something good. She doesn't like this kind of job.

A few parents, although certainly in the minority, indicated to their daughters a certain pride that they were trying something nontraditional. A welder whose father was in construction and whose mother had been a bus driver stated:

They are all for it, I think more so because I don't have a husband and they know there are so many things I want and you have to have a certain amount of money to raise a child by yourself too. They were real happy when I got the job, they were real happy.

An appliance repairperson reported that even though her parents wished she had used her college education, they took a certain pride in her nontraditional employment.

A lot of people have a lot of respect because it takes a lot to do it. . . . The ones that do it—our parents wish that we had another kind of job, but when their friends come over they brag, "My daughter works at Sears" and "My daughter's a truckdriver." I guess it's because it's the year of the woman, and they see it all over TV and stuff like that, and their daughter's a part of it. You know, they kind of question it sometimes, but I think they think it's okay.

CONCLUDING COMMENTS: EARLY PATTERN BREAKERS

I began this chapter with the assertion that people with a capacity for risk taking or making nontraditional choices are made, not born, and that the family is the first place where capacities, preferences, and potential risk-taking abilities are formed. By now it should be clear that this is usually not because parents *deliberately* set out to socialize their little girls into independent beings who will grow up outside of traditional sex and occupational roles. Rather, accidents of childhood, inadvertent granting of independence, family crises, and parental role models give rise to unexpected, unintended outcomes. Although most of the parents of the women we studied articulated conventional expectations for their daughters and the daughters themselves grew up expecting to conform to conventional patterns, the pattern-breaking experiences of early childhood opened up in them the capacity for pursuing another course. These women did not have predictable, secure childhoods. They could not count on constant care from parents for the cultivation of the dispositions, interests, and abilities associated with female socialization at home and in school. As young girls, most assumed responsibility beyond what is normally expected of children and adolescents. Most nonetheless had a sense of roots and stability from their parents, usually their mothers, but in some cases their fathers. Most reported hard times in childhood that got better or were episodic rather than never-ending and uncontrollable. They were enough "out of step" with other girls to know the world is not an absolutely predictable place and that their place in it as women was not something to be simply taken for granted. Most of them were called upon to be sufficiently independent to learn that as girls or women they were not helpless. Most had success models of one sort or another to give them the sense that things can get better if you work at it.

In contrast, the women in more traditional jobs had less of a sense of being in control, of having a secure and predictable base or set of relationships with which to weather their hard times. Such women, often victims of "hard living," were less in a position to explore certain kinds of occupational risks, both because they have fewer resources as adults and because they had fewer early opportunities to develop certain essential capacities. This is not to suggest that *all* occupationally traditional women are victims of "hard living." It does suggest, however, that women who have been victimized in childhood by structural economic factors beyond their control, or who have had relations with parents that are untrustworthy or oppressive, are far less likely to develop personal independence and risk-taking capacities, especially in the occupational world. On the other hand, women from more secure backgrounds who have never had to question traditional values or develop unusual independence are likely to grow up with little interest in boundary testing or risk taking, even though other resources and specific opportunities may be there for them.

Thus the pioneer in the blue-collar world tends to be a woman who has come from a family background characterized by a subtle mix of emotional security, predictability, and trust in critical interpersonal relationships, even though significant financial or family crises may be present. There is some security and hope for things getting better, even though success and happiness are tenuous and not taken for granted. The girl learns that, in her case at least, such things must be worked for.

Whether or not this general disposition is translated into a preference for nontraditional alternatives, much less a decision to pursue nontraditional employment, depends on later experiences. Adolescence and young adulthood are times for experiences and choices that may or may not reinforce the independence fostered by the pattern breaking early family experiences. This next stage in the life cycle is what we now turn to.

III

Roads to Adulthood

Just as the family and early childhood experiences of these nontraditional women were characterized by significant pattern breaking, so were their experiences in adolescence and young adulthood. For some of our respondents it was not until adolescence or young adulthood that their experiences first diverged from conventional norms and expectations. For the majority, however, the types of experience that made them different in childhood were paralleled in these later stages of their development.

Typical patterns of norms and expectations for girls center around the development of interests, skills, and orientations that reinforce domestic roles. By the time a girl reaches adolescence, much of her behavior has already become "family forming" in that it is directed at developing and preparing her for her *primary* adult role as wife and mother. Although the impact of the women's movement in the last decade may be changing the character of adolescent and young adult experiences— through, for example, increased access to shop classes, team sports, math and science, and the increased availability of contraception and abortion—the women in our study were all in early or middle adulthood by the time feminism began to influence the media, the schools, and daily life. They matured in an era when being attractive, having nice clothes, being well liked, not competing with boys, and pursuing vocational or avocational interests that could combine readily with domestic roles were the typical patterns for most girls. Extensive research has documented the extent to which girls, upon reaching adolescence, abandon many interests defined as boyish. By adolescence most girls simply don't make an effort to pursue interests or skills in areas that are socially defined as masculine or are perceived as not easily combined with finding and keeping a mate and rearing children. By adolescence, girls are already beginning to evaluate options and form preferences based on consequences for their ultimate roles in the family. Boys are already more self-directed, experimental, and individualistic. Boys are worrying about achievement and competency "in the world." Not only the activities that boys engage in, but also what adolescents value in people and situations, is differentiated along gender lines: girls value physical attractiveness, cooperation, kindness, ability to get along with people, neatness, and passivity; boys value strength, competitiveness, toughness, power, and drive or aggressiveness. In adolescence, boys and girls begin committing themselves in earnest to activities and roles that express these socially prescribed and valued characteristics.

Breaks in these patterns of traditional expectations can be intended or unintended. Parents may encourage an athletic teenage girl self-consciously and deliberately. Physical unattractiveness or a shabby wardrobe because of poverty are events over which neither the growing girl nor her parents have much control, but which nonetheless throw her out of step with other girls' experiences. Atypical interests or responsibilities resulting from the necessities of family life—full-time jobs through high school or the presence of a strong, successful mother—may also create circumstances that contrast with and therefore call into question the supposedly typical patterns for girls and young women. In the course of our interviews, three key questions triggered responses that provided insight into the special character of the women's interests, needs, and experiences. The first had to do with childhood interests and fantasies; the second, with significant turning points in their lives; and the third, with describing the point at which the kind of work they really wanted to do fell into place. Building on our conversations about these three issues, this chapter will describe the roads to adulthood of nontraditional women in terms of (1) the adolescent's world, (2) turning points, and (3) stabilization of work role identity.

THE ADOLESCENT'S WORLD

A few of the women we interviewed had what might be considered fairly typical adolescences. They described themselves as having good friends, doing okay in school, being reasonably attractive, dating at least occasionally, being active in some school activities, maybe having a part-time job, and overall having a relatively happy time as teenagers. Such women went on from high school into college or full-time paid employment and had experiences somewhat later in young adulthood that were critical to their dawning realization that they were responsible for themselves and might be interested in nontraditional options. Sandra Wong, the successful machinist with a university degree and middle-class background described in Chapter I, is one such example.

The majority of the women we encountered, however, did not live through that kind of adolescence. Although only a few remembered their adolescence as an unhappy time, many recalled feeling different from other kids. A small but significant number reported having little time for the intensely peer-related activities associated with the teenage years because they had already made the transition into adultlike responsibilities. This was either because of the families' need for their full-time employment, because of leaving home at an early age owing to family conflict and unhappiness, or because of an early marriage or pregnancy. A few of the women we interviewed reported living through their adolescence with a dawning realization of homosexual preferences that made them feel different from their peers and created an early sense that they would live adult lives different from those of most other women. The largest number of women who described themselves as different from other kids their age, however, attributed that difference to a number of distinct but sometimes related factors that we can lump under the heading "being tomboys." These include such factors as (1) a keen interest in athletics and particularly team sports; (2) brotherly or asexual relationships with boys their own age, with little dating or sexual contact except perhaps with much older boys; (3) a certain self-consciousness about their physical appearance, primarily because of being over-weight or, as a number of the women described it, "not know-ing how," or not being able to dress in ways that they felt fit in with the other girls. It is possible that feeling overweight and improperly dressed is the preoccupation of *every* teenage girl, no matter how slender, well dressed, or popular she is. How-ever, the association of these comments with other factors such as an interest in team sports, dating older boys, and feelings of being different from other kids creates a picture of likeable and competent girls who were just a little bit "out of it" when it came to cliques and school dances, peer group parties, and girl-ish interests in clothes, hairstyles, and boy talk.

Being interested in sports, being a tomboy, being outside the dating mainstream; having a full-time job or a husband or baby by age fifteen or sixteen; or dealing with a marginal sexual preference such as homosexuality: these are not in and of themselves sufficient to divert an adolescent girl in an unequiv-ocally nontraditional direction. What these factors all do have in common, however, is that they "break pattern." The girls with one or more characteristics or experiences such as these were forced to define themselves as different from other girls and began to have some practice living in the world as a person for whom all the ordinary or typical rules do not apply—as a person who must develop both cognitive and behavioral alter-natives to what are considered typical experiences. Such out-of-the-ordinary characteristics are but steps in the larger and longer process of developing an identity as a woman, particu-larly as a nontraditional woman. Nonetheless, they occurred with enough frequency in the backgrounds of the women we met that they appear to be important experiential building blocks.

Once again, sharing in detail some of the descriptions of the adolescent years of nontraditional women makes this point far better than a social scientist's summation. Let's look once again at the early years of Jan Spencer, the successful chief mechanic. In addition to early access to nontraditional skills, employment in her early teens, and periods of economic insecurity in her family background, Jan had many interests and feelings in adolescence and young adulthood that set her apart from other teenage girls in the Midwest.

I had some trucks and I had little toy people . . . like cowboys and Indians.

I was involved in sports. The whole social activity around my neighborhood was seasonal . . . football, baseball, and whatever. Whoever was oldest in the neighborhood at the time was sort of the social director. Everyone in the neighborhood participated in that. But I didn't like high school much.

I didn't like being thought of as weird. For example, my appearance in high school bothered me. I wanted to look inconspicuous and what my mother wanted me to wear would have made me look like a sore thumb. She would pick out flashy colors, something different from what the kids were wearing, not that I wanted to look like everyone else. I just didn't want to be seen, I wanted to blend in with the woodwork. And I would have to wear the same thing over and over again to school. I would have to dig something out from the corner somewhere and wash it out by hand and iron, and I could do that only once in a while—it took a lot of time. My mother would get resentful about it and troop around the house about—"wasn't she a good enough mother and did I think she should spend her whole life taking care of kids" and stuff. Not that I would care that she didn't do that stuff [but] she would get upset every time. About two years in the middle of my high school they bought this restaurant and decided they were going to have a small business of their own, and it failed miserably, but while they were doing it they had to work like sixteen hours a day over there. We never saw them for two years straight. So I really took care of myself.

Jan went on to say about dating:

I went out with this guy for about two years. My folks didn't like
him, it's not that they thought he was objectionable—they thought
he was a drip. He was—I knew it. I didn't want to go out with
boys at all—I was going out to get some of the pressure off. My
mom said she knew I was gay all through high school. I was also
going out with girls, but I thought I had that hidden, but I guess
you can't hide something like that from your mother, but I did have
it hidden from others. It was supposed to look like just some girls
going out together, but she knew what was going on.

A woman not unlike Jan in her adolescent interests and fantasies is Wanda Hellman. Wanda is a black welder we interviewed in Los Angeles who grew up in a large family about
whom she has very positive feelings.

I'm from a large family. I have seven brothers and four sisters.
Well, mostly I grew up with my brothers because my sisters—
there's a gap between all of us. Well, not then the sister under me—
is much younger, so I really didn't have many sisters to grow up
with. I was—as they say—a tomboy. When I was little I was jus' like
a tomboy—you could see me climb trees, play softball. That's what
I mostly did, play softball, I love to play softball. I could play that
all day long—all summer long as long as it was light I would play
that an' jacks, an' I like to run a lot. Oh, what do you call it—hide
an' seek or run and go one, two, three red light—an' things like that
—marbles. I use to play a lot of marbles. An' even in high school I
wore pants. I wore a lot of pants, my brothers' pants because like it
would snow, or if the weather was cold an' it would be snowing and
you had to wear pants a lot—snow boot. I didn't date much—let
me see—high school? No, not in high school, I might have had one
boyfriend in high school, I'm the type of person that I—I consider
myself mature. Like the guys—I'm just not attracted to 'em. Like I
go for older guys. Like when I was in high school, like—I might
have had one boyfriend so my parents wouldn't be suspicious or
anything. An' I, like, I went with a few guys about twenty-one or
twenty-two. I was about sixteen.

Wanda shared her ideas about what she saw in her future when
she was a teenager:

I had always wanted to be ah—an airline stewardess or else to go into the Navy. I mostly wanted to go into the Navy, but ah—I was goin' in there but I changed my mind. My daughter was two an' like I didn't want to leave her, so—that changed my mind. Other than that I would have went in the Navy. I got the idea of going in the Navy from ah—my brother-in-law, 'cause all my sisters when they married they married guys from the Air Force. I would see them in their uniform and I would think they would look nice on. I mostly wanted to go in the Navy to travel an'—to make a career of it. But I haven't went yet. I know I don't want to be a secretary or typist or anything like that. I really always wanted to be somethin' that would be different—I would take a man's trade because I wanted to—I really wanted to take up the job of electrician like my brother—so I know I couldn't get that, so I jes' went for weldin'. I'm in weldin' mostly 'cause they pay you good. Like—you don't see many womens in it, like they say—"it's a man's job, let a man do it." I feel that women is for cookin'—men cook—so if they can do the job, why not if they can do the job why not let 'em do it. I feels the same way about women's doin' men's jobs.

Almost all of Wanda's jobs had been in nontraditional fields, and though we only interviewed her once we learned through a friend of hers whom we did reinterview that she was still pursuing nontraditional employment.

A chef's apprentice who by our third-year contact was working in a major New York City hotel is an interesting contrast to Jan and Wanda. Erin Kelly's parents' separation in the ninth grade disrupted an otherwise conventional middle-class childhood. Erin also thought of herself as a tomboy, but this disruption of her teenage years seemed to be her most significant pattern-breaking experience.

I feel that I made a lot of my own decisions. I've been supporting myself for a long time. I worked in junior high school and high school baby-sitting and then I got a job when I was in high school. And I was a tomboy. We played army, my girl friend across the street and I were the rowdies in the neighborhood and we played army a lot, both being from army families. We played kick the can, hide and seek, stuff like that. In high school I was having a lot of trouble in classes—as I said, I really can't pinpoint why I started to do bad in high school. It's hard to say; I had a teacher who was just basically a big help to me. That was right when my parents split up and trying to cope with that and then moving back to California—I think it's really traumatic for most people to move right before you graduate from high school. You're at an awkward age to meet people and going through the whole change is quite a change. I didn't date and I only had a few friends. My parents' separation changed my life a lot, because if they hadn't I probably would have graduated from the high school I went to back East in the place that I had lived for the longest up until that point in my life, and then I probably would have gone right into school, it would have been a more settled life-style, so I think that definitely had an effect over it. I think—that was probably the major thing.

Erin shared some of her teenage dreams with us:

I wanted to be the first lady astronaut. I love flying. I'm going to take flying lessons when I can afford it. I used to want to be an anthropologist. That's about it.

Another woman, a college dropout from a Catholic working-class family who remembers her mother as the only employed mother among her peers, is a successful installer for the telephone company in Southern California. She described the persistent conflicts she felt as a young adult between what she was interested in and wanted to do and what she felt she was expected to do.

She asked me, it was the kinda counseling your senior year where you, you know, kind of . . . you know, they wanta give you some kinda directions an' I'm sitting there, I mean just, a dump you know, I mean, the furthest image from an airline stewardess that they could have. And . . . I was good at languages. I studied Spanish and French and I was gonna start German and I told her I was real interested in languages and I wanted to do some kind of an interpreting thing at that time. But she said, no, you should become an airline stewardess, right, because that's . . . you'd enjoy that a whole . . . a lot more, wouldn't be hard you know; I couldn't understand her counseling at the time because I was academically doing really well, but that's what counseling I got. A friend of mine wanted to be a doctor and they tried to push her into being a nurse and she'd really sit around and get bitter about it. When I was growing up, I wanted to work, I wanted to be a fireman . . . and—I—that was when I was real young, like when I was four, I remember that real clearly. From the time I was in the fifth grade on, my thoughts were geared in that direction, and I basically accepted that I was gonna be a schoolteacher, in fact, that's, I mean, that's what I really thought I was gonna do up to about six months ago . . . in my younger days I thought, I was going to be an interpreter and go to, you know, off to Brazil or something like that. . . . Another thing that I wanted to do was work in, I can't remember exactly what I wanted to do, but I wanted to work for the forest. When I was real little, we used to go up to Big Sur every summer when I was young, and it was so pretty and I would sit there and just think "I'd like to work here," that kinda thing. And I also read *Charlotte's Web* . . . it took me out of . . . it's a farm story and it took me out of a city setting, an urban setting, into the country and gave me a realization that I did not have to accept working inside. Well, it's real hard to describe because it's like I had accepted that I would be working inside, you know, as a teacher primarily but, that as a girl, you know, and, and the role image that I had is my mother, who was a nurse, you know, and so I had, I had this acceptance, I was gonna be working inside but yet this book took me outside, right, um, and that was real important influence, um, I would read the Hardy Boys, I read all the Hardy Boys, and that again was very adventurous and took me outside again and um . . . Robin Hood, too, influenced me a whole lot when I read that. Adventure, out of doors, all that stuff was *really* important.

A final example of an "atypical" adolescence is the experience of the UPS driver who was a competitive skater, Penny Widmer. In addition to having a hardworking, frequently absent mother and athletic interests, Penny remembers feeling socially and economically inferior to the kids in her upper-middle-class suburban high school, even though she was involved and popular.

I started skating when I was five years old. I quit when I was nineteen, and during those years I competed in California and nationally, made a U.S. Olympic training team, won some national championships and stuff. That was my basic goal of growing up—to be an Olympic skater, which I never made. I played softball in the summers, single A, double A. I was always doing something extra. I skated in the winter, trained in the summer. I rode my ten-speed fifteen or twenty miles a day just to keep in shape. Even so, I had lots of tools, I loved them. I loved to read also, although I read mostly Golden Books or comic books or something like that . . . I didn't like novels. I enjoyed reading, but I wanted something I could just read like within a week or something. I never felt like an outsider with the other kids. I was one of the lucky kids who had an easy time going through school. But when I look back on it now, what I liked least about it was the pressure to think that you're financially better off than you are. For me it was a very bad thing for me to go to that high school because the kids I hung out with had a lot more money and the school was basically an upper-class school. I didn't like all that kind of pressure. I drank real heavy in high school. I had big parties. They'd come and tear my house apart, but when they'd have their private dinner parties, I wouldn't get invited. So there was a lot of class hurt through high school when I look back on it.

I started drinking at age twelve. By the time I was sixteen I would consume, at a party, a quart of tequila or vodka or whatever I decided to get at the time or two six-packs of malt liquor. I would drink three to four times a week. I was basically an alcoholic. I really felt pressure about my appearance and stuff like that. In my peer group these things were very important. I'd make my mom go in hock so I could have a nice dress or a nice pair of shoes. Everyone else would have twenty nice dresses and twenty nice pairs of shoes. She busted her ass to buy me nice clothes. She knew the kind of school I was going to and she knew my friends. My mom isn't alive now, but I think it was hard on her during high school. My friends had such an influence on me in high school that it reflected on how I treated my parents when I went to an upper-class high school.

These extended comments are meant to give the flavor of how the majority of the nontraditional women remembered their adolescence. Some, like Penny, were pretty much in the mainstream except for feeling marginal because of their appearance or their family status (relative income, parental alcoholism, or employed mother). Most, however, felt very much out of it, like Jan Spencer. Many of the women you have met in other contexts—Ardath Hoover, Polly Nichols, Elaine Elmer—described periods of profound feelings of isolation and difference through most of high school. Some of the women even reported having changed schools, dropped out of school, or graduated late because of social and behavioral problems related to their feeling like "misfits." The picture of adolescence that emerges is by no means tragic, but it is clearly one in which many of the women who grew up to make nontraditional choices began both to experience and to live with the fact of being "different."

TURNING POINTS

Most people, when reflecting upon adolescence and early adulthood, can remember certain critical turning points in their lives: personal experiences, significant relationships, or special events that touched their lives in a way that they began to see and feel things differently thereafter and often began to live quite differently. The end of adolescence is a predictable time for such experiences. Until the last decade, the most critical turning points in girls' lives have usually involved the selection of a mate. The women we studied grew up at a time when girls who were not college-bound married and started a family within a year or two of finishing high school. The girls who were college-bound often dropped out before finishing a degree in order to marry and/or have a family, or they married and had a family within one or two years of completing college. Many female high school and college graduates of their generation had brief periods of employment before marriage and raising a family, but such employment was rarely regarded as a fundamental commitment. Until very recently most women stayed home in the early years of marriage to rear young children. If one is to believe the sociological research and popular press to date, the real crisis periods or significant turning points

for women do not happen until mid-life, when a woman faces
the "empty nest" syndrome, divorce, or widowhood, and thus is
forced to make a social and economic place for herself independent of her father or her husband. Some of these "typical"
patterns may be changing among younger women today, but
they are an accurate description of the social context in which
most of the women we met matured.

In contrast, boys at the end of adolescence and upon college
graduation, although also choosing mates, are coming to terms
with fundamental questions about who they are in the world,
what they want to be and do, and in what arenas they will per-
form for a livelihood, for community service, and for personal
stature. These preoccupations became crystallized and reinforced in a man's adolescent and young adult experiences
through such things as an increasing interest in academic subjects (in contrast to the female's decreased interest), increased
performance in academic subjects (in contrast to the female's
decreased performance), a continuing, even expanding interest
and participation in team sports and competitive athletics, and
for some a period of military service. Girls, for the most part,
do not participate in these experiences. They are not on the
athletic teams, they are not in the shop classes and math
classes, they are not in the military, they are not seriously involved in the paid work force, and so the experiences that
could potentially be critical turning points are quite different
from the boys'. Unless there is something about their circumstances, abilities, or interests which pulls them into those "masculine" worlds and demands that they "take charge," girls have
very little such opportunity outside of their own family experiences.

What, then, makes a woman "take charge"? Has the woman
who by her middle twenties or thirties is on an occupational
path that takes her beyond traditional expectations had some
critical turning point as a young adult that helped to move her
in such a direction? The interview responses suggest that this
was frequently the case. Some of the women we interviewed

had such experiences in mid-life, but for the majority they occurred in young adulthood.

Turning points are key experiences, relationships, or events that usually have the following three qualities: (1) they represent opportunities or demands for new sets of behaviors and perspectives; (2) they involve having to make often difficult or conflicting choices, and then acting on those choices; and (3) they often involve shifts in responsibility for oneself or for others. For women, turning points can also involve relinquishing control to a husband or even children. These nontraditional women, however, whose work is characteristically similar to men's, experience turning points more similar to those of men.

Increased responsibility for self and others is a critical aspect of the transition into the adult male role. Taking such responsibility is not necessarily voluntary. It's a simple fact of life for most men. It can be delayed, but unless a young man is very rich or very lucky, he is usually required by the late teens or early twenties to take charge of things, no matter how effectively or ineffectively. The woman left at home with a child is in a parallel situation. No one has really told her how to do it, but suddenly the baby is there and it is up to her to figure out how to pull it all together and do the best job possible. The analogue for this experience for a man includes not only feeling responsible for the livelihood and well-being of himself, his wife, and his children, but being involved in a variety of spheres in which he is expected to "come through." He may have to come through as the quarterback for the team, as the untrained lieutenant commander on a new ship, as a son expected to handle a deceased father's business for a helpless mother, as a salesman in the field, as a skilled electrician or engineer expected to keep the power going, or as an airline pilot expected to land the 747 safely. In countless ways, men have experiences that equip them both to understand and to deal with this kind of responsibility. Possibly, women in this society are increasingly having such experiences, but until recently such women were the exception, not the rule. Women have been bystanders and supporters but rarely "in charge."

One woman who found herself forced to take charge is Penny
Widmer, the competitive skater, who grew up in the upper-middle-class suburban neighborhood described in the previous section. When we asked Penny if she could think of any important
experiences or turning points, she responded:

Two important events—when I was fifteen and I was skating, I was
in the Midwest staying with a friend who was in her twenties. She
was a very exciting woman and very popular, and during that time
I figured out why people liked her so much, so when I came home,
I didn't become her, but I saw what she did and I changed myself
and it worked and more people liked me. The other thing that
changed my life was when my mother died. She died of cancer. She
had a brain tumor. I was taken out of college—well, I came back
from a college in Wisconsin and I had only been there for four
months, and I took care of her. My father had left, my brother was
married, and my father wasn't coming back and I decided I would
take care of my mother. I came home and my aunt and uncle and
their two kids moved in. My aunt and uncle are also alcoholics and
their two kids were young—five and six. Basically I took care of
my mother, who was blinded by cobalt, and my aunt and uncle,
who were alcoholics, and their two kids, who got more than their
fair share of punishment for things. I was always in family fights
during that period. I don't suppose you have ever lived with anyone
who has a brain tumor, but what it is is deterioration. The person
deteriorates in front of you. Because we didn't have any money my
mother stayed home as much as possible and then at forty-three she
went into a home and after one and one-half years—it was very
painful—I withdrew and ever since then it's affected how close I get
to people. I don't like loving anyone—I don't like being close, but
at the same time my best friend since first grade was killed one
month before my mother in a car accident. She was, up until that
time, my biggest support with my mother. A lot of my friends left
me during that time because they couldn't deal with pain. That is
what basically changed my life. I dropped out of college, I went to
work. I've been working ever since—it changes you. When you are
nineteen and you lose a parent—that's just when you begin to understand what a parent goes through or something and it's those
kinds of lines of communication. It has definitely changed my
whole outlook on life.

Having to take responsibility for another person was a frequent theme in the young adulthood of the nontraditional woman. Only a few women cited parents or siblings. The primary event giving rise to this feeling of responsibility was the birth of a child, often out of wedlock, for whom the woman felt solely responsible. A press operator described it this way:

My daughter—she made me grow up. When I had her I understood things so much better and it was very important to pull myself together and do something. I went to trade school for two years and I got out of college in '73. I just hung around for a couple of years. After I had her, it was like she just said, now you've got to pull yourself together and get yourself an occupation and go back to school or something. I signed up for vocational school to be a nurse, just anything. I had to get myself together. She hit me harder than anything. She got me off into politics—I wanted to know what was happening everywhere.

An auto mechanic who eventually became a computer analyst also talked about the importance of her daughter's birth in her life.

When my daughter was born—I was about twenty-one and not married, so suddenly I changed from somebody single to someone who had an awful lot of responsibility. I had been working at Defense Industries at the time and was going to school at night, working on a math degree, and I probably would have continued on and gone to school at that time, but when she was born, it was a little too rough to be going to school and taking care of a kid—I think they need a certain amount of attention. In fact, I didn't go to school again until she was about five years old. Then I went to school at nights.

She went on to describe how, after so many years on her own, her marriage and eventual divorce were also important turning points.

When I got married she was about six years old and that was a change I guess. Most people, when they get divorced, get emotionally upset and everything, but my husband and I are parting friends, we get along and see each other occasionally. Now I definitely have to support myself. In the past, well, I've been going to school up until the last five or six years—up until last year, I was working on my master's degree, and working on a master's degree you don't make a lot of money, you know. I was a teacher's aide and I had starvation wages, I think I made two hundred dollars a month. So I will not finish my master's degree until I find a job and then all I have to do is write my thesis, and take one other class, which I have to take during the daytime. So now I have to get a job. My husband makes a lot of money, but I don't think it's appropriate to support me. He has offered to help me if I need it in order to find an occupation that will give me enough money.

She went on to describe how getting married changed the direction of her life.

My idea of a wife was someone—it was probably very similar to my husband's—he was raised in Texas also—so we had kind of similar ideas about how a woman's supposed to stay home and do this —although he said I could work if I wanted to—but I know what he really expected and I tried to be domestic—to pretend like it was fun sweeping floors and washing dishes, but I went nuts and couldn't stand it. I went through a really bad depression and I didn't understand why. At the time I thought there was something wrong with me 'cause I couldn't stand to stay home and cook meals and my husband is a really neat person, he's never mistreated me in any way, but I just couldn't stand it. The only contact I had with people was with my daughter, who at that time was only seven years old—you can't talk to a seven-year-old and expect to—then I went back to school and I really enjoyed that. I was working on a math degree but ran into an anthropology class, which I really enjoyed, and my B.A. is in anthropology, math, and genetics and I've learned a great deal about myself and society in general.

Older women are sometimes forced by an unexpected divorce to assume full responsibility for their children, "jolted" into taking charge after many years as a traditional wife and mother. The best example of this is Molly O'Hara, the engineering draftsperson.

I'd say the biggest and most traumatic experience was getting a divorce after eighteen years of being a navy wife, 'n' ah, all of a sudden I had to raise three children. My oldest son Jake was sixteen going on seventeen, Willard was twelve, and Clem was eleven. That's thirteen years ago. . . . I think that was the biggest thing. Getting married and traveling and being a navy wife, I just seemed to fit right into the pattern and I liked it. We had a happy life and a good life—and then, ohhh, then things kinda fell apart.

Molly survived the divorce and is successful in a well-paid nontraditional job. In her early fifties, she is a budding women's-rights activist.

Only about 20 percent of the women described having to assume full responsibility for other persons. A much greater number described assuming full responsibility for themselves as a significant turning point. Some moved out of the family on their own because of tension with parents or a desire to be independent. Some moved out in order to escape the social and financial limitations they felt. Others were simply set loose by their parents upon finishing high school. In all these circumstances, the women were learning to be self-sufficient before committing themselves to a long-term relationship with a man.

The self-employed plumber, whose well-educated parents had hoped she would go on to college, described her turning points in this way:

I can see points in my life that were definitely turning points. One of the ones I can think of right now is when I decided not to go to college. That was a big load off my mind. Another was moving out of the house. That was my first big break and I've always been glad I did that. The week after I graduated, I moved out and lived in the Bay area. Quitting my first real job was another big turning point. Deciding to live the independent life for a while. Then I started thinking about what I wanted to do with my life and realized that when I quit the next shitty job that I had, what was I going to do. I had no what I would call marketable skills and I realized that for the rest of my life, if I had no marketable skills, I'd be down on the bottom of the job market, making at the most three dollars an hour. This is not where it's at. So that was the major turning point as far as my career. Being pregnant was a big turning point. I had a job as a machinist and that kind of gave me a start on thinking about marketable skills and what I could do with my life and how I could support my kid.

In contrast, Polly Nichols described herself as having been left on her own when she had actually been expecting help from her mother.

When I went into college, things began to change gradually and that change was accelerated at a certain stage when my mother said I would have to earn my own keep, so to speak. She had always told me she would support me through college, and it was always unspoken but understood that to repay her I would support her in her old age. I never agreed to that and never thought it was a fair deal anyway. Anyway, that didn't happen, thank God. She moved away and I had to support myself and this is when I started taking electronics classes and this was only like starting about a year or two ago. That's when my change started becoming accelerated. It has recently become much more accelerated because I started working at the lab.

Four of the nontraditional women we interviewed moved out of their parents' houses before completing high school. In one instance the parents decided to change their residence and lifestyle, but their daughter wished to finish high school in the community where she had grown up. This woman, an office machine repairperson when we met her, frequently referred to the significance of her learning to live alone at age sixteen. She described her initial decision this way:

Probably when we moved to a different class—that had a great effect on me. It was when I was sixteen. My parents made a new life-style choice. They consulted me about it when they wanted to do it. They thought that maybe moving to that rural area would be better for my brother. They asked me if it was all right with me and I told them—yeah, it was fine. They thought I was going to come with them, but I couldn't handle living out in the country so I lived in that house and I didn't go. First I moved in with a friend in that peer group, and her parents had separated and they had four daughters in the family and the oldest one had just gone away to college at Berkeley and my friend was next in line and she was really looking forward to having the power in the house and I came and I took it away and so she harassed me and harassed me for six weeks and I couldn't take it anymore. So then I moved in with a friend of my mother's for a while until I moved in with that family. I was a junior in high school then. In my senior year I graduated a semester early and I lived in kind of a raunchy apartment down in Torrance by myself. I always had a car and could get around by myself. I think I had three visitors the whole time I lived down there and it was only fifteen minutes away from school. I really isolated myself.

Other instances of moving out of the parents' house were precipitated by the stress and conflict the women felt at home, either because of differing life-styles or because they felt hemmed in by a small, crowded house with no privacy. A woman who was successfully progressing as a machinist over the period of this study described her circumstances:

When I was in high school I usually didn't like these little cliques in school, I didn't ever try to get into that stuff or anything like that, you know, like the cheerleaders and the football players and how they were in their own little cliques, and the people that were in that kind of stuff I never cared for so I never worried about it.

I flunked the eighth grade and had to go back. And you can't miss more than five days, and I missed two weeks, so I had to repeat the eighth grade again. I never did any of my homework, because there were too many people around and it was noisy and the other kids were there, so I never bothered to do my homework. Then when I was seventeen, I moved out of the house and I was by myself, and it was quieter and I think that's the reason that my grades went up. That was the biggest turning point in my life and I think I probably changed my attitude a lot since then. My boyfriend and I started living together, so I just moved in with him. I was still in high school, so I did want to complete it. At first I was going to drop out, you know, but then I said, "No, I don't want to do that, I'd rather complete it." This was my last year, you know, and I had spent all those years in school—the least thing I can do is get the diploma. I'm married to him now. I had known him—he had been a friend of the family for a long time and he's a real nice person and everything. Then we started dating and he moved out and wanted me to come and live with him, so I said okay. Great.

For a significant number—as many as 20 percent—of the non-traditional women, husbands, boyfriends, or male friends were identified as critical in the transition from adolescence into adulthood. The men were considered important not simply for providing affection and security. Much more frequently they were described as having helped the woman decide who she wanted to be and what she wanted to do in the world. Relationships with supportive and encouraging men represented turning points for many women. Contrary to popular stereotypes, men were often a positive asset in establishing an individual identity for blue-collar women.

Of course, in many of the lower-middle- and middle-class blue-collar environments from which these women emerged, employment of adult women is very common. In white-collar middle-class environments and among upper-middle-class business and professional people the question of whether or not a woman "works" is still problematic. It appeared to us that for many of the women we studied, whether or not you were going to be employed was not a question. Most expected to work as adults. The more significant question was what kind of employment they would seek and with what level of commitment. Because the employment of women is more typical in these blue-collar milieus, it is not so surprising that the young men many of the women dated or married helped them to settle down and focus on what they wanted to do. In white-collar and professional families, men and women were less likely to work out these issues unless the effects of inflation hit the family or the woman's need for meaningful work outside of the family began to emerge. For a small but significant group of the younger women we interviewed, boyfriends and husbands were helpful even in the late teens. Elaine Elmer, the production control trainee, who grew up in a family of twelve children, described her husband thus:

When I met my husband, boy, he really did a lot for me. I don't smoke anymore. I told you about when I was a senior in high school I lost a lot of weight and after I graduated I moved up to South Dakota and I worked for about six months and I was really unhappy and I gained it all back and when I met my husband I was pretty heavy again and like I said, he helped me quit smoking and he took about thirty-five pounds off of me. You know, just helping me and working right with me on everything—being understanding —and when I met him I was in a clerical type of position doing a type of typing that is taking the place of keypunching and he got me interested in this training program—he had gone through it before I got into it. He's just really done a lot for me—a lot.

Ardath Hoover, the gas service repairperson, also saw her husband as a critical influence in getting her to settle down as a teenager and later in finding the kind of employment that really satisfied her.

My husband had a lot of influence on me from age sixteen because he helped mellow me out. I lost contact with boys from about the time I was thirteen until about sixteen. Before, they were my major playmates, we used to climb trees or whatever. He really mellowed me out a lot and my emotional state more than anything else. Of course, my mother had a lot of influence on me just understanding life. We talked a lot about that kind of stuff.

For another small group of nontraditional women, the turning points had to do with more radical shifts in values and lifestyles. The political climate of the sixties, the burgeoning of the women's movement and feminist consciousness, or the realization of a homosexual preference resulted in some of the women taking stock of their lives, deciding on a new course of action, and ultimately feeling more in control.

An Amtrak employee who had dropped out of college described her change in political consciousness:

When I went to college I got politically conscious. I got into a NOW conscious group and that changed my life overnight. I started reading things that were happening in the world—like the coup in Chile—and started putting pieces together. That really started changing my life. I had been in school for a while. I was studying English literature.

A pipe fitter in her early thirties who had been very attached to men through most of her early life described her dawning appreciation of women.

I was married for seven years and one of the main effects that it had on me was that his family was a lot more emotionally open than my family, and also the women in that family—they sort of took each other seriously and gave each other a lot of support and were very close, and so I got to spend a lot of time with my sisters-in-law and with my mother-in-law and I guess I learned some way of being with people and being different from them but feeling accepted and tolerated and loved in that kind of atmosphere. They had a very strong family life and it was very emotional—they used to have fights with each other and it was okay, and my family was not like that. Fights were considered—it was something that was not supposed to happen. Everyone was always supposed to smile. I think the other big thing that happened to me was that I got into the women's movement and the main effect that had on me was I got to be friends with women. I got a lot of support from women and had a lot of free space to kind of figure out what it was I wanted to do and a lot of support for doing it and practical help in doing the things I wanted to do with my women friends.

A young apprentice surveyor who is supporting her daughter and is determined never to marry felt growing up in the sixties was really significant for her. She had taken a lot of drugs, had been sexually liberal, and until her daughter's birth could be very "hang loose" about what she wanted to do in the world. For her, the most significant turning point in life had been witnessing the political strife of the sixties.

At the People's Park, I saw police beating people. I think politically that changed my life a lot. I saw a lot of injustice. I felt that I was always seeing the weird side of life. Not good or bad, but weird.

An appliance service technician in her middle thirties who had lived her young adulthood with a great deal of uncertainty was finally able to pull herself together after psychotherapy led her into a women's group. Three of the nontraditional women we interviewed had comments similar to this:

Therapy . . . when my stepfather died. The therapy in the hospital wasn't so great. It was mostly shock therapy. And when . . . I got married when I was twenty-four and I hadn't been dating . . . I hadn't dated very much. Then I was getting depressed a couple of

years after I'd gotten married and I didn't know why and I knew
that I could kill myself or I could get into therapy. So I got into
good therapy with a good therapist. He was really a trippy guy. I
think he must have been a bisexual because he was a really open
person. I became a feminist after I'd been to him. He helped me
get into myself and the whole woman's thing and start exploring
and growing and I just developed from there. . . .

For 10 percent of the nontraditional women we met, coming
out as a lesbian appeared to be a key turning point. Although
we did not probe the respondents for how they felt about being
gay or what they felt might be the relationship between their
sexual preferences and their nontraditional occupational interests, certain things became clear from the overall tone of their
interviews. The relationship between gayness and nontraditional work roles is far more subtle than the assumptions many
people harbor about gay women. Nontraditional work for gay
women is not an exercise in "role reversal"; it is not an effort to
assume a masculine identity. It appears rather to come from a
concern for lifelong financial livelihood and a desire to find interesting and lucrative work. Being gay, like being divorced or
abandoned, forces upon women the reality of *having* to work.
In addition, being gay makes a woman marginal to mainstream
female culture and as such gives her practice at living with the
problem of "being different." Practice at living as an outsider
cannot help but improve her ability to succeed at a job where
she has to be able to survive a certain amount of initial harassment and isolation. The issue of gayness is introduced here because it is pattern-breaking and practice-giving, not because of
any special connection between alternative sexual preferences
and alternative occupational preferences. The women who mentioned coming out as a turning point did so for the most part
rather matter-of-factly.

A pipe fitter who had grown up in a middle-class family with
a mother who had never been employed, and of whom it was
simply assumed she would go to college (preferably to a presti-
gious eastern girls' school), described it this way:

Turning points, okay, let me think. I spent a year in Mexico and
Guatemala and I think that was a real—I mean something about

that year . . . it was the happiest and probably the heaviest in my life. I lived in Guatemala with this woman from Canada and it was the first time I ever had a real relationship with anyone. I mean, where we talk to each other and we worked out problems and we cared about each other and where there was some kind of mutual response which I had never experienced. I didn't even know it was possible, and so that was a turning point in my life because then I came back and I got into therapy after that and I really started to pull it all together.

An auto mechanic described her coming out as part of a larger process of opening up and understanding the world from a different perspective than when she was growing up.

Yeah, certain things that happened in college. I got more disillusioned with the system. I took LSD and that changed me a lot—not necessarily permanently, but it changed me more than ever. It brought out feelings that I have, I was always real inhibited with my feelings and it made me more in touch with my feelings. Then coming out as a lesbian changed me a whole lot. Then moving to Southern California—the people I met here taught me about class differences—that changed me a lot because they made me feel like I had to reject my middle-class background. A lot of things they believed were misguided, but it did change me a lot in a lot of good ways.

Ann Baker, the gay activist mechanic whose ideal job would be "playing beautiful music for lesbians," described her first affair with a woman as a critical step in her decision to drop out of private college and pursue a life-style different from that of her conservative, upper-middle-class midwestern parents.

A major turning point was—let's see—I fell in love with a woman when I was a junior or sophomore—must have been a junior in college. And that was a real big deal for me. This was a church-related school and neither one of us could deal with it—I mean we could not even mention the word "lesbian." The reason I'm having trouble figuring out where it fits here is because we both blocked it for a long time—a long time. But the fact that it happened is important. Something else happened later that started easing that tension. I eventually left school, had a lot of different jobs, and ended up out here.

Turning points—assuming responsibility for others, becoming financially self-sufficient, dropping out of college, having a child out of wedlock, acting on a homosexual preference—are all events requiring decision and action and eventually leading to more self-direction and control. These are the significant events of young adulthood. Only a very few nontraditional women named selecting a nontraditional job as a turning point. This suggests that coming to terms with general identity questions, such as those resolved through the experiences just described, may be a necessary and earlier step in the process of developing nontraditional interests and selecting nontraditional options.

PATTERN BREAKING SUMMARIZED

This chapter has moved us beyond early childhood and family contexts into a discussion of adolescent and young adult experiences. Both differentiate the nontraditional women we met from other women growing up in America in the 1950s and '60s. Many things about their experiences broke pattern with most young girls of their times. Virtually all the nontraditional women continued to have a great deal of personal independence through adolescence. The majority were only marginally involved in school cliques and school-related activities. More than half of the women described themselves as not particularly attractive in adolescence, as not dating, as not being boy-conscious and clothes-conscious the way so many girls were. In addition, many worked through high school—filling their nonschool time primarily by earning money. Finally, a number of the women were living with boyfriends or husbands, or were pregnant before finishing high school. It was the rare woman who described a cheery, carefree adolescence full of school activities, parties, and boyfriends. Adolescence is hard on all kids, but the women we met lived with a special kind of marginality and separateness that went beyond the predictable anxieties and loneliness tied to the transition into adulthood. It is possible that learning to live with that special kind of differentness contributed to their ability to be occupational risk takers later.

After completing high school and leaving the family home, which the majority of the women we met did by age seventeen or eighteen, these women embarked on a whole new phase of their lives—finding meaningful adult roles at work and establishing their own families. The early work experiences these women had, how they made the transition into nontraditional blue-collar work, and what their experiences as blue-collar workers have been like require lengthy discussions that are the topic of Part Two of our story, "Working in a Blue-collar Job."

PART TWO

WORKING IN A
BLUE-COLLAR JOB

IV

The Stabilization of Work Role Identity

INTRODUCTION

Part One introduced some common themes in the childhood and background experiences of nontraditional blue-collar women and considered how these experiences contributed to the capacity for and interest in occupational risk taking. Part Two will emphasize the world of work itself. It will examine the work histories of women in nontraditional jobs, the factors influencing their decision to pursue a nontraditional job, how they feel about paid employment generally and what they like about their specific jobs, what their experiences on the job have been like, what and who has helped or hindered them, and the factors affecting success as a pioneer.

We shall begin with a look at the experiences of the women as they moved out of adolescence and into adult responsibilities, and in particular into full-time paid employment. By the time we met them, the majority of the women we talked with had a fairly clear sense of the kind of work they preferred and an expectation that they would always be employed. This sense of oneself as a permanent member of the paid labor force, with definite likes and dislikes for particular jobs and job settings, is what I will refer to as "stabilization of work role identity." But a stable work role identity emerged only after a number of on-the-job experiences and trial and error experiments. The work role identities of the women we met and the processes by which these women came to have a clear sense of the work they wanted is the subject of this chapter.

Even though most of the women we met grew up learning to be autonomous and expecting to be employed, they also grew up facing traditional expectations and limited opportunities. Very few women grew up having a clear sense of what work they wanted to do as adults, or prepared themselves to pursue a particular vocation through either schooling or on-the-job training. In other words, most of the women did not plan their careers. Rather, they moved from job to job as opportunities presented themselves and most frequently discovered interests and capacities along the way. Many of them reported having a clearer sense of what they *didn't* want to do than what they did want. For example, many women said they didn't want a sit-down job or an inside job; they didn't want to clean other people's houses or do typing; they didn't want a job that required a lot of schooling or spending money on clothes. Thus, their search for work as young adults had some direction, but it lacked the focus of young men going off to college to prepare for a profession or graduating from high school with an eye on qualifying for an apprenticeship in a skilled trade or craft.

The women interviewed followed three different kinds of career paths. The first involved simply finding a job, any kind of job. These women graduated from high school and weren't going to college, or were single parents, or had parents who could no longer support them. Over time, they defined their vocational interests, but at first they needed any job. A second kind of career path involved women who went to college without clear occupational goals or with a conventional objective such as teaching or nursing. Many of these women dropped out of college because they realized it wasn't for them, and many who completed their degrees found—when it came time to look for work—that the only jobs open to them were the same that they would have gotten as high school graduates. The final type of career path is represented by a small number of women who began their adulthood with the expectations that marriage and motherhood would be their primary roles. These women entered the job market later in life as a result of husbands' unemployment, divorce, or financial stresses, but their experiences in entry-level jobs and the process of finding work they really cared about was not very different from those of the other two groups.

For the women interviewed, most of whom entered the paid labor force in the sixties and early seventies, some a decade earlier, initial vocational options and experiences were remarkably similar, regardless of their educational backgrounds or motivations for working. High school graduates, college dropouts, and college graduates could get jobs in service areas such as waitressing and housekeeping. They could get assembly jobs in factories. They could get jobs in sales areas such as women's clothing or flower and gift shops. They could get jobs in clerical areas as receptionists, typists, or executive secretaries. With the exception of a few highly trained women who became teachers or librarians or nurses, practically every woman we met spent most of her occupational life in the world of semiskilled jobs earning minimum wages, or in clerical positions averaging $500 or $600 a month. For the vast majority of the women, the job they currently had—a nontraditional blue-collar job—represented the best pay, benefits, security, and opportunity for advancement of *any* job they had had. This, by the way, included teaching, according to some of our respondents. Even though after three years a number of the women left nontraditional jobs, only two, a computer analyst and a bookkeeper, were in jobs that paid more than the blue-collar trade. The self-employed tradeswomen were struggling but still making more money than the majority of employed women.

What all of this suggests is that the traditional failure of girls and young women to clearly articulate an occupational direction and a vocational "game plan" is as much a function of limited opportunities as it is of seeing paid employment as something to be combined with, or secondary to, marriage and a family. The women we studied had expected to be in paid employment for most of their adult lives. They also articulated needs for interesting, challenging, and well-paid work. They also knew what kind of work they *didn't* want to do. Their problem was that *they didn't know what kind of work they did want to do.* What ultimately differentiates them from millions of other women workers is that as information became available and opportunities opened up, they opted out of the conventional track and tried unexplored territory. Previous discussions have suggested some early pattern-breaking experiences that helped them opt out. But the woman who from the beginning was interested in unexplored territory was rare indeed. Most arrived there only as real opportunities opened up.

WORK HISTORIES

Despite the fact that women entered the paid labor force for different reasons, at different stages in life, and with very different family backgrounds and experiences, their early employment experiences were remarkably similar. For example, Molly O'Hara worked for only a brief time before marrying her husband at the end of World War II. A successful engineering draftsperson in her early fifties, Molly had held only traditional low-paying jobs before her apprenticeship. She described her employment experiences this way:

My first job was right after high school in the 1940s. I worked for an insurance company in New York City two blocks from Wall Street. I got the job through a friend. He told me they had an opening. I did typing, policy typing and things like that. My starting salary was $75 a month, and I was there for about a year and a half. I was making $100 a month when I quit. The reason I quit was I planned a vacation to California to meet my intended in-laws. My husband was from here and I was gonna take two weeks' vacation and two weeks' leave of absence, and the day I picked up my railroad ticket they told me I couldn't have my two weeks' leave of absence, so I quit. . . . With my father's permission, of course. I was nineteen then and I came to California on a two-week trip, stayed three and a half months. I finally went back to New York and went to work for a manufacturing corporation. Very foolishly I told 'em I could type and do clerical work, so I got the job of a girl that left a clerical job to go on the bench. We were also in testing equipment, she made four times as much money as I did. I only stayed there a year and I came back to California in 1945 to stay with my future mother-in-law. She had had a severe heart attack and so I came out here and the war ended and we were married here. My husband was a career navy man and I didn't work again until, um . . . twelve years ago when we got divorced. Well, I did work part time for a while before my husband retired from the Navy. I worked for a florist here in town part time. I had a friend at the flower shop and while my husband was overseas I worked part time and learned some of the business: making flower arrangements, but mostly it was delivery all over the city. I was with them off and on for three years. I worked during the winter, my son would work for her during the summer, I think. Then I went to work at Military Island. It was eleven years ago last month I went over there as a temporary. I was looking for a job then, I needed to go to work and my sister worked there and she told me that they needed clerks, typists. I got a temporary job for $700. It's eleven years last week . . . I'm still there, that's how I got started and that's the only employment I've really had. I've been in this apprenticeship with them almost two years now.

May Rogers also went to work after being a wife and mother. Her marriage lasted five years. Like Molly, when she was divorced, she had to support her three children with no vocational training. She was an apprentice electronics mechanic when we met her, but had fifteen years of work experience, which she shared with us.

When I was a secretary in high school at age seventeen I was getting $.50 an hour working two hours a day. After that I got married and had my three kids and when I had to go to work I went to work in the local garment factory. I think I was making $1.00 an hour there. I was working full time and I was twenty-two. I was called an inspector, but we just looked at the finished garment to be sure the stitches were right. And then from there I went to work for a contractor—they typed up stock lists and things for the government. I started out making $1.25 as a typist and then I went up to—I must have stayed there about a year or so, because it ended up at about $1.40 an hour. Then I started for the government and passed the clerk test, and started as a file clerk. They put me on special projects and I started at $1.68 an hour as a GS-3, and worked for about three years. I was divorced by then and I resigned to marry a captain in the Air Force who was assigned to France. When we came back to Texas I went back to work—that was in '64, when I was twenty-eight. I went back to work as a GS-3, clerk typist, continued to work there until I got another job in the purchasing office as a clerk typist—ended up a GS-4 in the purchasing office and then I got another divorce. I divorced him in '66 and then I was still working there. I had met a guy at the air force base before I went to France—just a real good friend, and when I had been divorced about a year or so I heard from him and we started corresponding and ended up getting married in '68. So then he retired in '70 and we moved out here and I continued to do clerical work in civil service until I got into the apprentice program in '72.

Both Molly and May took clerical jobs, not because of a strong preference for that kind of work, but because there were no alternatives. Twenty years later this was still the case for most women. Even young women with college degrees found themselves confronted with only clerical jobs requiring one or two *high school* classes, not college training. As college graduates with no interest in traditional women's jobs such as teaching or nursing, such women had nowhere else to turn for a job in the middle and late sixties. Sandra Wong, for example, seems very different from Molly and May, but her work options were not that different. Here is how she described her situation:

I guess the first job that I had was baby-sitting for friends and I'd get $.50 or $.75 an hour. I didn't have to earn my own money when I was a kid so I worked just for fun or extras. I worked a concession stand at the zoo on weekends. I didn't work in college except when I came home in the summers and then I would work full time in clerical jobs, typing, filing, stuff like that for minimum wage. The two years I studied in Hong Kong I also did some part-time tutoring of English. After I graduated from college I came home instead of going to New York City with some friends. I got a job on a special project at a mental health clinic. They paid me one lump sum of about $400. I was twenty-three by then. I had finished college, I'd studied in Hong Kong, and I had to find a *real* job and you guessed it—the only job I could find at that time was as a secretary with the city through the CETA program. I made $3.00 an hour on that job. It was the only thing I could do—typing. I told you about that job and how much I disliked it. So, anyway, I decided to try to find something different and went for some career counseling and I ended up as a machinist trainee in this steel mill. Here I've spent four years in a great university and I go to work in a factory and now I want to—it's not to become a professional, but now I want to have a skill instead. *And* I'm already making more than my friends who are teachers.

Sandra's experience was echoed in the vocational experiences of women who entered the work force immediately upon high school graduation, women who were college dropouts, and college graduates. All reported employment opportunities limited primarily to clerical jobs, waitressing, housecleaning, and factory work. One college graduate interviewed had a much lengthier work history than Sandra because she frequently interrupted her schooling to take full-time jobs. When Ann Chew finally finished her education at twenty-eight, a major manufacturing company was looking for women to hire for nontraditional jobs, and she decided to try tool and die making. Ann was a machinist apprentice when we met her. She liked the field and despite her college degree felt it held the brightest prospects for her. She described her work experiences:

My first job, I was fifteen, and I worked after school in a restaurant as a waitress. I think I made $.70 an hour or something. The next job I had was a summer job at a restaurant as a waitress. I think I was about sixteen years old and I worked for the summer months, two months, full time, and there I made $.70 an hour plus tips. Then I don't think I worked until I left Goddard, which is the school I went to for a year and a half. I went to New York and I did all sorts of odd jobs. I never did land any full-time jobs. I did typing here and there and I remember working for a place that codes research studies—marketing research. For the next few years I had all kinds of odd jobs. I moved around a lot. I had a baby when I was twenty in Illinois. When I left the father of my child at around twenty-one I had all kinds of odd jobs around a university.

I usually worked part time and got about $2.50 an hour. I did this straight through because I was going to school at this time and I went to school in the summer. Then I dropped out of college. I didn't have my bachelor's degree yet. I started working full time as a production typist for a management consultant firm and I must have turned twenty-five in there sometime. I must have made $650 a month—full time. I worked there for a year and I quit and went back to get my master's degree. I was getting my master's in teaching English as a second language. I could get my B.A. at the same time since I only had three hours to go. So I dropped out of the master's program, but I got my B.A. Then I started looking around and I went to the manufacturing company and they offered me an apprenticeship in tool and die, but before I got the tool and die apprenticeship I had to get some training. It wasn't really like a job, but I did get paid for it by the state. It was a CETA program— maybe that was a federal program—I never can remember. I was getting full-time training—machine shop training. I worked there for five months and that took me up to last May. I made $84 a week. It was peanuts, but it was nontaxable and better than nothing. Last year I was twenty-eight. When I finished the training for the tool and die apprenticeship, the apprenticeship fell through because the company had a big cutback and they decided I had to go. Then I decided to come to California and I was on my way and they called and told me I was back on as an apprentice, but I told them it was too late. I job-hunted for about a month and then I sort of accidentally fell on this job. I started at $4.39 an hour as a machine operator, and when I became an apprentice I got a raise to $4.59 an hour. I know now that I want to go into a mechanical field. What I would branch into—the actual direction in the machine field I don't know. I do feel pretty strongly about being a machinist. I think it's something I'll really enjoy once I really get into it.

Another woman we met had finished two years of art school in New York City and couldn't find the kind of work she wanted. Over time she revised her work goals to the point of considering an apprenticeship in woodworking so she could eventually be a furniture maker. She ultimately settled for a position as an apprentice welder, which she was enjoying a great deal when we met her. Like Ann, she was still in her trade by our third-year follow-up. Katie Jenkins described her employment as follows:

At age eighteen I was a census taker. Then I went to art school and I worked in a garment factory making children's clothing for three weeks. I worked as a salesgirl in a dime store for about one year and that was part time and I earned minimum wage. I worked in a shoe store for about one and a half years and I was nineteen to twenty-one years old. I was a clerk and I did stock and that was part time and I earned $2.00 an hour. Then after that I cleaned houses for about one and a half years. That was when I was twenty-one to twenty-two years old. Worked for myself and I subcontracted a floor waxer; he had a van and stuff and I'd get him to polish people's floors for me. That was full time and I set my price at $20 a day instead of hours. I made $100 a week, so I had a different house each day. Then I was in training in welding school and I did that for eight months and now I have this job.

Kim Fargo, a very shy woman, was a cable splicer for the telephone company. Like most of the women we interviewed, she had jobs baby-sitting and in food services through her teens. She was very religious through high school and went to nursing school upon graduation hoping to be a medical missionary. She described her experiences:

After high school I went into nursing school. My counselor helped me get in and everything, and it was really a good nursing school and they didn't accept many people, and I was in that for a year. But then I became an atheist while I was in nursing school, and I went to nursing school because I wanted to be a missionary, so with the biology and psychology I was taking, it just didn't go with my beliefs at the time. I dropped out of nursing school, and went to Arizona for a summer and went to school there, then I went back and went to Ohio State for the fall and I was in social work for . . . six months. I was raped at the beginning, in the fall, and became like, I just couldn't handle it and I went into therapy again at that time. I just, I couldn't live, and he helped me get through that and get out of school and everything. And uh, become, y'know, I got a full-time job with the telephone company—information operator of all things, God, that was terrible. I was twenty-three by that time and it gave me the money to get out of the house. I'd been living at home and the therapist helped me out of the house. I started driving a car—I bought a car, and I had my first date, quote "date," started dating guys, and he helped get me into the socially acceptable area where you know . . . I hadn't been there before . . . and functioning . . . into maybe middle class, so I was in the telephone company nine months and I moved to Arizona. . . . In Phoenix, Arizona, almost everybody works at the electronics company, and my aunt and uncle in Arizona helped me get on there, and I met my husband there. I worked semiconductors there. I made semiconductors, using microscopes, sitting at a microscope eight hours, putting these little wires on pads. I did that for . . . about a year and a half . . . make parts. My husband really wanted to move to California. He had lived here, and I came out here and I happened like when we were married it just happened I was off most of the summers, I didn't really work full time permanently. When we were married, it was like my job wasn't that important. I'd worked at a pen factory for a coupla months. I think I went back to $1.98 an hour inspecting pens. That was a horrible . . . all women, mostly, uh, Mexican American or Latin Americans. After my husband and I separated I got into nurse's aide training in a hospital in the L.A. area, and I think I started at $2.35 an hour. I was twenty-six then and I did that for four years, a nurse's aide, I went up to $3.62 an hour, $3.65 an hour, and I . . . working part time mostly because I was going to school during that time, first in child development, then psychology, and I dropped out of school . . . January, this last January. I decided that I wanted to start earning a living—a real living now.

Another woman, who dropped out of a highly competitive university after two years, was a gas service repairperson. In our third-year follow-up, she told us she liked her job so much she doubted she would go for the early retirement she had initially planned. The daughter of extremely well educated, affluent parents, she described her career development in the following way:

I took care of the animals in a Natural Science Center in New York. I was sixteen and I was paid $2.00 an hour and I worked four full days a week—twenty-eight hours. I guided people around and answered questions. I kept it clean. Job number two I was seventeen, this was also a summer job, I worked for the Housing Development Administration in a big eastern city. My dad worked for the city and he knew the people that were hiring me. They were conducting a study of people who relocated by urban renewal and I worked for the group of people who went around to the relocating offices and looked through the files and put down certain data. I put the data on a coded sheet and a keypunch person—I think I made $110 a week. Then I went away to school. After my sophomore year I moved to California and in the fall I came out here. I took any job I could get, which happened to be a salesgirl at Saswell's. I started at $2.00 an hour part time. I worked there for three years part time. In the meantime I had three other jobs—also part time—Singer Fabrics for two weeks and then they cut me down to two hours a day and I decided it wasn't worth it at $1.85 an hour—I was taking my bus fare for my salary. When I first came to California I had a job collating papers for two weeks for $2.00 an hour in a printing plant. The reason I got the job is that I had a friend that worked there. I worked for the Metropolitan Transportation Authority—I'm not sure when this was. It must have been in the spring of 1973. I was a traffic enumerator for three days a week, eight hours each of the three days. I had this little punch thing and as the cars went by we punched the ticket for how many people were in the car. You only worked twenty minutes out of every hour—it was really very easy I got a tan mostly. I made $3.00 an hour there, and that lasted about two months. Then for one fall my boyfriend had a job taking care of an apartment building and I took it over for him one fall and that was five hours a week or $65 a month. I swept and did gardening and that sort of thing. That was probably the fall of '73. Then we went to Seattle for the summer of '74. For three days I had a job selling books on the telephone. Then I guess my next job was working for the phone company from November of '74 until March of '75. It was a temporary job for four months and I took out telephones. I took the job with hopes that I would get a full-time permanent job with them, but I didn't. Last September '75 I was hired at the utility company where I work now, and I make $231 a week. I think I'm in a job I'm really going to like.

Examples of women dropping out of college and jumping from job to job are numerous. Up until the point of nontraditional employment, the work histories of the college graduates and dropouts we interviewed were erratic and unstable—six months here, three months there, and so forth. Many observers have looked at such employment patterns and said that "women don't know what they want. You can't rely on them to stay with a job. They aren't career-minded." Our data suggest that, given an opportunity to be trained and to earn good money and benefits in a place where advancement is possible, women settle down into their jobs and commit themselves to their work.

The experiences of young women seeking employment after high school mirror those of the college-educated women just described. The chef's apprentice, Erin Kelly, is an interesting case study.

My first job was working at this army base, at a beach. I was like a handyperson and I did jobs, depending on where they were short, like sometimes I'd sit at the gate and let people in or working in the mess doing hot dogs. I was fourteen then and it was full time during the summer. I got about $2.00 an hour. Then I moved out to California and I was fifteen and got a job at a place called Speedy Burgers, and I did try fry-cooking there. I worked there until I got out of high school. I think I got $1.75 an hour. And it was part time after school and on weekends. Then I started cooking in a little tiny restaurant and I made $3.00 an hour. And I was seventeen. Then they sold the place and the people who bought it brought their own cooks, so I became a waitress and made $1.00 an hour, but the tips were really good. I worked there about one and a half years. Then I went back East and worked as a parts manager in a motorcycle shop and I don't remember how much they paid me but it wasn't very much. I was eighteen, and I worked there about six months. Then I went back to being a waitress until I moved back out to California and the money was really good there. I got paid $2.00 an hour and the tips were fantastic. I used to take home $200 a week. I worked full time during the school year and then during the summer I only worked three days a week. Then I moved back out here and worked at a bootleg tape factory making these cassettes illegally—eight-track tapes. That didn't pay very well, but it was money under the table so that was nice. I worked at a pie shop in Sacramento part time. I was almost twenty and I didn't work there very long either. Between the tape factory and the pie shop it was only about six months because that's all I spent in that area, then I moved down to the Bay Area and have been here ever since. That was the summer I turned twenty. I made about $1.25 an hour. Then I went to Berkeley again and I worked for the manager of the apartment building I lived in. I think I got $2.25 an hour. I used to clean the apartments and stuff after people moved out. That was for about six months and then I moved over to San Francisco. Then I started off with this company and I started off at $2.24 an hour or $2.50, but I started off as a cashier there and then I became a cook and when they moved over to a new plant I became the manager of one of the shifts there. I was making around $600 a month and then I started the apprentice program. I was twenty-one then. In the apprenticeship you start off at $23.40 a shift, and you get a percentage of all the other cooks' wages and now I'm up to 85 percent and I get $33.06 a shift and it's full-time work.

A young woman who was working in production control in a military manufacturing and repair activity was quite ambivalent about her job the first year we interviewed her because it didn't deal with "people" but with "things." By our third-year follow-up she was still in her job, very enthusiastic about the nature of the work and very optimistic about staying and advancing in her field. Before getting this job she had had a string of unskilled jobs, each of which lasted only a short time.

The first job I had, I was fifteen, I worked one day a week, Saturdays in a café as a waitress, I was paid $1.35 an hour. I also worked around that same time—my stepfather opened a record store and I worked in the store selling records, stocking them, and that sort of thing. I made about $1.50 an hour. That was two or three days a week. Also while I was working at the record store I was writing three articles a week for the newspaper and I got paid $10 a week for doing that. The waitress job only lasted three or four months. And the record job lasted three or four months and I got fired from the newspaper after four or five months. They didn't think I could write very well. Then not too long after—I think I was seventeen—I started working in a hamburger place as a waitress and cooking hamburgers and I made $1.60 an hour when I started and then went up to $1.70. It was full time, weekends and evenings. It lasted about seven months. Then I went to work at a retirement home as a waitress serving the tables in the dining area. That was part time and I made about $1.75 an hour and that lasted three or four months and I quit that 'cause that's when I graduated from high school. Then I went up to Washington State and was there for the summer and worked in another hamburger place and made about $1.50 an hour. That was full time for the summer. Then I came back to Southern California and went back to work at the retirement home and made the same—$1.75 an hour, and I worked about seven or eight months and then I quit and went to Chicago for a while and I wasn't working. I came back to Southern California and went to work for the Parks and Recreation Department as a recreation leader on the playground. It was a temporary job for the summer and I made $1.65 an hour. Then I quit there and went to Chicago. I think I was nineteen or twenty at that time. I worked at another hamburger place and worked there for three months full time and I earned about $1.80 an hour. I came back to California and I was twenty-one by this time and I got a job tending bar and I tended bar for about eight months and made around $2.00 an hour. It was full time, and I quit there and went to work at Military Island, where I work now. I've been here two years.

With the exception of one Asian woman, these work histories reflect the employment experiences of white women. Those of black women are somewhat different and need to be described separately. While the white women we interviewed held a wide range of clerical jobs, the black women had much more domestic service work and factory work. This was also true of most of the other minority women. Nonskilled or low skilled domestic and factory work was all that was available to the minority woman high school graduate looking for employment prior to the early sixties in this country. Even clerical jobs were difficult to get outside of the liberal urban centers. Kelly Lincoln, a successful black foreperson, had a twenty-year work history that was apparently scattered and unfocused, but as opportunities opened up in the late sixties, her heretofore unrealized outstanding abilities and motivation helped her successfully complete an apprenticeship as a roto-blade mechanic. She summarized her work experiences:

I started with baby-sitter jobs when I was about thirteen. I had different day jobs during my junior and senior years. I think I made $.50 an hour until I was sixteen. I tried to work five days and it would be about three or four hours in the afternoon. After high school I went to Oklahoma City and worked for a lady on a live-in job.

I think I had that job for about four months. I went to Oakland and I got a job at a diner. That was full time and I was seventeen. Then I went to work in a cannery. I was canning peaches. My next job was a waitress in Oakland. I didn't have another job until I came to San Diego in 1949. I was about twenty-one. I got this baby-sitting job. It was full time. I made $20 a week. That's mostly what I did, baby-sitting and house cleaning. I even took my baby with me places. My husband was messing up, so I decided to find a better job. I went to school for Defense Industries. They told me I had no experience and so they asked me if I had worked during the last war. I said no, but the way things were going I am going to be too old for this one. I said don't you have a school to send me to? That is how I got into school. Then Defense Industries hired me and I got $1.11 plus, the night shift. So I made $1.19 an hour. I worked there from '51 until the first part of 1955 and then I went out on pregnancy leave and then I went back in 1956 and stayed until 1958 and then I got laid off. When I went back the second time I went back as an assembler. I learned it on the job—I don't know what the pay rate was then. It couldn't have been much more. Maybe two dollars something an hour or thereabouts. I worked at that kind of assembly line stuff until the middle sixties, with layoffs here and there.

In 1965 I was about thirty-seven and I made $2.37 an hour. They were fixing to lay people off where I was and I got a call from Military Island. I didn't know what a sheet metal worker was but I took it. I went to Military Island in 1966 and I have been there ever since. I have been a sheet metal worker and a journeyman and then I was picked up on an inspection and then I made foreman. They changed our rate to rotor-blade mechanic effective date 1975. I was making $7.56 an hour and now I think I make $8.56 an hour.

Another black woman, twenty years Kelly's junior, had a similar work history. The employment programs of the sixties gave Connie Johnson an opportunity to break out. Over the three years we were in contact she had held four different jobs but was sticking to a nontraditional track. By our third-year interview, Connie was working as a laborer on a construction crew, earning close to $8.00 an hour. She described her work history:

All through high school I cleaned hotel rooms with my mother. She would give me $10. She didn't tell me, but that was a lot of money for me. She would say, "Now is this enough," and I would say sure, you know, and then after I finished school I got a job of my own and I was working as a maid and I was making $40 per week and she wanted to take it but I wouldn't give it to her. When I finished working as a maid, I told my mother and I talked to her before, and I said, "You know, I'd never take my daughter to do that type of work because I know when I finished school I was used to doing it." I got right out of school and went doing this and then, then I did it. But I also, well afterwards, I got married when I was twenty years old and I went right on doing it. I worked hotels mostly all the time and then I came out of—I got married and I was doing maid work then, and my husband was always telling me, "Why don't you try and find you something else, why you wanna do that?" I just did it because that was the first thing I had experience in and afterwards I started working at a shirt factory as a armhole creaser and presser and I felt so much better not cleaning. It was a big step for me, you know, working as a presser, it was good, plus I would be making—well, the most I ever made was $2.00 an hour as a maid, which the pay went up, minimum wages was $2.00, so I think I was only making about $1.65 when I started working at the factory. I think it was $1.65 for the starting wage, but then I went all the way up to $3.00 maybe, and even more. It was according to how fast you worked with your hands and so I a . . . you know, I was armhole creasing and I was collar pressing and my husband liked me working there. When I stopped working for two years, you know, I got pregnant and I stopped working for two years and I went back but at the time they weren't hiring, they were laying off. Then I went to work in a restaurant as a cashier and a fry cook. That was full time and I worked there a long time.

I worked at a spa also as a janitor for a year. It was more or less, I would help the ladies in the Jacuzzi, it wasn't much of anything, I would assist them with a robe and the steam cabinet and I'd clean the spa. And then for a while I was off there, and then I went to work as a nurse's aide in this convalescent home.

Me and my husband wasn't together and I was trying to hold onto my house and everything and I went to the spa but eventually they laid me off and then I went to work at the barbecue for six months. And then from there I went to the Women's Store Front and they helped me find a job as a meat cutter at a grocery store, but it only lasted for two weeks. Then I went into the bus driver's training school.

Some younger black women we interviewed had employment experiences and options closer to those of white women. The experiences of an apprentice who had entered the trades upon completing four years of military service is an example of the somewhat expanded opportunities and work experience.

Okay, at sixteen I worked at a restaurant. Length of employment would be three years full time after school and I'd get off about two o'clock in the morning, but I worked from four to two and go home and do my homework at work—it seemed like it was go to work, go to school, go to work, go to school. I was earning about . . . I started off at $.95 an hour at the time and I quit there in 1967 at the age of nineteen and I went in the Air Force. My job there was inventory management specialist—that was my career field that I was assigned to and I was sent to technical school for the special training, which was four months, and my hours—it varied, being in the service. I was averaging about thirty-two hours per week and when I got out I was earning $306 because I lived off base and you get extra money for separate lodging.

I got out of the Air Force January 1971, after four years and eleven days' duty time. After that I went on unemployment for three or four months at the most. Then I worked in a jewelry factory back East in Rhode Island at $1.90 an hour because I told them I refused to take any less, because some of the women working there were still only making $1.55 an hour at the time. This was in 1971, which was still shocking to me even then. So they hired me but they didn't want to because of my background of being in the service, 'cause they felt I'd be there a little while and then go off and get a better job. Well, I wasn't making enough there to live, so I had to go get another job besides. So I was working in a garment factory making bras and girdles and things like this. I was doing that as a sewing machine operator. I had both of those jobs for three or four weeks because I had registered with the State of Rhode Island with the Disabled Veterans and I registered at the unemployment office, so they called me up and asked if I could come in for an appointment down at the unemployment office 'cause I told them if they heard of anything to get me a better job, I'd like to try it. So myself and a couple of girls—we were all three registered—he called us down and asked if we'd like to have a job with the government, building instruments. We went down to the naval air station there, and we met a guy in personnel. This was when President Nixon had opened up this job program for veterans, 'cause there was nothing for us except for these creepy jobs. So they said, well, can you come back tomorrow and be interviewed by the board to see if you qualify for any of these jobs or whatever? We saw a lot of different jobs there and they gave me a bad time about some of the ones I said I was interested in. I finally got into an apprenticeship in aircraft instrument repair, which is the job I have now.

What should be clear from this sampling of work histories is that for large numbers of women, particularly the kinds of woman we met, vocational interests and preferences evolve and become stabilized as a result of on-the-job experiences and employment opportunities. Specific interests and work commitments grew out of their employment experiences; interests and commitments did not lead the women to the jobs. This appears to contradict what we understand to be the experience of successfully employed middle-class women (and most employed men). It is usually assumed that a certain amount of interest, planning, and preparation precede actual decisions about employment.[1] Most of the literature on vocational interest development emphasizes how parents, counselors, and teachers are crucial in helping a young person define interests and pursue a chosen career. In contrast, the experiences of these women in the workplace and their exposure to opportunities seemed more crucial to the development of their vocational interests than advance planning, preparation, or reinforcement from a teacher, parent, or counselor.

We have pointed out that the women described themselves as having a range of interests and potential skills, but as having received very little clear vocational direction from others. At the same time they described themselves as always having expected to work at something. The assumption that they would always work appears to have derived in part from the fact that 60 percent of these women had mothers who worked full time and in part from the fact that, with one or two exceptions, all of the women were engaged in odd jobs or some form of part-time employment by their early teens. The majority were out of school and in full-time jobs by age seventeen or eighteen as a financial necessity. Thus it is not surprising that the women described their interests as having grown out of work experience and new employment opportunities rather than from a set of earlier preferences. What nontraditional interests or abilities the women did have for the most part lay dormant until some kind of employment opportunity presented itself.

This may seem like an obvious point, but given the generalizing tendencies of the rash of current studies of primarily middle-class and managerial women, one might easily overlook this interesting difference between women of different backgrounds. To some extent (and this may be changing with increasing inflation), middle-class and professional men and women appear to develop interests and capacities independent of their work experience. They seek out employment through which they can express these interests and abilities.[2] The great majority of working women, however, appear to develop interests and capacities in the work environment, and to increase commitment and explore options in the context of the work itself rather than in the process of self-exploration and education. (Often this leads us to assume that these women do not have complicated feelings about work and personal identity.) Conventional middle-class women do not or are not encouraged to take paid employment for granted and are more likely to see it as an option, not a necessity. Therefore they are more likely to believe, correctly or incorrectly, that they should wait for a job that matches their interests. In contrast, women who must find paid employment will take whatever work is available. Thus the relationship between vocational interests and vocational choice is not a simple one-way relationship, wherein attitudes and interests lead to specific choices. It varies by class, by race, and by other factors limiting the number of life-style alternatives available. As the pioneering sociologist Everett C. Hughes pointed out, the process of moving into jobs is a complex interaction of personal orientations, structural opportunities and events, and probably a certain amount of luck.[3]

THE IMPACT OF OPPORTUNITY ON INTEREST IN BLUE-COLLAR JOBS

Many have been pessimistic about the gains of the women's movement and of recent federal legislation enacted to foster new skills and more equal employment for women. The figures are discouraging. Women still occupy a very small percentage of higher-paying, responsible positions. Nonetheless, what little action there has been appears to have been a direct result of the aggressive efforts to equalize employment opportunities. These efforts have resulted in certain guidelines and policies that force employers to admit women into nontraditional fields. More important, from our point of view, they have created a climate of expectations and readiness which for a small group of women has opened the door to increased opportunity. Eighty percent of the women we talked to were involved in some sort of vocational school or on-the-job training program. Most of these sorts of programs and jobs had opened up to women only recently. The women were quick to describe the significance of the pressures on vocational schools and industry to hire and train women. Many of them indicated that, had the opportunity for this kind of work been present a few years ago, they might have tried a nontraditional job sooner. One woman stated:

It's only been the last few years there has been any affirmative action. I'd never have had this job if UPS hadn't been forced to hire women. It wasn't out of their own good will that they hired us. They are doing everything possible to discourage female employment, and if it continues—I would think literally thousands of industries have not had a suit brought against them. If you are a woman and you want a job outside the usual female work, it's hard to get it.

A press operator who was very successful at her work repeated what many women said to us in the first year.

I think they really hired me 'cause the government says that you have to at least give a woman a try at any kind of job that she thinks she can do 'cause ah—I don't think they really intended to let me get that far, but I'm really doing okay at this.

Until recently, women did not pursue numerous trades and crafts jobs, less from a lack of interest or desire for more satisfying, well-paid work than from a complete lack of knowledge of such jobs or from a very realistic sense that they were not wanted and probably would not be given a chance to try. A number of women we interviewed said they had no prior knowledge of the jobs they currently held until someone came along and gave them an opportunity. Maggie Patterson, who began as a keypunch operator at a military installation, moved into an apprenticeship with only the vaguest idea of what she was getting into.

After three years it just got to the point where $3.25 an hour was just not worth it. Some people came around to the keypunch area, which is all women, and said they were looking for some women to apply for the apprentice program. Well, some of the girls had husbands who were in the program or who had been in the program, so we knew a little about what it was—that it was a four-year deal and they sent you to school and you came out of it with an A.A. degree, and we figured if they could do it, we could do it, so three of us went down and took the test and I was the only one that passed it. I could have killed them, because I didn't want to go by myself. I had no idea what it was going to be like working with all guys after working with all women for three years, and I knew nothing about any of the jobs they had available.

Molly O'Hara described her decision to sign up for an apprenticeship in drafting in much the same way.

I was trained in clerical work. I took shorthand and typing in high school and so naturally went into the clerical field when I started to work for the government. I had hoped to get a job as a budget analyst with the Navy. They were having some job opportunities and I thought that this would probably be my field; even though I'm terrible in math, I like figures. When this job opportunity came up to be a draftsman, it was just something out of the clear blue. I didn't plan on it, have any idea or know anything like that was available. My son is an architect, so I had some idea of blueprints and I worked in the industrial planning division where blueprints crossed my desk all the time that the fellas made 'n' I had to send out that type of thing, but as far as doing any of it, it never entered my mind.

A woman working as a production control trainee in the aircraft industry said the same sort of thing:

I didn't know anything about aircraft other than to see them fly . . . they just called me to this job and I didn't know what to expect, but I knew that I would be trained. You take a test first of all when you apply. You go down and see the listing and I just saw whatever was vacant and I applied for the test. This is the test that I scored the highest on that I called in to, but as far as planning to get into the aircraft field, I never had any idea that I'd be doing this, because really I wanted to be a medical technologist. And that went down when the babies started. You really have to devote all your time to school in that field.

In the past the few women who *did* have some sort of knowledge and interest in nontraditional skills and a desire for blue-collar work either had to be superwomen who made it on their own or lucky enough to latch on to a skilled crafts- or tradesperson who would help them learn the ropes. We came across some of these "lucky" women in the course of the research. However, it was not until training, apprenticeship, and employment opportunities opened up systematically that it became possible for larger numbers and more diverse types of women to enter nontraditional fields. Some of the women we met who had strong interests in specific jobs, prior to getting the job, described a long and discouraging process. Until recently these motivated women had been very frustrated.

The experiences of a self-employed plumber underscore this point.

I think I'm going to stick in plumbing for a while. I think it first occurred to me when I was working in the variety store. That was the day that I was sitting there in the part with the cookware and the tools—the two things I'm interested in. I happened to look at a pipe wrench, and I thought who makes more money than me. At $1.80 an hour a lot make more money and I started thinking that plumbers make a lot of money and the more I thought about it the more I wanted to be a plumber, so I went to the union and I went through their whole screening and I'm on their union list in this county. Out of 94 applicants I was 52. They were taking the top 10. I made a special plea to them to let me in because I was a woman—the only woman out of 252 people that had taken the test and gotten this far—and they wouldn't do it. They wouldn't make a special category for women, which has just been changed after my three years of hassling. They have finally changed that. I spent one year on my time off talking to the plumbers in Berkeley and asking everyone and telling everyone that I wanted to be a plumber—will you teach me. I mostly got a lot of belly laughs. Finally, when I was working at the discount store, I happened to meet this guy and he was the first one who didn't laugh, so I snatched at the opportunity.

I'm going to stick with it. I've been with it almost three years. You can't keep jumping around from job to job, which is the main reason I wanted to get something I would like. I do like it.

Another woman described how her growing interest in nontraditional work came from job experiences and access to tradespeople but was never fully realized until government programs created real opportunities.

I was interested in the trades when I was still in North Carolina. I did some fix-it work at the day care center I worked at. When I came out here I fell in with some women who worked in the trades and they had some potlucks for women in the building trades and I went there and saw all these women and I was real excited—I thought, "Oh, yeah, that's who I am, I'm like those women over there." Of course, it's taken a long time for me to actually be able to support myself as a tradeswoman.

The few women we met who had some prior interest in nontraditional jobs were pleased to finally have a job more suited to their interests. However, more than half of the women interviewed indicated no particular prior interest in nontraditional work, and they described their movement into nontraditional fields as directly related to the appearance of better opportunities. Thus what appears to be the crucial factor in pursuing a nontraditional opportunity was a growing sense of what they ideally wanted to get out of work *in general*. The women were not highly committed to a particular skill; what they had was a desire for challenging work and good pay. A few samples bear this out.

I didn't even know it existed. It was all by chance that I got into this particular thing. I had no idea what I'd be doing. I'd heard a lot about the chances for women to be able to advance and work in civil service jobs and the benefits that civil service offers, and the pay that the job started at was better than I had ever made before, so I decided to try an apprenticeship.

Another woman commented:

Good money. In fact, that's a big plus factor. When I get really discouraged, I think where else am I gonna make this kind of money. Because even though it's not that skilled a job and essentially I'm outside being a janitor, I'm getting $3.89 an hour.

That's very good. I look in the papers and what do they offer?— $2.50, and I've worked sometimes at what I consider a skilled job— well, receptionist or secretary, and they start off at $2.50. And I started at $3.89 right off. That's not fair but that's because it's a man's job, too.

Another woman indicated her reasons in the following manner:

Right now I really want to get into something that was interesting to me. Waitressing is not in a way bad, but it is physically wearing and this is why I decided I wanted training in appliance repair. I had been thinking about some kind of trade I could get in, and this seemed like it was the most interesting. I enjoyed the training—there's enough to fixing machines so that it's something to work at, you know, it's just not something you automatically do, you think it over and figure it out and this is the kind of work I want to get into because I think I'll enjoy it more, than just more routine, routine—put it into a slot and turn it over and stamp it—that sort of a . . . thing.

The stereotype of an employed working-class woman focuses on her inconsistent work patterns, desire for sociable and non-challenging work settings, and ability to do boring, routine work for long periods. In contrast, these women had done boring, routine work and had not been satisfied by it. One wonders how many of the women workers supposedly "preferring" and "content with" their routine low-paying jobs are actually resigned to a lack of opportunities.

QUALITIES OF EMPLOYMENT VALUED BY WOMEN

What these highly work-oriented women valued in their employment was essentially the same things men value. The need for full-time employment and a regular paycheck was the critical reason for working for all but a few of the women. This is true for most employed men also. For these women, however, a job was clearly more than a paycheck. Anyone who has closely examined the work lives and family lives of blue-collar women has noted this. Nearly twenty years ago, Mirra Komarovsky, the well-known Barnard College sociologist, commented in her book on the blue-collar family that

the economic motive for taking a job is universally acknowledged, but it turns out to be not one but a cluster of motives. The women work, of course, because they desire what money can buy—but the sheer pride of earning is itself another reward.[4]

In a later passage, Komarovsky expands on this observation:

Apart from money, the working wives mentioned other rewards of working: the enjoyment of social life on the job, the pleasures of workmanship, the bracing effect of having to get dressed up in the morning, some relief from constant association with young children, and "having something interesting to tell my husband." A job apparently need not be a highly skilled one to yield the worker some satisfaction from its execution.[5]

We were able to identify five recurring themes that give some insight into what these women value in their jobs (in addition to the money): (1) *productivity,* in terms both of identifiable "output" of goods or services and of feelings of "accomplishment" based on internal standards; (2) *challenge,* most frequently described as "newness" and "variety," but also as "problem solving" and attempting something "unusual"; (3) *relatedness,* which the women expressed as feeling in the "swim of life" and as having daily contacts and relationships which provide "sociability," "recognition," and "feedback"; (4) *autonomy,* or some form of "control" over the pacing of the work and "discretion" as to the sequence and frequency of tasks; (5) *well-being,* in terms both of "mental and physical" satisfaction and of the "spillover" effects on self-identity and personal relationships.

PRODUCTIVITY

Productivity was a value expressed by many of the women in both traditional and nontraditional jobs during our first-year interviews. It was described in a variety of ways: a feeling of having done something constructive, of having accomplished something with one's time, of having an output, a product that people noticed and valued. Along with a desire for challenge, this was the most frequent spontaneously mentioned value. It was far more important to the cross section of women working in skilled jobs than values such as friendships in the workplace, convenience, or simple and clear tasks. For example, a young pipe fitter stated it this way:

Yeah, I would say that for me it's real important to have something, some productive work that I feel that I do every day and, like, sometimes, you know, you're just feeling depressed for whatever reason—some friends move out of town or someone you know is very ill or you're having hassles with your friends. It's just nice to be able to go and do something like, install a toilet which works. I feel I like to have something concrete that I can do and feel something's going right.

A welder in airplane repair expressed a similar sentiment about her work:

I don't like, you know, being around the house, I'd rather be out doing something constructive, something that I can account for all my time, I just enjoy it. I get satisfaction out of seeing something accomplished.

Even the women in more conventional jobs felt similarly. One cosmetologist talked about the sense of gratification she got from transforming the women who came into her shop.

I enjoy it, I really do. It gives you a sense of accomplishment when you make somebody else look better. When they come in sometimes they're all a mess, they're very depressed. But after I finish them, they leave here feeling a lot better.

For many women, a sense of productivity is tied to a sense of making a concrete contribution, as expressed by this electronics mechanic:

Um, it's important to me. I have to have a sense of accomplishment or a sense that I'm actually contributing. And, ah, I think I am, and, ah, it's important to me.

A woman training to be an auto mechanic expressed it this way:

I just feel that I want to make some sort of contribution. Maybe that's the best I can put, you know. And I just don't feel like cleaning toilets in particular. It's no contribution, it's just something that has to be done.

CHALLENGE

The women also had a great deal to say about the ways in which they found their jobs challenging and the elements of the work process that made a job interesting and satisfying. A challenging job is one that is varied, that is a new or unusual experience, that requires a woman to stretch herself, to reach, to grow. It involves for many women a sense of problem solving or mental challenges. Many women, however, also value physically challenging work.

The challenge of varied work was expressed by a young welder:

Well, it pays pretty well, the pay scale here is pretty low compared to other companies, so I could be making more someplace else, but the thing that I like about it is the job is interesting. You do something different every day.

A telephone installer described her varied and satisfying job with the following comments:

I like working on my own. I like going into people's houses and dealing with the different situations that I find there. Talking to different people and having to, the interchange that I have to do, deal with what they want and get it done. If they start hassling me about something, dealing with that in a way that feels good on both sides. I like the technical part, just learning about phone, learning about electricity, you know, why things don't work and why they do work. I like the physical part of, you know, just screwing screws in the wall plus lifting things up and down. I actually love climbing telephone poles. I'm just ecstatic about that. And it's really, I mean if there's a pole that needs climbing when I'm working with somebody, oh, it's no problem.

Related to the notion of variety is the fact that for many women the tasks involved in paid employment are new and thus there is the sense of learning something all the time. One woman, working in electronics repair in the communications area, was quite eloquent in her enthusiasm:

Well, I like learning about communications. I mean, the field of electronics is one that has interested me for a long time. It's so complex. I feel like I don't know very much and if I knew more, I know I would enjoy it more. I have this insatiable curiosity, and it's really interesting to understand what happens when you pick up this little box and talk into it that makes somebody else a mile away able to hear what you're saying. You know, what those little things do in there. I mean, that's really interesting to me. Um, so, I like that, I like learning about that even though I don't understand it completely. I like that. I like working with um, real precise, well-made equipment. One of those machines alone costs five or six thousand dollars. Where else am I going to be able to come in contact with that kind of stuff?

The newness and unfamiliarity of certain kinds of jobs and the chance to master skills that once seemed totally remote were also valued by many of the women we interviewed. This feeling was summarized well by an auto mechanic:

Um, I think it's very important the fact that I'm learning to do things that at one point seemed completely above me . . . certain kinds of knowledge, like working on cars or something, at some point in my life, it seemed like I'd never be able to learn things like that, and now I'm gradually doing it. It's fantastic!

The problem-solving character of many jobs was also appealing to women. It represented a kind of challenge that they described as keeping them mentally alert and constantly interested in what they were doing. An auto mechanic in Northern California expressed it this way:

I've really learned a lot about how to solve problems. I mean, that's like a lot of what fixing cars is about, is that you get the symptoms of a problem and you have to figure out where it comes from and what you can do to make it go away. Working with my hands, being able to see the results of my labors . . . is the kind of satisfaction I need to keep doing it day after day. It's also never the same. I mean I could do a thousand tune-ups, but each one is different . . . it's not like being on the assembly line where you punch the same rivets day after day.

A woman who was an auto mechanic and had previously been a computer programmer described both of these jobs as appealing because of their problem-solving dimensions:

The diagnostic work is what I like mostly. Once I find out what's wrong I get bored. Just fixing, I don't like turning wrenches or changing points. You know, I really don't like that. It's the diagnosis that I really enjoy. I walk up to a car that won't start and try to figure out why. And it's probably the same thing that's attracted me to computer programming, that's the same type of thing. So that's what I like mostly.

Many women were seeking physical challenge in their work, as well as variety and mental stimulation. A welder we interviewed was very direct about this:

I get a lot of exercise. I get to do a whole lot of different kinds of things. . . . I get to move around a lot, I get to drive a truck, I get to drive a forklift. I get to use all kinds of different tools, I get to climb up and down ladders and work off of scaffolding and walk around on the roofs and everything you know. So there's a lot of variety and that's really good and I love the physicalness of it. You know, I like really doing physical kinds of things. You know, keeps me in shape and that's what I like about it.

The value of challenge in one's work and its multifaceted dimensions—mental, physical, and variety—were perhaps best summed up in the following comments by a young auto mechanic which were presented at the beginning of this book:

I found what I really liked when I was working in the shop was that my body felt better, I was getting exercise, and I need exercise really bad because I'm so out of shape, and that was really important to me, that my job wasn't a sit-down job, I liked that. It got hard at times, you know, where your body was pooped out, but then it feels good because you felt like you had exercised so you had more energy in the long run. And doing something with your hands was kind of cool, because you could see what you were doing. Actually see the results—when you fixed a car it ran—the immediate satisfaction, and that's something I never have had on a job. In a factory you don't see where it's going or anything, so that's cool, plus you know that you did it. It's like solving a puzzle—when you get the answer—yeah!

RELATEDNESS

Another value that emerged from our interviews is what I define as *relatedness*. I have deliberately chosen this term because I feel it is general enough to encompass the often discussed need for sociability that paid employment fulfills, as well as the less often discussed problems of feeling as if one's "in the swim of things," in the "mainstream" of life, rather than isolated from human contact and activity. In addition, the need for feedback on performance and a desire for recognition are typically realized in the process of interacting with others. My choice of the term *relatedness* is an attempt to get at the more subtle symbolic aspects of social interaction, which in turn are fundamental to a person's sense of rootedness in the world. A plumber's apprentice who never completed high school expressed it this way:

I think for me, having a job for me means having some kind of real contact with the world. Like when I was laid off last winter, I mean sometimes I would just totally go into hibernation or something, you know, and I feel totally out of contact with people and cut off . . . so when I'm out working and making a salary, you know, even though I don't like the job or whatever, you know, at least I'm out there performing, you know . . . so it's really important to me to ah—be ah—just to have some kind of connection like that through work.

A middle-aged woman in training for a nontraditional job said:

It's, it's, well, I don't mean to say it's everything, but it's almost everything. When I'm unemployed I can't, I feel useless, I feel, I just don't feel, I feel half. It's awful.

A gas service repairperson interviewed in Northern California made the following statement:

Oh, I feel that work is the natural rhythm of life. I feel, people have to work, I mean, not all people. Some people are stay-at-homes, but it's keeping in with the rhythm of society, you know.

These and many similar comments suggest that paid employment is not simply a source of income and challenge, but may be intimately tied to how "connected" and important women feel. The comments on well-being, discussed later in this section, suggest this particular dimension of relatedness may be very important.

There were, however, other aspects of relatedness that were important to our respondents. The opportunities for sociability, for relationships with adults, for shared experiences and projects were all characteristics of paid employment that the women in our sample valued. A UPS driver stated it this way:

Being out on your own all day. Um, the money, and some of the people you contact are good. You have a lot of resources out there. See a hundred different people every day, you have a lot of contacts you know about other jobs and stuff like that.

A mechanic talked about the people she met at work in very positive terms:

I don't like feeling cramped. I don't like feeling pinned in. I don't like not being able to discuss something with someone, where when you're in a house you can't. So with a job, I have the contact of most of the time of my peers, or someone, a lot of times with intelligent people. I enjoy the idea that . . . that there is something special I can do. I never found a manual-type job that I can't do. I'm extremely good with dexterity-type jobs. The plus of the job where I am is that I have something that I can do and people I can talk to.

Relatedness also encompasses feedback and recognition from others. For many of the women, previous jobs or housework left them feeling unappreciated, and one of the things that they want in their work is to be appreciated. Even a woman working in a conventional female job, electronics assembly, felt better just because she was working.

I feel better, ya know, better. Because my son, he hurt my feelings . . . he said I was so dumb, ya know, kids. I said, "Well, that's why I wanted to better myself, ya know." It makes me feel better. I now have something to offer, to succeed in.

A woman in auto upholstery described how pleasing others pleased herself:

The good thing is that you can see what you're doing. The pleasure it gives people when they see something that comes in with the stuffing showing through or the foam showing through and you recover it and put in new insides and you sit on it, you see that they're pleased and you're pleased with yourself.

A plumber described how she liked the fact that people were excited because she was a woman in a nontraditional job, and went on to describe how she also felt she was providing people with a valued service:

I usually enjoy meeting the people I'm working for. I like to, ah, it's really a good thing when I get . . . do whatever I do and have it work and then that gives me a good feeling about it. I really feel like I'm providing a service, a necessary service.

An engineering draftsperson described her sense of satisfaction at having the engineer sign his name to her work:

I enjoy the work, and every day is something new. It's challenging and when you're creating something like a painting, of course I'm not an artist, but doing a drawing and making it look like something and having an engineer say, "Boy, that's good," and him signing his name to it, gives a sense of satisfaction.

AUTONOMY

Another value associated with paid employment was autonomy. Earlier autonomy was described both as control over such things as pacing and timing and as discretion in the sequencing of tasks and assignments. It also means freedom from supervision and a chance to work independently. This is another value that usually has not been considered important to women. It has too long been taken for granted that women prefer sociable work environments and tasks that have a human service component. Our research suggests that many women enjoy working alone and like a feeling of control over the work process, in particular the opportunity to make their own decisions.

The enjoyment of freedom from supervision and the opportunity to direct their own pacing was expressed in a variety of ways:

Well, I like being on my own more, I did have some opportunity to go out by myself when I was a trainee and I found it very satisfying to tackle a problem by myself. I liked not being supervised directly, mostly what my foreman does is a little bit, it's kind of sheepdog activity. [A gas service repairperson]

As a job, one of the good things about it is that I don't have anyone breathing down my neck all the time. I'm by myself all day and make my decisions about where I'm going to go next and what I'm going to do next. [An office machine repairperson]

I enjoy the kind of work I do and one good point to me is the fact that I do enjoy it. I don't think, oh, I have to get up and go to work today. I really like going there—it's um, creative and it's loose enough so that I'm my own boss to a certain extent. [An apprentice chef]

I like it. I like doing, ah, physical work. I like the freedom having my own truck and going from house to house and I like my customers pretty much. They're pretty excited about my job. [Another appliance repairperson]

Over and over we heard how positively the women felt about jobs where they had this kind of freedom and how unhappy they had been in previous jobs where they had had close supervision or had "to punch in and out." Similarly, many of the women described periods of being a housewife as times when they had very little control or discretion over their hours and the work they would do. This is somewhat surprising in that we think of housewives as having a great deal of discretionary time and a good deal of control over the organization of domestic work. However, such an image may flow from a middle-class perception of the nature of housework. Where discretionary income is limited, where laborsaving devices and convenient transportation are not available, and where there are no resources for child care, domestic work may be more constraining than many types of paid employment. Certainly for many of the women we encountered in skilled and semiskilled jobs, this was the case.

A final way in which autonomy was described by many of the women was as a desire to work alone. This desire stems less from a lack of interest in other people than it does from a desire to be fully responsible for the pacing and execution of a task, as the following comment by a pipe fitter illustrates:

I think one thing I like about it is that I have a lot of physical mobility and I have a lot of choices about how I do my work, like the order in which I do things. I can, if I need to . . . I can get help or advice from other people or I can just tell them to go shove it if I want to. I am pretty much, you know, in some usually, in some deserted corner where there are maybe other people around but of another trade so I can kind of just sit down and figure it out and make some choices about how I'm going to get it in. If I put it in wrong, you know, I can take the rap for it but I am responsible for something.

A telephone installer commented:

And I like working outdoors. I like, what else do I like . . . I like walking around all day, you know . . . and I like working by myself a lot and being answerable to myself.

A welder interviewed in San Francisco described the following situation:

I mean, I love to weld, I like to weld so, like last night, I welded all night long. I burned and welded all night long and that was fun and I liked that. I like it when I can do jobs where I work by myself.

These spontaneous comments from the women suggest that women value work that is both varied and complicated. It is important to emphasize that these comments are what women themselves identified as important, rather than responses to fixed alternative questions. The women could have talked about work they could combine easily with family life; they could have talked about convenient hours, about work that made limited demands on their time, energy, and attention. They could have talked about social relationships and opportunities to serve others. Some did. But most, when given the chance to respond in their own words, at their own pace, articulated the values just described.

WELL-BEING

For women, as for men, the quality of the work they do is very probably linked to feelings of competence, satisfaction, and general well-being. As one woman phrased it, "If you don't like your work, then you don't like the world around you and you just don't like yourself." The majority of the women we met liked their work and themselves, and that was almost entirely due to the fact that most of them had jobs in which they could enjoy feelings of productivity, autonomy, challenge, and relatedness, and for which they received good financial rewards compared with prior jobs or unpaid work in the domestic sphere.

The kind of work one does clearly has spillover effects for the way people feel about themselves, and the women's comments echoed this sentiment again and again. One woman stated it this way:

God, when I'm not, whenever I'm at a really shitty job, it really depresses me. You know, I really feel bummed about myself, I really do. . . .

Another in this way:

I think the work you do affects the way you feel about yourself. If you're doing, like, say if you're doing some kind of work that would be degrading to you, you wouldn't feel good about yourself.

For the vast majority of the women we met, work has had a positive effect on their self-concepts. It was not simply that they were confident and pleased with their ability to do the work, but that their ability to master job-related tasks spilled over into their *general* sense of confidence, mastery, and well-being. A woman groundskeeper offered the following comments:

If I sit home a great deal or if I'm very unsatisfactory in my employment, like for instance—maid work, which I've had to try, I drink more because I am bored. I get insomnia and all kinds of jazz like that, which I don't do when I'm working at something I enjoy working at because I'm satisfied. I'm doing something and I feel good about myself and you can't be bored then. You're busy and you have to use your time more efficiently. It's a good thing, the more I'm doing, the more I do.

A number of women described how mastering a particular job gave them confidence in other spheres:

I think I'm more confident. I think I'm more open-minded. I think that I would be more willing to try different things now. Once you've had some sort of success . . . you are . . . more confident. [An electronics mechanic]

When I started I couldn't even put up a shelf on a wall. I had never done anything with my hands. My out-in-the-world experience had always been academic and things I could do with my head. I thought I couldn't learn about machines, but since I started it, I realized that I had just as much common sense as anyone else and that that's where most learning comes from. I feel that I could do anything occupation-wise now. [A woman in custom woodworking]

I always lacked self-confidence in myself, and this is helping a lot because it is something that I want real bad. I'm pushing myself a lot on it and I'm showing myself I can do things that I didn't think I could do. I'm starting to think . . . fantasies that I've had all my life are attainable. [A young woman working as a cable splicer for the telephone company]

Taken together, the comments on these pages suggest a number of things about the experience of women in skilled jobs. They had high levels of job satisfaction, defined their work as interesting and challenging, and reported increasing levels of competence and self-confidence as a result of their experiences. In addition, they reported that these feelings positively affected other roles they play. This was particularly true for "pioneer" women. However, even among the women in the more traditional jobs such as cosmetology, operatives jobs, and small-parts assembly, the vast majority reported paid employment was a very positive experience, and for the most part preferable to domestic roles.

CONCLUDING COMMENTS

This chapter has provided an overview of the work experiences of women in blue-collar trades, as well as a look at the factors that enabled them to opt out of traditional female jobs and into nontraditional ones in the early and middle 1970s. It has also provided some insight into the quality of the work experience that women are looking for, and some feeling for why, in addition to good money and benefits, blue-collar jobs are so attractive. For women whose employment options have been severely circumscribed (regardless of their family background or educational attainment), skilled blue-collar jobs represent a marvelous opportunity to do something more challenging, interesting, and autonomous than the limited occupations traditionally open to women.

In the Introduction, I suggested that women seek the same things from their work that men do, but because of different histories of labor force participation and a different range of contemporary employment options, the types of jobs women see as providing the sorts of challenge and independence they are seeking are quite different than those men identify. To be sociological for a moment, it is possible to understand the *true* significance of paid employment in the lives of women only by understanding its relationship to the previous paid and unpaid work experiences of women in American society. With the declining economic and social significance of housework, and the

continued routinization and limitations of many paid jobs traditionally open to women, we should expect to see a continued
influx of women not only into the labor force, but into nontraditional jobs. Paid employment is increasingly the sector in
which women in American society will seek opportunities for
challenging, nonalienating work and for a sense of personal
power and efficacy. Employment that is not particularly attractive from the social scientist's point of view may be highly appealing from the perspective of working women.

The achievement of paid employment itself, as well as the
occupational and extraoccupational opportunities such employment opens up, must be seen as a critical factor contributing to
the overall level of job satisfaction reported among *all* women
workers. Our findings suggest that women in skilled blue-collar
jobs are extremely, even surprisingly, satisfied. They judge their
present opportunities differently than do men or well-educated
women. It is not only because of the better money that they are
satisfied. It is also because of the challenging qualities the
nontraditional work experience offers, in contrast to traditional
women's work. Whether domestic or paid, traditional women's
work has become increasingly diminished and trivialized in
urban-industrial societies, and no longer offers these women
what they want.

V

Life at Work

This chapter moves beyond the development of general interests in nontraditional work and into the specifics of finding, learning, and keeping a job. It will show that, in addition to a strong identity as a working person and expanding opportunities, people need information about specific employment opportunities in order to actually get a job. Various formal and informal mechanisms provide access to specific jobs. Once a person has a job, particularly in a field that is entirely new, the process of learning the job begins—for some in classrooms, for others on the job, and for many in a combination of formal instruction and on-the-job experience.

Learning the job will be approached from four points of view: (1) developing job skills—intellectual, technical, mechanical, and/or physical; (2) learning the job process—the pacing and timing of the work, the independent and interdependent aspects of the job; (3) understanding work group norms, including informal power and cliques in the workplace, work attitudes, and sharing in co-workers' interests and hobbies; and (4) adapting to the work setting, such as the physical context of the workplace, the sexual composition of the work group, and the size of the organization. Any person entering a new job has to concern himself or herself with all these areas. The person entering a work environment, skill area, and work group that are totally unfamiliar has special problems.

Even if one does successfully learn these various aspects, keeping a skilled blue-collar job continues to be problematic. It depends on a variety of personal, work environment, and external environment factors. Understanding what these are and succeeding over time in any job, most certainly in a nontraditional job, can be described as "work savvy." We will use the three key steps—finding, learning, and keeping the job—as the organizing themes for our discussion of life at work.

FINDING A NONTRADITIONAL BLUE-COLLAR JOB

Based on the extensive first- and second-year interview data on the nature of the women's interest in nontraditional work and how they got into their jobs, I would like to present a very simple model that summarizes their job-finding experiences.

FLOW CHART: DEVELOPMENT OF JOB COMMITMENT

Need for Employment ⟶ Exposure to Spheres of Opportunity ⟶ Information on Specific Jobs ⟶ Access to Specific Job ⟶ Employment Decision ⟶ Work Experience ⟶ Clarification of Knowledge about and Interest in Type of Job ⟶ Commitment and Preference for Job or No Interest/No Commitment to Job

Need refers to the economic necessity of paid employment and the identification of oneself as a full-time, lifelong working person. *Spheres of opportunity* refers to the jobs available to the woman, given her sex and geographical location. (As the previous chapter discussed, ability, interest, and education or training are less significant than sex, geographical location, and the market demand for workers in determining the employment options available to women.) *Information* refers to formal and informal facts, ideas, and attitudes about opportunities and how to act on them. *Access* involves direct contact with a potential employer or indirect contact through an agency or personal relationship that enables a person to follow up on information and make a decision. The on-the-job or training *experience* then stabilizes commitment to the job. The occupational histories of the blue-collar women we met were characterized by the kind of sequencing of events just outlined. This sequence underscores once again the extent to which need, opportunity, and access, rather than well-defined interests and specific preferences, are the primary influences. Our data suggest that interests become focused and preferences articulated *subsequent* to on-the-job experiences and not prior to them. A woman working in aircraft maintenance after years in traditional jobs put this sociological point in everyday terms:

The good thing about working at this job is that I'm really learning a lot, like I said, every week I change what I'm doing and if I don't learn it well, they keep me there an additional week. They make sure that we know what we're doing and I really enjoy that because I feel like I'm accomplishing something, whereas before where I was working it was routine and you could not see anything from it, you know, you were helping somebody else, but you weren't helping yourself. With the training program, you really feel like you're learning something so you're helping yourself, you feel good about it.

With the job itself, the parts that we're doing, they go in the airplane and I've really been getting into airplanes and old movies and go to the library and look at the books there. I've really taken notice of this type of thing a lot more, so that's good, too, because I never really had a special interest that I really got into like I am with that. I had no idea what any of this would be like or how much I would enjoy it until I actually started training and doing it.

Sandy Harold, the successful auto mechanic from an elite New England family, described her growing commitment to full-time employment as a mechanic:

I never made a conscious decision to become a mechanic, y'know, for that to be my skill or my trade. I don't remember that happening. It is now. And I think this is pretty much my life's work. I don't envision . . . becoming a doctor again or a lawyer or any-thing like that. There's a lot of different things I wanna do with it. In the past, I don't really remember what, any one event that changed things. Even when I was going to school full time I kept saying, I don't wanna work in a dealership, I just wanna learn how to work on my own car. At trade school I guess was where I started really working full time, that was more than full time, 'n' I would work there sixty or seventy hours a week doing one thing or an-other. That's where I started to value my work and think that I could support myself doing it. It still wasn't very good support, but it was then that I started thinking that's the work I'm gonna do. I can see that I can do it, maybe not very well now, but you know, it's something to work with for a long time and I know I could eventually make good money.

A woman who after many years of hovering around garden-ing and landscape work finally abandoned teaching school in order to pursue landscaping and maintenance full time, de-scribed her progressive commitment to her new vocation in the following way:

It was real gradual . . . I just started getting interested in plants. I started buyin' plants for myself 'n' buyin' plants for my boyfriend's apartment. I don't know exactly when it came together, but I knew when I quit school when I quit teaching school that I wanted to work in a nursery or work with plants somehow. Also my vision of my body has been changing slowly over the years—I've always been pretty unathletic, then I started taking yoga classes a couple of years ago and getting more into that and thinking more about my body and that has a lot to do with—being in California . . . like, I knew that there was a little more money and the Women's Store-front was getting into more hardcore jobs . . . the whole night be-fore I was supposed to show up for work there, I thought, you know, I'm gonna . . . I won't be able to do it. I'm gonna be fired, laid off in a week . . . and it turned out it just wasn't physically that difficult. There was nothing overpowering that I couldn't do or that the men couldn't do if I couldn't do it, and it still wouldn't be a bad thing, you know. Now that I have that, I really want—I wanta be a gardener for the city or a gardener for somebody, you know, that kinda job.

These examples, along with those cited in the previous chapter, show the extent to which opportunity and on-the-job experiences affect job preferences and commitment. That is why it may be more important to look at the opportunities with which women are presented and the formal and informal relationships that provide them with the information and personal access they need to get a specific nontraditional job than it is to study prior occupational values or preferences.

The two primary and often overlapping ways the women we studied got their jobs were (1) on the advice of or with the help of friends, or family members (48 percent), and (2) through a direct referral from an agency such as a women's referral center or a special job referral or employee development program. The primary job referral agencies for women seeking nontraditional options in the early 1970s were special programs funded by local, state, and federal organizations to help individuals and employers find one another in an ongoing effort to meet affirmative action and equal employment opportunity goals in industry. The names of many of the women we interviewed were initially given us by these women's agencies. However, we also interviewed women we had identified through major employers and through vocational schools. Approximately fifteen of the women in nontraditional jobs reported that their move into a nontraditional job was an intracompany move precipitated by the company's push to get more women into apprenticeship. As mentioned earlier, more than half of the women also cited the changing social climate, the increased government pressure on employers, and the frequent attention to blue-collar opportunities in the media as important factors in helping them consider and ultimately try a blue-collar job. Given that social climate, however, each woman still needed a specific opportunity and specific information to move her along. This will be discussed from the point of view of (1) those who were sought out or encouraged to try blue-collar jobs, that is, intracompany recruits and family-aided recruits, and (2) those who sought the job—that is, those who got encouragement and/or went to agencies looking for help in locating a job.

The latter represents the experience of the majority of the women, but in both cases the women needed help in identifying and deciding on a specific choice. Let's begin with a look at people who were directly recruited or encouraged.

BEING RECRUITED FOR BLUE-COLLAR JOBS

Most employers initially "sought out" women for nontraditional jobs through outside agencies rather than from their own ranks. Thus most of the pioneer women we met obtained their jobs through the help of a government agency, a women's agency, or a friend or family member in similar employment. Nonetheless, of the eighty-two interviewees working or training for nontraditional jobs in the first year, more than a dozen had been recruited by their current employer from their traditional job into apprenticeship or shop learner programs. Civil service industries and public utilities were more likely to do this than the manufacturing and transportation industries, in large part because they had a larger existing female work force to draw upon. Industries dominated at all levels, including the unskilled, by men and industries with few clerical and office positions have fewer women to draw from. Thus the industry must hire from outside rather than inside. Government programs and women's referral agencies are a critical resource for such programs. They are important to the other industries too, though not as critically. Most of the women we met who had made intracompany moves were in some area of the civilian work force of the armed services support industry at various locales within the state of California. The best example of this was Maggie Patterson, who after three years as a keypunch operator applied for an apprenticeship because someone came around recruiting women and she knew it would mean more money and a chance for schooling.

Some people came around and said we are looking for women to apply. I talked to my uncle about it and he said it was a good deal and he knew a few people who had some contact with it. I think they came around because EEO or somebody was down on them to get more women in the program. So I applied and took the test and then I was called in for an interview, and like I said, I didn't know I was going to have to pick. I wasn't prepared when I went for the interview to say—this is what I want to do. I assumed from the tests— the nature of the tests to me seemed to be an aptitude-type test and I figured, you know, you'd either be a grease monkey or you'd be stringing wires in electronics, you know. I guess I kinda assumed that I would be in electronics or electrical, but like I said, I didn't know there were so many exact little names and groups that were that specific. Like just in electronics there's electronics mechanic, radar; there's electronics mechanic, test instrument; there's electronics mechanic, maintenance. I thought, you know, what's the difference and you know, you just do different things. I work on radar—specialize on radar and communication equipment—and the test instrument people work on test instruments. More like calibration-type stuff, not stuff that goes into the plane, but stuff you use to check the stuff that goes into the plane. And you know, I just really didn't have any idea there was that big of a difference. I did pick the dirtiest—short of being out with a grease monkey type thing.

Elaine Elmer was working as a clerk typist when she decided to pursue a nontraditional option. They were opening up to women in her industry and her husband was already in a shop learner program and encouraged her to try. She described her experience this way:

I knew a lot about it generally from working in the training office for a long time and because my husband was in it, you know. But actually, when I got into the program I didn't know that it was what it was. I knew that some of the people that had gotten in the training program that my husband was in started out as shop learners and helper generals, and when they opened up the production control training program that I had put in for, they had been highly qualified for it. The shop learner program gives them a lot of background training on it. I knew they weren't opening any training programs in production control, you know, and this shop learning thing was opening up. I wasn't satisfied with the work I was doing, so you kind of take what comes along, you know. You can't be very picky when it comes to switching jobs. So anyway, it was announced that they were opening up the shop learner, helper general program and I didn't even know that I could apply for it and take the test right there at Military Island. What I did was I took a day off from work and I went down to the civil service commission and I applied for the job and they called me back and I had to take another day off and I had to take a test. Later I learned I wouldn't have had to take the days off, I mean I was in the training office and nobody even knew about it—I mean nobody even told me about it, but I guess I didn't let anybody know, but I did it all on my own after I saw the general notice. Nobody in my office told me about it at all.

A woman who had been a civil service typist and secretary for seven years, from eighteen through twenty-five, moved from her last clerical job, where she was making $3.80 an hour, into an aircraft electrician apprentice job making $4.94 an hour. She described the transition this way:

One of the men I worked with told me of the apprentice program and the opportunities that you could have in it. My supervisors all told me—nothing. They pointed me in other directions, like draftsman, and illustrator—things that were opening for women, but they all said, "You can't do this other, they won't let you in the programs" except for this one person who had gone through the apprentice program and that was enough to get me going. You see, I felt that I was at such a dead-ended position and that I wasn't qualified or I couldn't get the jobs that I thought I was qualified for and I knew I had to get a trade background, because I want to go into white-collar work and I want to go into industrial systems analyst or something like that and you can't go in there unless you have four years of college, which I figure really doesn't give you anything of a trade background, and the only way you can get a trade background is to work in a trade, and the only way to get in the trade for a woman is to get into a training program.

A woman working as an apprentice airplane instrument mechanic said her employment was based on her desire for more pay and because she had always liked to work with her hands.

Well, I started working at Military Island—I was twenty years old and worked in an office as a secretary, never wanted to be a secretary but I always had the skill just in case I, you know, I had something to fall on. So I was working in an office and I like to sew and crochet and I like to work with my hands, so the men in my office recommended that I take the shop learner test, and I went to check into that, and shop learner was closed. Sometimes I used to walk around to the different shops and see the different people and what they did, you know, the different trades and what was involved. So that was closed—so I was told to go ahead and take an apprentice program. I was told I would not be taken because I was a woman— forget to even bother taking the test, but a couple of men in the office really helped, so I went ahead and took it anyway. Then I was called in for an interview and I got that job. I mean, I was in the right place at the right time, I guess. When I went for the interview to be in the apprentice program, I chose metalsmith and airplane instrument mechanic—a metalsmith, they really didn't want me in—they were "Oh, you're going to have to be out on the plane and you're going to get dirty" and they were trying to discourage me from wanting to be a metalsmith and they were trying to steer me towards being an aircraft instrument mechanic, so that was my second choice. That's why I got into it.

As noted earlier, friends, lovers, or husbands and family members were identified as important in job seeking by over thirty of the blue-collar women we talked to. Erin Kelly, the successful chef's apprentice introduced in earlier chapters, was an example of this.

I think well, I've always been interested in restaurants, I've always worked in them but I never actually thought I'd be in on the cooking, it's just kind of something that happened. I've always enjoyed cooking, but it's nice to be able to do it with a little bit of knowledge now. I cook a lot at home. I bake my own bread, make my own yogurt, and stuff like that. Basically my sister is the one who told me about the apprentice angle and it just seemed to have more of a future to it, I was going to look at things that way. With my sister's advice I took it from there and went after the apprenticeship. Of course, the lady at the apprentice office really did a lot to help me get placed. I mean, I'm one of the only two chef's apprentices in all of California!

A successful pipe fitter in private industry described how a friend influenced her move:

I came down here because I knew that women I had gone to trade school with were employed. And the women I knew in the trades in the Bay Area were mostly unemployed, so I thought maybe the economic situation down here would be different and I could get a job, so I went and interviewed all around town. A woman I knew was involved in this skilled trades readiness program, so like I would go down there and I didn't have any money and they had things like bus fare available for you to go on job interviews and they would actually call up places and set up interviews for you. I had known about it before because my roommate in San Francisco moved down to San Diego to be in the motorcycle program and so I knew it was there, but I heard from the people at the storefront that they were also doing something in pipe fitting. They didn't have anything special for women when I was there. I was in a class of about twenty-four and I was the only woman there and the exact thing that happened to me happened to every man in the class. They told all of us about openings now and then, and I just went down and interviewed for this one like everyone else and I got it.

Another woman who was training in auto mechanics when we first met described how she never considered a trade until she began seeing women in the trade. She was forced to consider a career change after moving out to California.

I had never done any work with my hands. I was surprised that I was able to do it. I rebuilt an engine about a month ago, and to this day I'm still stopping all the time and looking under the hood every time I drive it.

What got me started on this is that on my way out here, I stopped in Oakland to see a friend up there and she was in a welding program at the skills center up there and I met all of her friends, most of whom were in the skills center up there, one of whom was in auto mechanics. And in fact it's funny now looking back on it because I remember one of the guys saying, "Seeing so many women in auto mechanics and welders and things like that, can you ever imagine yourself in a nontraditional occupation?" and I said emphatically *"No,"* and two months later I was enrolled in an auto mechanics class. When I came down here and found out that they had the same type of program and I knew I didn't want to go back and be a secretary, which is the only job I could get, and I also knew—I had enough money to get me through Christmas. I signed up with the idea that I'll learn something, I won't feel like such an idiot, and it'll take up time in the meanwhile, because since I didn't know anybody I knew I would have a lot of free time. Then when I started doing it, I really liked it.

USING AN INTERMEDIARY TO FIND A BLUE-COLLAR JOB

Without specific options at her current workplace or the help of friends or family members, a woman who becomes aware of increased opportunities in blue-collar jobs must initiate her own search for information about access to specific jobs. A very small number of women reported responding to advertisements for jobs and a substantial number reported independently approaching unions and employers about opportunities for non-traditional employment. In the early seventies these direct approaches to unions and prospective employers proved to be unsuccessful for most of the women. They needed an intermediary, agent, or advocate to line them up with the right job. For these women, government employment programs, in particular women's job referral agencies in each of the three metropolitan areas we studied, proved an invaluable resource. The comments of a utilities company employee illustrated this:

Well, actually the way it worked out was—I was talking with my boyfriend about what kind of jobs I thought I could get and he said, "Oh, I know what you could be—you could be a telephone installer." And I remember how when I was a kid I thought that would be something that would be interesting to be and then at some point I heard of the Women's Storefront and I went over there one day and they had a pamphlet on jobs in the phone company. I went and talked to one of their women-in-apprenticeship people and the phone company had some kind of—maybe it was a contract—they had an arrangement with the storefront where they were sort of screening people in a preliminary sort of way and would recommend them to the phone company for a special hiring program for women. I wasn't hired for that program, but seven or eight months later I was hired for the temporary job which I took. And that's what got me started. After that I had the confidence to go to places—like the utility company—and I don't remember if I applied at East Bay or not. It's a municipal utility district. Um—I persisted in trying to get a job at the phone company, but I didn't. I went back to the storefront last fall and they told me the gas and electric company was hiring somebody for the gas meters repair position. They tutored me for the aptitude test—it was a mechanical aptitude test. They talked about what the interview situation would be like, and what to say and how to act and what to wear—just about any question I wanted they had an answer for or at least an idea about. It helped, because they only recommended two people for this one job so I had a fifty-fifty chance of getting the job and I did get it. I doubt if I would have gotten either of these jobs without the storefront's help, because I had applied to the utility company previously and they ignored it.

Another woman who had been with the telephone company as a cable splicer over three years described the importance of a woman's agency:

I found out through the Women's Career Center that the telephone company was giving a class. They open a class up once a year to twenty-five women to train them in cable splicing, without the guarantee of a job, and after you go through the twelve-week class, then it's virtually positive you're gonna get a job, but they don't know if they'll have openings. So, I went for the interview for the class an' they had four openings at that time, so they hired me on, without the class and without the training, and I did it because I wanted to learn to work with tools and I wanted a job where—that was new to women to get into.

Before taking the job, I had been in the center's nontraditional jobs workshop, which was real helpful, it kind of like, um . . . they had different games 'n' tools that you would use to look at what you thought you should be doing and what you wanted to do and what kind of skills you had from here that you could take over here, so that it became a real thing, that it was a possibility that I could try this over here. And at the same time they were getting job descriptions in, and so I went out on the interview.

A woman who eventually found a good job in landscaping began her movement into nontraditional work after getting advice from a women's center about training opportunities at a local community college. A number of women reported experiences similar to this one.

Well, about five years ago a friend of mine got a job in landscaping and I thought, "Wow, he's really lucky, working outside all day," and then last December, I met the women at the center and I told them I was looking for a job and not having very much luck—there's an abundance of office girls and I haven't worked in four years. So they said, "How would you like some training?" and I said sure, and they gave me a piece of paper with different classes they had at the skills center and told me to pick one and I went through the list and picked landscaping—I wanted to get into landscaping and they said okay and we filled out an application and six weeks later I started at the skills center. I was the third woman in the class and I went there for four months for masonry and carpentry on a small scale, doing outdoor work around the house, and a week before my training was up I called some landscapers out of the yellow pages and the third place I called said they were hiring and I went and asked them for the job and they gave it to me. That's how I got into it. They put me pulling weeds when I first got the job—a hard job, really hard, but now I have a project of my own, so pulling weeds isn't so bad. I'm still pulling 'em, but not all day.

A welder we interviewed described how a women's employment referral service got her into a CETA training program that eventually resulted in a full-time job.

I wouldn't say my interest in a trade is a truly new development, because my father was a machinist, so I think it's always been in my background. But I only thought of doing it recently. I majored in art in college and one of the classes I took was a metal class and we did some gas welding and arc welding, and after I got over being totally freaked out about the whole thing, I was a little scared, I got a little bit intrigued by it and then the class ended and that was that. But after that, more and more I knew I wanted to do something else—I knew I didn't want to be a secretary anymore so I thought about a few other things I could do in terms of more physical kind of work, and worked my way through those things—decided being a welder would be a pretty good thing for me. So when I really began thinking about getting into a skilled occupation

I went to the Women's Storefront and talked to them and then they sent me a flyer within a month and one of the things in this flyer was the welding and sheet metal program. So I called them and they said to go down and apply and I did and got in. They turned me on to that. And they also gave me a little inside information over the phone so that I could understand a little better what the situation was where I was applying.

GENERAL OBSERVATIONS ON JOB SEEKING

It is clear that special recruitment and counseling programs facilitated linking interested women with training and job programs in previously closed fields. In addition, these programs helped sponsor media and general efforts to inform isolated women of increased opportunities. Programs such as Advocates for Women in San Francisco, the Career Planning Center in Los Angeles, the Center for Women's Studies and Services in San Diego, and similar enterprises in practically all major metropolitan centers today became important channels of information for working women. Although programs of this type, because of staffing and fiscal limitations, were able to spend very little time with any one woman, 40 percent of the women we talked to indicated that they at some point had made contact with these programs, and a full 20 percent were involved in training or job experiences they had been referred to by the programs. Virtually all of the women we talked to were aware of and supported the efforts of these specialized agencies.

The experiences of blue-collar pioneers in seeking and finding work were not that dissimilar from those of all women in the labor force. The Department of Labor's recent Handbook on Women Workers reported the various methods typically used by women looking for work.

For women the method of looking for work that was used more than any other method was asking friends. This was followed, in order, by: applying directly to an employer, answering newspaper ads, asking relatives, applying to the State employment service and applying at private employment agencies—to mention the methods at the top of the list. . . . The method that got the most women their jobs was applying directly to the employer (35 percent). Asking friends and answering newspaper ads were tied for second place (16 percent), and private employment agencies was the next in order (8 percent). . . .

Generally, there was considerable similarity between women and men in the degree to which they used the various jobseeking methods and in the distribution of methods that got them their jobs. However, much smaller proportions of women than men reported asking friends and relatives, and using the State employment service and hiring rolls.[1]

One apparent difference between women seeking nontraditional jobs and other women looking for work is the importance of an intermediary—a government program or women's agency—in the initial identification of and contact with a prospective employer. Because so many unions and employers are still not interested in women or want women only for purposes of satisfying "quotas," the job-finding process is greatly streamlined by working through an intermediary who can summarize what is available where, and on what terms.

Before concluding this section, it is important to remember the significance of parents' occupations and of early exposure to skilled trades. The backgrounds of pioneering women had an indirect impact on their employment decisions. In addition to specific resources and information, the job of a parent, relative, or neighbor provided the growing child with some image of the world of work in general as well as the world of a particular trade or profession. Certain jobs and their requirements are thus to some extent demystified, particularly if the jobs are performed around or near the home. Children also learn about jobs if parents take them to the workplace or talk to them about their work. When a child does not see or share in the parents' work it is more mysterious. If the parents' work roles and access to other occupations are very limited, it is likely the child will see certain kinds of work as very special, mysterious, and inaccessible.

This is doubtless true for both men and women. However, as formal and informal expectations of men require that they be interested in and informed about work and employment roles, they are more likely to search out possibilities. The absence of such expectations of women makes *informal* access to learning about the content and nature of specific kinds of jobs more important. The world of paid employment and particularly paid employment in those numerous jobs typically closed to women needs to be demystified for women. As noted in Part One, a disproportionate number of women entering nontraditional jobs identified directly (about 40 percent) or indirectly (about 18 percent) an early childhood relationship providing access to and some learning about nontraditional work skills. This undoubtedly had some effect on their willingness to pursue skilled blue-collar jobs when opportunities opened up, and on their strategies for finding a specific job. To emphasize an earlier point, however, the women who identified some kind of access or foreknowledge about nontraditional skills in the main did not describe themselves as having compelling personal or vocational interests in these skills. They learned early that there were no opportunities for women in these fields, and they moved into them slowly.

It's possible that some early exposure sufficiently demystified traditional male strongholds so that, when opportunities opened up, women weren't quite as frightened or overwhelmed by the idea that the jobs required special skills, strengths, or aptitudes. From their informal access, they had a general feeling for the type of work and saw it as no big thing. Thus they were interested. They at least had some idea of what would be involved in the work; they had some sense of the better pay and greater challenge and they were not easily scared off by the claims that men's work was somehow more complex, difficult, and demanding. A single comment from a woman plumber summarizes most women's perspective.

I've always liked tools and I always liked to play in Father's workbench. It never occurred to me that I would ever be a plumber, until somebody handed me a wrench and said, "Hop to it." I just happened to run into that particular opportunity, but like if I happened to have met somebody who needed somebody to work with who did another kind of work like carpentry, I probably would have done that instead.

In conclusion, it is important to understand the overriding significance of opportunity, information, and access to job selection in order to sidestep the temptation of "blaming the victim" for the small numbers of women in skilled blue-collar jobs. Our society is still too convinced by the notion that if people, particularly women and minorities, are really interested in certain roles or occupations, they'd go after them. We use the fact that they don't go after them or participate in them as an indication that they're perfectly happy where they are. I have heard far too many professors of sociology, as well as union leaders and employers, make such comments for me to believe that the prejudices vary significantly across social or occupational lines. Our research clearly suggests that, in the absence of access and opportunity, only very few pursue fields that are for most mysterious and inhospitable. But as fields become demystified and open through both formal and informal mechanisms, surprising numbers and types of people begin choosing them.

LEARNING THE JOB

Once a woman landed a nontraditional job or training spot, what happened to her? The experiences varied widely. Some of the women found themselves literally set loose to figure everything out on their own. Others found themselves in highly structured training contexts. Others were lucky enough to find an individual supervisor or co-worker who helped them along, and still others had to face open hostility and harassment. By beginning with some descriptions of typical days at work we can get a feel for the flavor of the on-the-job experiences of blue-collar women. From these idiographic descriptions we can then draw some generalizations about the skills, process, work group norms, and work setting.

WHAT THE JOB IS

The range and variety of skilled jobs the women were working in were amazing and represented fields and skill areas about which I had absolutely no knowledge before embarking on this research. To me, a skilled tradesperson was a carpenter, an electrician, a mechanic, a plumber, or a machinist. The range of skills and variety of employment contexts available for tradespeople in a highly technological society such as our own is significantly broader than most of us realize. In order to give you a sense of this diversity I have selected descriptions of on-the-job experiences from a cross section of skilled trades and work settings.

Sandy Harold developed an interest in her trade slowly, but auto mechanics became a lifelong career commitment over the three years we knew her.

I've been working there about eight or nine months, I really like it . . . it's full time, actually it's more than full time, they don't pay me a lot of overtime, but I am there from eight to five every day and sometimes longer. And mostly that's because I'm doing . . . I'm sort of taking that on. Like I don't quite finish a job or I wanta stay and clean up something, that's sort of my . . . I feel pressured to do it, but I wouldn't have to if I didn't want to, and I sort of end up doing it. I am learning a lot of specific stuff about Volvos. And I'm becoming more efficient in my work. It's a four-year apprenticeship and I have to go to school two nights a week during those four years, an' that's really a drag. I'm back at the junior college that I went to years ago, when I was just learning about cars. The tables are really turned, like I'm . . . I know a whole lot more than some of the men that are there; 'n' before, I was just, y'know, a freak. I guess I'm still a freak, there aren't any other women in the night program that I know of, but I have a little bit more credibility because I'm an apprentice at a dealership, an' some of the guys are just working in gas stations an' trying ta, y'know, get into where I've finally gotten. But it's a drag, I'm not learning anything, school's a waste of my time, and I really resent having to be there two nights a week. I would lose my job if I didn't go into the apprenticeship school, though; the union has some deal worked out with the school . . . about money . . . it's part of the conditions of my apprenticeship, an' if the union withdraws my apprenticeship then I get fired from the job. I sort of resented being offered a four-year apprenticeship, I asked for a two- or a three-year one. I thought I would get some . . . time off for the work that I've done and the training that I've had, I think a lot of men could've walked into the same situation and succeeded in talking their way into it. But I didn't really have any choice an' since it was the only apprenticeship I'd ever been offered, I wasn't gonna refuse it because the terms were too long. But I think a man in my position coulda bought a buncha tools and rolled inta a dealership or a big shop, and convinced them he was working at journey level . . . without any apprenticeship papers. That's what I wanna be able to do, why I want to finish this apprenticeship program. Because I just wanna be able to go anywhere an' work. I wanna be able to rely on a skill an' I don't have any credibility without all those little pieces of paper, ya know. As stupid as getting that smog license was, I know it helped convince the people here that I was conscientious. It was a standard they could use to compare me with other people, and I did good, so I was worth it. I can't rely on the gift of gab or the image 'cause I don't fit inta the image an' I certainly . . . I didn't have the tools either for a long time, 'n' y'know, you can't work in the trade for four years without good tools, an' there was no way I could prove my four years', y'know, experience with a dinky little tool-box, which was all I had for a long time.

My normal workday begins about six-thirty, quarter of seven. I get up an' make coffee an' make myself a lunch for the day an' have breakfast. I have to be at work at eight 'n' I only live six blocks from where I work, so I walk . . . and usually punch in at 7:59, slide in, and work takes off slowly the first hour or so, people are just getting into their first jobs 'n' kinda waking up and the day sorta moves along. I might have a bad job or something that takes me a lot longer. I guess I could say a lot about the people I work with and the various things that go on there. I really like all the people I work with, I think it's an amazing group of people that are somehow magically assembled there. I work with six or seven other mechanics. They all help me and show me how to do jobs I'm unfamiliar with. We do lubes, repairs, that sort of thing. There's a woman at the parts counter. She's a first, too. She just got her journeyman papers today as a parts technician. She's neat, she just got married. I mean I really like the people I work with, but I'm not sure I wanna put energy out in their directions. I try to change the way they think, but it doesn't work, I mean overall most of those men see women as a class of subhumans, right, an' that. . . . They have their individual exceptions, of course, and that scares me 'cause I'm not sure what makes me different. I don't like to be separated from other women. There's still a lotta tits-an'-ass locker room bullshit that goes on, I mean after the first month or two, when I was outrageous, right, I just sorta gave up fighting them and a few weeks ago one of the mechanics asked me . . . what did he say . . . something about how whether I was becoming less radical in my older age or . . . you know, some sorta joke, but he was somewhat serious 'cause I just don't come down on people the way I used to any more 'cause it doesn't get me anywhere. I expend all this energy and everything stays the same.

In our second interview Sandy made no reference to the attitudes of her co-workers except to mention that things had quieted down. She was spending all her time and energy learning her trade and she was getting a lot of help and good jobs to work on.

Ardath Hoover, the ebullient gas service repairperson, was quite frustrated with her on-the-job experiences when first interviewed. By the time of our second encounter she had moved into work in which she felt she was learning more and which was also more enjoyable. This is what she had to say after just a few months on the job.

I have to be there before the damn buzzer rings, otherwise the foreman and assistant foreman are right there. That's at seven-thirty. Then I go into this low-ceiling, gray, ugly building and there's a lot of machine noises. You walk back and change to your steel-toed boots. You put solder guards over the bottom of your jeans so you don't get solder on them, you put on gloves, put on an apron, put on safety glasses, tie your hair up, put a bandanna over it, then I go back to my submerging station where I submerge meters and I start submerging meters. Flirt with the guys, get ribbed by the guys. There's about sixty guys in the shop. Then when the buzzer rings we go to the coffee machine and one lousy Coke machine and one lousy candy machine. I have found that we are some of the most poorly treated utility employees. The other people have it a lot easier as far as working conditions, amount of work that they have to do, strictness of the job, and a lot of other things. So anyway, we have a fifteen-minute coffee break and the buzzer rings and we get back on the job, do the job. I actually pick up the meters and the number I do varies. I did a phenomenal ninety today.

The sixty other people in my shop are repairing meters of one form or another—gas meters. In other departments they really get into some heavy technical things. I've spent a couple of lunchtimes with the big "tech" of the department and he showed me one of the big books with the information. I'm brain-starved, intellectually, at this place. When I took the job with them I thought it was in a more technical field and on the thing it said indoor-outdoor. So the job I currently have isn't exactly what I expected. If I can't get into that technical job soon I think I'm to the fed-up point where if it doesn't happen I think I want to relocate my family. You see, what I really want to get into is transmission and regulation. It's technical and I'd be starting out as a helper and it would take me several years to get on as an apprentice. But the journeymen calibrate and regulate the main gas flow going into the Upper Peninsula. That's what I'd really like to do. It's not dealing with the public, which I have learned is really a drag, and it's slightly technical and some of the journeymen are known as technicians.

By the middle of her second year with the utility company, Ardath was working in a new, "more technical" area.

You know, my work time is just a total change. I guess maybe just because it is outside. I was pretty unhappy last year. I've never worked that long inside. The skills I'm developing have changed too. I've been working in two basically, totally different departments, which was totally different from what I was doing before. In fact, I was working in the meter shop. I have taught all the guys . . . I was working leak crew outside. Many of them—it's a very large department, the street crew . . . street maintenance, gas, um, decided that they could use my skills at convening the meter shop and instructing the rest of the gentlemen on a few things about meters. And, let's see, ah, I don't know, it just seems like I've come up some, been beneficial to them—so it's worked all the way around.

Ardath went on to describe her feelings about this kind of work:

Good things are: the number one best asset of the job I have right now is it's a man's job by far and away. Secondly, it's outside. Thirdly, it pays good money. Fourthly, I'm able to express myself creatively—or that might even be first, over and above the gentle-men, yes, it is. The bad things are: I have to deal with the public, I really don't dig it, and I don't know, I'm very very pleased with it. I mean, I've had a few jobs, worked for the post office for a couple of years in Northern California, I've worked for the Renaissance Faire, total creativity, total ego, absolute lack of security, not a great deal of money—drive you nuts. This job is just the opposite, takes forever to get anywhere, but as long as I'm learning, then it's on the uphill and you can't beat the security.

Ardath was one of the very few women we talked to who was forthrightly flirtatious and delighted to be working with men. As will be seen in the next chapter, the relationships between the men and women at the workplace were very uneasy, partic-ularly in the first year. Most of the women saw traditional "macho" blue-collar men as a problem. Although Ardath had her share of hostility and harassment, she seemed actually tit-illated a bit by the byplay. This most certainly was *not* the case for the vast majority of the women we met. For now, let's con-tinue our look at the general work environments.

A welder working for a major California ship builder de-scribed the work she does quite specifically, beginning with the type of gear she needs to do her job.

Well, right now since I'm a beginner as a welder, I'm just doing arc welding. I put on leathers, which protects my body from all of the stuff—all the flying flak and sparks. So I get dressed and put on my hard hat and all this other business and then these goggles for gas welding. I have a hood for all types of electric welding like arc welding. The hood completely blacks out everything. Like if you put it down you couldn't see anything at all. You can only see the arc—you can only see where you are welding. I get all my para-phernalia together, all my tools, and then when the whistle blows at eight I go out of the locker room.

She went on to describe the kinds of job she did working with other skilled workers such as electricians, carpenters, pipe fitters, and shipfitters.

There is a million places you can be working at on a ship and so I'd go with my co-workers to where I was going to be located for the time being and then you proceed to get set up, which includes finding a welding machine somewhere on this ship, you have to connect the cable and drag it to wherever you're going to be and you have to hook up the manifold with oxygen and acetylene 'cause you have to do some burning—some cutting of metal—and you do this with a combination of acetylene and oxygen. And then you get set up. After that it would depend on what I would do. Sometimes I'd be told to do some cutting of metal. Cut through a bulkhead, cut some hangers and then weld them up, and the pipe fitter would maybe lay pipe and these hangers would hold the pipe, or again, if I was working with the pipe fitter, he would stick a pipe through the bulkhead in which I cut a hole and then I would have to weld around it, and then sometimes I would just be relaxing if my co-worker was working. I would do my thing and then they would do their thing and the day sort of proceeds like that. Lunchtime is half an hour and you go out and eat your lunch and then come back—about the same thing until about knock-off time and you leave there at four-thirty.

A free-lance plumber we met in Northern California described the kinds of jobs she was able to do based on training she received as an "assistant" to a black plumber. Although this plumber was a journeyman plumber, he was not a union member. Thus Nannette, who had no luck with the unions anyway, was not in a formal apprenticeship.

I was lucky, when I started working with him, he had a lot of jobs and that was really to my advantage because I could see a lot of different things. I sometimes feel like I might go and pick up ten toilets in ten days and you know the eleventh one will just throw me and I'll be there the whole day when the rest of them took a couple hours apiece. I was with him, and I'd see the same thing happen to him. Now he's been plumbing as long as I've been alive, and still some little thing'll hang you up all day. It was nice that way. He always was real good. He'd say, "This is my assistant,

Nannette, she's a plumber too," and women would go, "Oh my," you know, and he introduced me to the people he does business with as far as buying supplies. And he says, "Treat her as you would me," which give me instant credit with those people. I only just started realizing what a big boon that is. I mean, I can order hundreds of dollars' worth of stuff from them and pay them when I get paid, which is great.

Now I'm on my own and I might have a drain to unstop, for example, which means using an electric snake. I don't own a snake, but fortunately this man that taught me plumbing lets me have full use of any of his tools that I don't myself own. Plus I can call him at any time I get stuck and he'll give me advice. He'll even, if I'm really stuck, come over and unstick me. He's a black plumber. Back when he wanted to be a union plumber twenty-five years ago they didn't want any blacks, so he never joined, and later only had one hassle with them and he told some guys, "Well, listen, when I wanted to be in with you guys you didn't want me in and now I don't need you and leave me alone." And they've never hassled him and I'm sure that someday I'll be in the same position where they're hassling me to join and I'll say fuck you, which I'm really actually looking forward to telling them to get fucked.

Anyway, I might have a drain to unclog or I might have a toilet to repair, maybe it's leaking, maybe the inside flush assembly isn't working and I have to replace it. I had a job last week where I picked up a toilet and I took it up off the floor where it's bolted down and the woman's son had thrown a candle in there and I had to get the candle out and put it all back together and down again. Once in a while I get an installation of a gas dryer or washing machine or a gas heater or a water heater or a drippy faucet—I get a lot of dripping faucets, maybe faucet replacement, maybe just replacing washers. It really varies. That's one thing that's really nice— you don't do the same thing every day.

A majority of the women we talked to mentioned how much their job varied from day to day—what tasks needed doing, where and how it was done, and with whom and how many people it had to be done to. Jan Spencer, the chief mechanic, described her job the second year we met:

I do repair work and preventive maintenance work on rapid-transit vehicles, on their motors and their air-conditioning systems and electrical systems and air suspension and hydraulic systems. They have a pretty wide variety of technical problems we work on. We always work in teams. That's what I am now, a team chief. I'm usually assigned one or two, sometimes I work with other team chiefs. I'm in charge of seeing that it gets done—helping the others, who aren't supposed to be as skilled and things like that. In repair work, it's just an infinite variety of what it can be; it can be pulling down a two-ton motor alternator from a car which needs several hands, or it can be just changing the oil and giving lubes and checks for preventive maintenance. There's a lot of things one person can do.

Jan shared some opinions about the differences between being a mechanic on large transit vehicles and in an automobile dealership:

The kind of work I'm doing now is easier than the kind of work I was doing at a dealership a few years back. I had doubts about the work in dealerships, but this kind of job, for one thing, has a strong union and the union is present in the company, not like the union visiting you once every month at a dealership. The dealerships, you have to like lift four-speed transmissions which weigh—oh, I don't know—100, 150, 175 pounds. And they don't have the equipment to do it. In this place, there's something to pick up everything. If somethin's too heavy, you go and you push a button on the end of the ship and down comes this forty-ton crane that'll, you know, pick it up for you. There's a jack somewhere or there's fourteen guys who'll come and help you. They're not under any pressure to get their work done, so, you know. And there's tools everywhere, there's three-quarter-inch impact wrenches, you don't have to worry about splitting a socket, all the equipment is there. But in a smaller shop, the stuff you're working on is smaller. Like these things we take out of here are mammoth. The alternator is six feet long and this big around, it's really huge. A car alternator, like say, take a compressor—an AC compressor is only this big and this big around and it might weigh forty pounds, but you pick it up with your hands because you pick up everything on a car with your hands except for the engine. But you don't pick nothing up there that's too heavy for you—so the stuff is bigger, but it's better handled and there's a safety engineer around to scream if you do anything that's remotely dangerous.

There is an infinite variety of types of mechanics, from auto mechanics to rapid transit mechanics to a number of instrument and electronics mechanics working on high-technology transport such as jet planes, nuclear submarines, and radar equipment. An apprentice working on navy fighter jets described her job this way:

Okay, my title is electronics mechanic, radar—apprentice. It's basically the radar and communication-type equipment that goes onto the navy fighter jets. Right now I'm working in the plane in the cockpit, checking all this stuff that I used to repair. It comes in from the fleet and for one reason or another it doesn't work. You plug it in to whatever your test set is—you have a book with procedures to go through—you know, if you push this button you should get this indication on a meter, or if you do this you get that indication—and you just follow along, and then when something goes wrong, then you have to repair it, and get out the schematic and figure out why you're not getting this output when you should and replace parts, which include soldering and taking things out, putting things in. And all these little black boxes, you know, from little tiny things to great big one-hundred-pound things that I can barely get off the bench and they all end up eventually out in the plane after going through all the other shops—what they call feeder shops—do these individual boxes. Now I'm out seeing how they all finally work in the plane. You check out the radar, mainly is what our job is, and you sit up in the cockpit and push buttons and watch the radar move around and make sure it works right and you're getting all the indications. The same things, you go through a book and you're supposed to get this when you do that—then you figure out why it doesn't if it doesn't work. And you have to fix it. A lot of the time out on the plane you can just take the box back in to the original shop and make them fix it or have them give you another one. You don't have to do a lot of it out there, which I like, you just have to get it narrowed down to one little box, which is easy.

A woman working in a similar job on nuclear submarines described her work in the following way:

What I do is overhaul and repair electronic instruments in submarines. I start working on my equipment—I pull out all of my tools first, I see them as my play toys. Then I just start working on my equipment. It varies a lot. A lot of it is cleaning, a lot of it is actually electronic work, tests and repair and troubleshooting. I take things apart, drill holes, a lot of mechanical work. A lot like machinist work. I usually don't take many breaks. I work at a very slow speed. I'm very meticulous. I break my day up by going to get tools or supplies or taking care of business in other departments, walking around and things like that—or going to the head, which is usually a distance away, there aren't enough women's heads. Then I break for lunch, read my book, eat my lunch, sometimes I go sit in the sun if it's nice. Then after lunch it's the same thing. We leave promptly at 4:10. The training itself is very good since you get a lot of different sections. The schooling isn't terrific, but you do get schooling at work, which is unlike the unions where you have to go at night, so I really like that aspect. It's a big advantage, not having to go to school at night, and getting paid.

A woman we met in another city was working in a related context, shipbuilding, but in this instance it was for a private company, not civil service. She described her experiences as an apprentice pipe fitter:

I work as a pipe fitter. We work building ships, I'm working on a commercial oil tanker. Some of the time I've worked on steel pipes and what that means is, you have to be able to read blueprints—see how far up the pipe is supposed to be like up from the deck and out from the bulkhead and use rigging equipment to position it, and then, basically you're responsible for where the pipe is, and then telling the welder when to weld it when it's exactly where it's supposed to be. Right now I'm working on the silver brazing crew, you work with smaller pipe. I'm a helper, so I prepare the joints and lay the pipe out. I do lay out on the floor with the chalk line and work with the welder setting the pipe hangers. When you work with a welder, you're responsible for where everything is and all the welder does is weld it and so, like you use—oh, I don't know, hammers and wrenches and hand pulls. I read blueprints and I use rigging equipment, and basically I'm responsible for where the pipe should go and I tell the welder when to weld.

We also met women working for the telephone company in the three cities in which we interviewed. These comments from a cable splicer suggest the kind of nontraditional work some women are doing.

Okay, cable splicers for the telephone company—oh, God, how do I describe it? Okay, you have a telephone pole with a telephone cable running along it, right, and the line workers will put up the telephone poles and they'll put up the line and the cable splicers will come along and connect the cables to different cables. You have the starting point for a cable which is a central office, and it leaves the central office and goes down underground into a manhole, and at that point that cable, which is, like, the main cable for connecting, service, is connected to other cables. So that would be like one thing I do, I go down there into the manhole and I connect the main cable to different cables, and it's just connecting cables to cables to cables to cables. The installers will come along and they'll put the telephones in the houses and that kinda thing. I work on poles occasionally, but right now I'm mostly in manholes. I'll open up my manhole, put up all the safety gear and everything and go down there and open up the cable. What I did today, for example, was really dirty work. The line workers will put the cable through the conduits under the ground. They have tunnels that they put it through and it'll just be put into the manhole and then the splicer has to go down there and arrange the cable in the manhole, and this particular manhole had about three feet of water in it, and I pumped the water out of it, but there was still wet on the bottom, and so the cable I was working with was getting wet and it was just a mess. It was hot and just *yuk*. It's real bad, but I set it up, I set up real good and I'm real prouda that.

Clearly, even though many skilled blue-collar jobs are highly technical and precise, virtually all of them involve at some point or other physical, often very dirty work. Many of the women, however, were quick to point out that they actually liked that aspect of their jobs, as you can see from the remarks of this welder:

I'm a welder mechanic and I'm in the machinists' union. I'm a trailer mechanic, that is, I'm a trainee trailer mechanic. And ah, what I'm learning to do is to repair trailers, which are big boxes made out of stainless steel and aluminum that can either go on as boxcar service on the railroad or container overseas or on a trailer chassis bi-truck. So, that's what I'm learning to do, is to repair that, and I'm also learning to do some chassis work. I work swing shift. I punch in and punch out. I work Monday through Friday, three-thirty to midnight. I work by myself, but a lot of jobs require two people and so then I'll work with someone else. There is a journey-man who is sort of . . . I'm sort of assigned to him, like if I have questions, he's the one I ask. I'm going to stay with it. Welding is a real good skill to have. I might not work on the trucking industry, you know. I might do some other kind of welding, but I intend to use the skills. That's why I'm learning it. I can tell you one good thing about the job—it's great physically. I mean, I've always been strong but, I mean like, I'm really getting strong. I get a lot of exer-cise. I get to do, um, a whole lot of different kinds of things . . . I get to move around a lot, I get to drive a truck, I get to drive a forklift, I get to use all kinds of different tools, I get to climb up and down ladders and work off of scaffolding and walk around on the roofs and everything, you know. So there's a lot of variety. And that's really good. And the physicalness of it I love. You know, I like really doing physical kinds of things. You know, keeps me in shape and that's what I like about it.

Another job that is quite physical is gardening and land-scaping. We talked to three women working in this field. The comments of one woman captured the essence of all their expe-riences.

A lot of it is just general cleanup as far as plants go. Like today we were cutting ivy off trees, trimming off the dead parts of trees and shrubs. We work at reservoirs, you know, so it's mainly to keep up what's already planted at the reservoir lookin' decent. Cutting off with the handsaws or electric saws or whatever different pruning things that need to be trimmed up and then loading that into the truck. Some days, it's just litter pickup like a . . . there're a lot of beer cans and things that are dumped on different sites and it's just . . . you know, you spend the day just picking up trash that people have left. One job that we're working on off and on is like a new reclamation center that is being planted and we've planted one side and we go out there and it was really hard soil and we had to use a jackhammer to dig holes, and then we'd dig the rest by hand. Then it gets to the point where you're mixing the dirt up and planting five- to fifteen-gallon trees on the site. We went out mulching one planting we did, and then watering it after we'd done the mulching and fixing up basins around the plants. On rainy days we do drain checks, which is you go out and you make sure all the drains are cleared, and there're like ducts, I guess they're called drains too, cement. You just rake leaves out of those. What else . . . cutting down diseased trees, then cutting up the parts of the trees.

We met a number of women working in a variety of jobs as electricians, particularly in the repair and maintenance of complex electrical machinery. One example is this woman working in an aircraft industry.

Right now I'm working on the airplane out on the test site—working on the test line running up the airplane's full power taking down the electrical systems, all the electrical and hydraulic systems. We check the whole airplane so the pilots can take them. We go over each airplane and make sure it's safe and all together for pilots.

Right now my hours are from 2:45 to 11:15 in the evening. And, ah, if I worked on the day shift it would be from 6:30 to 3:00. We work at our own pace and do our own things and out on the test lines there's almost no supervision at all. I mean there's someone there, but there's no one telling you what you have to do or when to sit down, when to have a cup of coffee. We don't even have whistles.

A rapidly expanding skilled field is office machine repair. After six months of classes and work with a partner/trainer, a woman in this new field described her work to us in this way:

Ah, my job is, let's see, my job is to repair machines that break down during the course of the day. I work with an answering service and customers will call into this number and say—my machine is . . . you know, this is our name, this is our address, and you know, this is the problem we're having with our machine. Sometimes I'm able to help people over the telephone and not have to go out. Most of the time I'm in my car, driving around from one place to another, repairing equipment.

They're paper-handling machines, which is what I work on, or mail handling machines. Um, mail stampings, sealing. I work on a machine that, say, seals and stamps 170-odd envelopes a minute.

Um, I work on letter openers, I work on folders, I work on inserters. Um, they tie systems together for billing. I work on basic office equipment with the exception of typewriters and calculators. You know, copiers, folders, letter openers, embossing machines, um, what else do they make? That's about it. I'm supposed to make approximately eight calls per day. Um, to be productive and be doing my job as it should be done. I work alone mostly and I only know of one other woman doing what I do with this company in the Bay Area.

COMMON CHARACTERISTICS OF BLUE-COLLAR JOBS

Given the incredible diversity in skills and work settings these women represent, what, if any, common themes emerge from the detailed information we have on life at the workplace and the types of classroom and on-the-job training women are getting in skilled jobs? I can answer that question in terms of the four critical areas of "learning the job": skills, process, work group norms, work setting.

Skills. With the exception of a few women who had had some brief prior job experience or trade school or classroom instruction, for most of the women their new jobs called for a whole new set of skills. These were for the most part mechanical or technical in character and also physical. Most of their skilled jobs required some diagnostic or design competency: analyzing if a machine or instrument is functioning properly, identifying malfunctions, repairing, maintaining, and sometimes designing alternative operations or parts. It's the kind of work that calls upon analytical skills aided by mathematical abilities, blueprint reading, drawing and drafting, and the ability to use measurement-sensitive tools. All of these skills must be learned either on the job or in the classroom in order to go about the routine daily business of the workplace.

In addition, certain physical abilities have to be developed or at least creatively worked around, so one can work in the nooks and crannies, at the heights and depths, and in the odd physical positions often required to do such things as fitting a pipe while on your back, evaluating an instrument in the cockpit of a plane, or leveraging a heavy part or piece of equipment into place. None of these is simply a matter of brute strength, size, or muscle mass, but more of knowing how to use one's body in varied ways. In addition to knowing how, one must also build up strength and endurance by practice.

Process. The process of executing skilled blue-collar work is also quite different from that of the jobs most of these women had prior to entering a trade. Interestingly, it is not that different from what many of us identify as characteristic of professions and at times even of housework. The jobs these women are working in involve a great deal of autonomy. Work groups are very small, for the most part two or three persons, and often work can be done alone. They are not closely supervised jobs. They are not easily timed jobs. Because so much is maintenance and repair, the nature of the problem determines the length of time required on any one job. Because they are specialized jobs done in small work groups, the interdependencies are few. One can pretty much control one's own pacing. One is not too dependent on another person's pacing for how one executes work, and does not have someone breathing down one's neck, waiting to do his or her part. Compare this kind of pacing with the lot of a person on an assembly line, with that of a secretary in a typing pool or of a waitress working a busy lunch counter, depending on the cook to get orders out fast.

Another element of the work process in these jobs is the intimate relationship between the worker and machinery and tools. The execution of the job depends on knowledge of equipment. One is much more likely to be slowed down or thrown off schedule because of faulty tools or a broken machine than because of the work habits of particular people. It helps to know how to fix them or who to go to to get them fixed, to be good at the job. Women moving into skilled jobs have to figure out all of these aspects of the work process and to some extent be comfortable with the self-paced, often isolating "person to machine" process of getting the job done.

Work group norms: In the next chapter a great deal of attention will be given to this topic because of one problematic aspect of blue-collar work norms facing women in industry. That is the norm that skilled blue-collar work is essentially *man's* work. How a woman deals with that norm and finds acceptance over time will be discussed in detail later. There are other norms, however, suggested by the women's descriptions of their jobs. One has to do with when and how much you work. Overtime is extremely common in skilled blue-collar work, and a willingness to work overtime is essential. Multiple shifts are also common, so a willingness to work swing shifts (4 P.M. to 12 midnight) and graveyard shifts (midnight to 8 A.M.) is also essential. Catching on to when you take breaks, how long you can take for lunch, when you can stop at a coffee shop, when you can have a beer, is part of the informal work norms.

Beyond this, knowing how to ask for help and be an active learner is of critical importance. The on-the-job training that takes place depends entirely on the willingness of a journeyman or supervisor to share information and instruct and the ability of a new employee to ask good questions, pick up information fast, and remember well. Apprenticeship and on-the-job training programs are for the most part extremely unstructured and unspecific, and it is possible to sit around for four years and not learn anything. Becoming competent in a trade requires both helpful co-workers *and* an assertive personal style. In some industrial contexts the latter has been referred to as the ability to "step up to people"; in others it has been referred to less appealingly as "having balls." Whatever the case, the women themselves pointed out time and again how important helpful, information-sharing people were and how much of an active role they had to take in order to be taught and to learn. I'm convinced this norm applies to men and women equally in skilled blue-collar settings. It may be harder for women to get journeymen to take an interest initially in training them, and it may be harder for women to be assertive, active learners because of their lack of background and unfamiliarity with industrial/technical settings, but the norm is that "you ask questions, pull your own weight, and pick things up fast or you'll be left behind," regardless of your sex.

Work setting: Finally, the place, the environment in which most skilled blue-collar work is done, is totally alien to the experience of most women. It possesses none of the niceties one associates with office work, hospitals, churches, or even housework. It is not just that the work itself is dirty but that the environment is frequently noisy, too hot or too cold, barren, and depressing. The nature of the work is to work on the inside of an oil tanker's hull, to string underground cable, to repair engines where tools, heavy equipment, and grease are unavoidable. Outdoor work frequently entails bad weather, hazardous heights, or unappealing emergencies such as broken sewer lines or gas leaks. Most skilled blue-collar work requires a good deal of time in such physical settings.

In addition, the nature of the product with which the company works and the size of the work force are important. The product line can be large or small, mechanical or electronic, and each has an impact on how the work is done and experienced. Work force or company size, as Jan Spencer pointed out, can affect a company's ability to have certain kinds of tools or equipment available that can make the execution of work more or less difficult. Size of the work force can also affect the ease with which a new employee can learn a skill, the strength of the union, or the methods for grievance when a worker feels wronged by the employer or a supervisor. Also the sex role composition of the work force is an important characteristic of the work setting, for it affects how new women will be regarded and treated at all levels in the organization. Finally, there are external factors impinging on the work setting that structure the opportunities and experiences of pioneering women. A worker has to figure out the environment and to some extent take control of it if he or she is going to last.

Each of these aspects of the job had to be learned and understood, for the most part, within the first year on the job for a woman to begin getting a clearer sense of her own competence and develop a long-term interest in the work. The first year was also enough time for the employer, supervisors, and coworkers to begin accepting the woman in a nontraditional role.

We were frankly quite surprised at how positive the women's overall evaluations of the quality of their work experiences in the first year were. Although there were numerous problems on the job, when we tabulated the types of reactions and evaluations we found that 45 percent spontaneously mentioned positive feelings about their earnings, 50 percent offered positive statements about their co-workers, 49 percent reported feeling they were being adequatly prepared, and 38 percent felt they were already competent at their new job. Another 49 percent spontaneously talked about how much they liked the physical and technical nature of their work. When we probed for what the women felt were the negative aspects of their job, 48 percent mentioned uncooperative, indifferent, and sometimes downright hostile relationships with their co-workers; 43 percent, the nature of the work, particularly the physical demands and work setting. The most often mentioned criticism (68 percent) was the haphazard way they were being trained, especially poor instruction in the formal settings and not enough exposure to a variety of skills and operations. However, many of these same women reported getting what they needed either on their own or with the help of a responsible supervisor or a friendly co-worker.

A majority of the women in their first year felt they were getting poor formal training and having difficulties with male co-workers because of being the first or one of few women on the job. Fully 67 percent cited having to deal with this issue in the first year. Nonetheless, close to half still felt they were learning something, becoming competent, and developing positive relationships on the job. Fifty-six percent of the women felt they had an adequate general knowledge of their skill, and 51 percent were optimistic about keeping their jobs, in contrast to 21 percent who were pessimistic.

In sum, the experiences in the first year were mixed for most women. There were some good journeymen and some bad ones; some good instructors and some bad ones; harassment from some people, encouragement from others; the jobs were physically demanding and dirty, but on the other hand challenging and interesting; the hours were long and hard, but the money fantastic. There was, however, one critical factor differentiating the eighty-two women we interviewed in the first year, and that was the nature of the employment or training setting in which they were working. It became quite clear by the second year that probably the *most* important factor in sticking with a nontraditional job after that first very difficult six to twelve months was job security, i.e., employment in a place or program that was permanent or lengthy. Such things as apprenticeships or company-initiated on-the-job training programs were better for pioneers than experimental, time-limited, or exclusively classroom-based training with only tenuous promises of employment at the end. This was in part because the former facilitated better skills development over time, but also because they established the sense that both the employer and employee were making a *real* investment in developing a successful skilled worker.

We lost twice as many of the women who were simply in training or time-limited employment programs such as CETA as we did women who were apprentices, on-the-job trainees, or skilled workers in a "real" job with a stable employer. The other women still had to face finding jobs and establishing credibility, and without an intermediary to help them get employment they disappeared, at least from our sight. The few who did go on to stable employment reported either having had the help of an instructor or friend or going to an agency that helped them get a job or an apprenticeship. The woman who tried to get a job on her own with only trade school behind her was at a disadvantage. More than a dozen such women were back in traditional jobs by the second-year interview.

What can we say about the women who succeeded in spite of the very mixed experiences they had when first entering a skilled blue-collar job? About 25 percent of the women we met were no longer working in a skilled blue-collar job after fifteen months. Some of them just couldn't learn what was necessary, some decided they weren't really interested, and others very probably were driven out of their jobs before they had a fair chance to learn. We reinterviewed only a small number of the women who had moved back to traditional work or were unemployed. Our estimate is that close to 75 percent of the women were actually employed in full-time skilled blue-collar jobs after fifteen months, and we interviewed in depth three-fourths of these, or forty-seven women. Of that group of forty-seven, 75 percent were still in a skilled blue-collar job at the end of three years. What factors contributed to that success and how they mastered the four essential elements of the job just described is what will now be addressed.

WOMEN WHO SUCCEED: KEEPING THE JOB

Whether or not a woman in a nontraditional job slot keeps her job is a function of three distinct but interrelated factors. The first is good job skills, that is being really competent at the various aspects of the job. The second is understanding how to behave as a worker, especially how to fit into the culture of the new workplace, which can be referred to as work savvy. The third is the development of a real commitment to the job, because of the compensations and benefits and/or because of the gratifications of the work itself. The forty women interviewed who were still employed in nontraditional blue-collar jobs by the end of the second year and an additional twenty nontraditional women we were able to track down by phone at the end of that year had many of these qualities in common. By the end of the third year, we were in direct contact with forty-one of the original group of nontraditional women who were still in nontraditional jobs and they still emphasized the importance of these factors.

It is clear that competence, savvy, and commitment were the keys to success and that for pioneers in a field the burden of responsibility for success was placed on the individual. This was certainly true for the first wave of women in skilled trades. It was the perseverance and sensitivity of the individual, rather than any programs or commitment on the part of institutions, that assured success. Beyond a general readiness to allow new people to enter previously closed fields and once-exclusive classrooms and work sites, there was little active encouragement or help at an institutional or small-support-group level. The women tended to be isolated or found friends and supports on their own. Understanding how they did this may nonetheless provide some guidelines for how institutions and groups can facilitate the success of second and thrid waves of women workers and reduce the still-large number of failures.

What, then, can be learned from the individual experiences of the women? Once again, I find myself turning to Jan Spencer. Jan was enormously successful and yet at every step along the way had to face and overcome obstacles (even though her family background and early vocational choices gave her a significant edge).

But this particular job has been unreal. It's like a fairy tale, you know, just no problem. I could just be lulled into thinking life was simple for women mechanics at this job, you know. But other women who're at this transit company don't have that experience. I think that part of it comes from—you know, I went through a lot of jobs before I got to this one, too, before I learned how to deal with men, you know. Every time you start to deal with men in a certain way, then you're stuck with that technique in dealing with that same set of men. It's not easy to change after you once start dealing one way, then you gotta stick to it or if you try to change, there's no respect for you 'cause they don't think you know your own mind. Even if you're just trying to experiment, find your way, work things out with them, and I've been through so many ways, I think I have a way down pat now to know what to say, what not to say, but I don't know if I could ever explain it . . . a lot of areas that would create instant havoc, confusion and hate and discontentment. I try to let people live their own lives, you know. I try to understand and have respect for other people. You know, that's one thing, I think politicals get very intolerant of anyone else, which is the exact opposite of what they're asking for. But as important as all of this is the fact that I consider myself to be a professional, you know. I worked long and hard at it, served an apprenticeship, most of an apprenticeship, went to trade school for two years. Before that, I was in the Army and did electricity there and, ah, I'm not stupid, things come to me pretty easily and I've had some great instructors . . . some really old-time mechanics. Masters who've been in the trade, worked at it, took a shine to me, and helped me out even though I was behaving like a fool . . . 'cause I thought I was going to need the best training possible, you know. And I've had some good breaks as far as getting top-flight instruction and I had the intelligence to be able to work with it and just a knack to pick it up. And that has gotten me a long ways because you can blow so far, and you can carry affirmative action so far, but your skill has to take you the rest of the way. The skills and abilities are technical and most women aren't trained, they're not trained to get them. They're not encouraged to go after them and, I mean, it's obvious that they don't have them. They just don't have . . . they don't go into the armed forces. I mean, half the guys on a crew learn their skills in the Navy, you know, I went into the Army. I learned my electrical there. I've learned a lot of things from men, if it hadn't been a situation where I was working with men all the time and doing the technical things, and other stuff. About diesel engines, I never worked on diesel engines but I know a lot about 'em from talking to guys back and forth, you know. About six months ago, they took me out and I learned to drive Mack wreckers, three-quarter-ton trucks, over-the-road diesels, and tractor trailers, and . . . I have every license that California offers right now. And that's because I'm in a male job. Because I'm around them all the time and express an interest, they said okay, you know.

Another woman we followed over the three years worked in an extremely difficult industrial setting, a private steel and shipbuilding company that employs thousands of skilled and semi-skilled workers. The first year we met Tam Cullen she had had some experience and training as a plumber through community college classes and had been working for about a year in shipbuilding as a pipe fitter trainee through the federally funded jobs program CETA. A year and a half later, she had become a permanent employee, and by our third-year contact she was a journeyman pipe fitter doing heavy construction jobs on oil tankers. She endured a great deal of hostility in her first year, was working in a physically taxing and hazardous job, and yet really enjoyed the trade and intended to work in it for a long time. Here are some of the comments she shared with us:

I work generally with one other pipe fitter and a welder or alone with a welder and we install piping systems on ships, mostly commercial oil tankers that are about as long as a football field. And the pipe is usually steel pipe, sometimes it's copper or nickel, and so, like, I'm responsible for reading blueprints and getting everything together so the job can be done. If scaffolding has to be built I have to go to the right people to get that done, and if we need repairs, or whatever, I have to see that that gets done, and then I mark and cut the pipe and show the welder what to do. I'm feeling pretty good about the job this year. I would say that I've had some good breaks in terms of people helping me out when I was starting to get into the trades and of, you know, meeting other people who were convinced that it was perfectly reasonable for a woman to be able to do the job. So when I later got in situations where I had to fight harder to, like, insist on being trained, it was easier because I had already been in situations where I had succeeded in learning similar things. I would say also I tend to have hung in with the job because of, you know, knowing other women in the trades and so I can kind of get some support from other people and also I'm somewhat involved in union activities. And, you know, kind of have some friendly relations with my co-workers off of that. You know, when I was starting off just doing plumbing, I used to worry a lot about whether that was something I could do. I figured I could figure out how the job was done, but I wasn't sure I could do things like, is it hard to cut three-inch pipe with a hacksaw, or am I strong enough to disconnect joints that are corroded together? I've learned I can do all those things. I like it a lot now and I get along great with the guys.

Tam Cullen and Jan Spencer had a lot in common. They were truly competent, for the most part because of their own initiative and a few good co-workers. They had a deep interest in and enjoyment of the work they do and where they do it. Just as important, they had a sympathetic feeling for the attitudes and life-styles of their co-workers. I am tempted to use the word *compassion* because both of the women suffered a great deal of harassment, but their response was to interpret the behavior of men with an understanding of the social and economic position and pressures of blue-collar life. In addition, both of these women were quite small, five foot two, but strong and agile. They came from rural backgrounds and had had some early exposure to tools and problem solving of a mechanical and technical nature. Both, however, began their work lives in traditional jobs and slowly ventured into the trades as opportunities opened up. Jan and Tam were highly skilled, well integrated into male-dominated blue-collar work groups, comfortable in an industrial setting, and challenged by solitary problem-solving mechanical work. They were also persistent, hardworking, and interested in making good money.

These themes were echoed throughout the second-year interviews and third-year telephone follow-ups with the successful women. "I need the money"; "I don't like to be a quitter"; "This is the best job I've ever had and I'm going to make a success of it."

An electronics apprentice in a naval shipyard emphasized these things and described having stayed with her job for the following reasons:

Let's see, the money thing. I'm making good money and to quit now, to take any other job would be ridiculous, you know. Unless it was a job I just really loved. And I can't think of anything like that at the present that I love that much, you know, that really draws me to pursue it. And I wanted to finish the apprenticeship so that I'll have something when I finish, you know, out of my time spent there. I'll have something that will be worth something. If I quit now, I'll just have maybe some work experience. And if I wait till the four years is finished, it's like having a degree, you know. And $7.34 is really good pay for a woman. It'll only get better.

We talked by phone shortly after she had become a journeyman and she still emphasized her desire to finish something she had started and not to reflect badly on other women. She said she didn't really like the people she worked with although she felt the job was pretty easy and the money was "incredible." She finished our phone conversation with, "It's impossible to know where I'll be three years from now."

Perseverance and proving you can do it was a theme among many of the women. As a result of this tenacity, most of the women also reported that they had become more interested in and committed to their work. A free-lance plumber who had had more than her fair share of problems when she started out was convinced she would stick with the trade. By our third-year telephone conversation, she reported she was working on getting her contractor's license and concluded with, "Things are just getting better and better."

A forklift operator who, after three years on her job, reported being an example held up to all the new women, shared the reasons why she was making it:

I have too much pride. I won't let nobody put me down. I've just worked at it. I won't let somebody ruin my life for me. Also, the problems have become fewer over the year because everybody got used to me. They knew they couldn't get rid of me and they said, well, either take her or leave her. I'll probably even move up next into management. But it pays good. I'm used to the money. And the job there is really secure. Like I don't have to worry about a job at all. I feel more secure now than I did last year and I guess it's just that I've been there a long time now and I know that I can do the work. I don't have to worry about anything. In fact, I can load more than the guys I work with. I guess they don't try to, they can if they want to but they don't try. But it's a lot better this year than last year. And we got rid of some of the bad people, too, that used to give me problems. But mainly, I did it myself, I wanted to move higher.

The overriding need for a secure job and desire for a good income is not to be underestimated. Virtually every woman still in a skilled job by the end of the third year was a single person or head of a household. The few married women remaining were older, with grown children. Thus circumstances either demanded or allowed the investment of the time and energy required to be a successful skilled tradesperson. A welder in private industry summarized the significance of a secure job in a way that captured the concerns of many of the women.

I do it for the money, you, um, it's the first legitimate employment
I've had in a long, long time, years and years. I'm doing it for the
money and I'm doing it because I need a skill that I'm going to be
able to get jobs at wherever else I decide to travel to. I'm saving a
lot of money on my job. It's about the most secure job I could have
gotten. It's not the job I thought I wanted but it's turned out to be
the right one. I've had to fight for my training and I mean fight for
it, but I really think they now want to keep me because I'm willing
to do anything they give me and I've learned the job. I mean I love
to weld, I really do. And you know, I need the money. I'm never
going to inherit anything. I own nothing. I've never had anything
and it's always going to be that way, so I've gotta keep working.

There are more quantitative indicators of factors the women
identified as contributing to their staying on the job for more
than two years. In response to the question "To what do you
attribute your stable employment over the last two years?" 46
percent mentioned money either in terms of good pay or in
terms of "I can't afford to make a change"; 46 percent commented on the good job security, and 80 percent on very good
prospects for future employment elsewhere. Nonetheless, over
30 percent complained about the difficulty of the job and the
limitations of the work setting (although I would venture to
guess that blue-collar tradesmen have similar complaints).
The most frequently mentioned factors contributing to success,
offered by over 80 percent of the forty-seven women, were personal characteristics such as perseverance, their interest in the
work, their satisfaction with the skill, their desire to prove to
themselves and others that they could do the job. Eighty percent of the women gave an overall positive evaluation of their
job. Compared to the first year, the job setting and co-workers
were perceived more positively. Fifty-two percent reported being more satisfied with their jobs at the end of the second year
than they had been in the early months of the first year when
we first interviewed them.

In the second year, as in the first, the aspects of the job the
women were concerned with in their conversations with us were
the skills involved, the nature of the work setting, the quality of

the training, and the earnings and benefits of the job. They said very little, negative or positive, about hours, location, convenience, or simplicity. They focused on tasks, mobility, and pay. This kind of orientation to their work contradicts portrayals of working women in some studies. Such studies have tended to minimize the seriousness with which women take their work and to downplay the significance of intrinsic rewards for women in work. The women's concern with skills and rewards also explains why they succeeded. Because they were interested in work-related issues, in doing the job well, in learning new techniques and ways to do the job, in taking pleasure in the execution of the work, and because they saw their work as dignified and complex, and as a lifelong career, they had a better chance at making it. They began not only to increase their own levels of commitment to the job, but also the respect and affection with which their co-workers regarded them.

Although I personally am concerned with humanizing the workplace and changing it in ways that accommodate the legitimate claims of new waves of workers, it appears that for pioneer blue-collar women a key to success was to like the work the way a man does, do it the way a man does, and not let any background limitations or sex-related problems get in the way. If a woman can do a craftsmanlike job and reasonably adapt to the work group norms and job setting without making any special claims as a woman, she is probably going to make it. Such an attitude was essential in the *first* wave of women workers. Their success and experience can be used creatively as a basis for designing more effective recruitment, training, and evaluation procedures for future waves of women workers. This is not yet the case. It was very clear even after the second year that the quality of training and evaluation continued to be haphazard and very poor and that the women were still constantly hustling to learn things on their own and feeling that there were many things they hadn't learned. The system is not really working beyond providing an initial opportunity. What is happening in trades today, as in law and medicine a decade ago, is that a few risk-taking, persevering pioneers are making it because of individual ability and commitment. What we can learn from them is that a woman with a little background, a lot of social marginality, and a great deal of perseverance can make it. Since there are not too many women like that, it is necessary to be more systematic at the developmental, organizational, and training levels if we are to ensure there will be competent tradeswomen in the future.

WOMEN WHO DON'T SUCCEED: LOSING OR QUITTING THE JOB

A number of the women we met in our first year were in time-limited training programs on the job or in community college classrooms which were *supposed* to result in permanent employment but which only did so for a few. We also met a number of feminists and gay activists who admittedly were trying a skilled trade as an alternative work style that promised more pay and more challenging tasks. Many of these women eventually became bored with the work or outraged by the climate at the workplace, in particular by the attitudes and values of the men with whom they worked. Another small number of women were clearly unqualified and unmotivated in the first place and were filling their own time or were placed in slots simply to fill affirmative action numbers requirements. Some of these women were squeezed out, some quit, and others were being carried along in less-demanding skilled jobs.

Four of the unemployed women we reinterviewed had been in government-funded training programs to which they had been referred by a women's agency and after which they were unable to find permanent employment. In the year since our first interview, three of them had continued to have erratic employment experiences similar to those that most of the women we met had before finding their skilled jobs. Two of the four women were black and also had less education than most women we met. Three of the four had not graduated from high school. The absence of positive background characteristics, and an unstable job or training opportunity in the first place, worked against these women. An unemployed woman who had trained as a machinist described her experiences in the following way:

I finished the program and I got my certificate and everything. But then I found that getting a job in that particular training was an altogether, you know, different ball game. I think one of the primary reasons for that was that they require a minimum of three years' or so experience. And when you tell 'em that you just have five hundred hours of machine shop they don't consider that a very good recommendation. I went to several places trying to find a job, and none of them were interested in taking on more of a trainee type person. And then I think also one of the, in fact, it was my age because one of the places they had a sort of like, on-the-job training position, slotted for the age group of eighteen to thirty-five, and that's true also with some of the apprenticeship programs. I've worked briefly, you know, not as a machinist. I worked as a—I worked for the Bayview Hotel. As a maid, back to the maid bit again. I've been employed from that hotel about two months now. I quit. It was just too hard for me. The constant bending and I'd had some previous, you know, female problems and it was just too hard for me. I'd come home, you know, all pooped out, you know. And it was just too hard for me to do. Minimum seventeen, eighteen rooms a day. I'm not too optimistic about getting a job, not like going through the training. I was really, you know, gung ho about it and everything. Then people back you, you know. It came to light that I hadn't really examined if I could really get a job. I have been investigating, you know, whatever possibilities that, you know, like if somebody tells me about something or going to the unemployment and looking on the board and seeing and calling from time to time, you know, my instructor down at the center to find out if he's, you know, heard of anything. But it seems that I, you know, really don't have much choice but to go back to the type of work that I've always done. Like doing maid work, or cooking or something in that . . . something along those lines, or hospital work or something that I can at least say that I've had experience.

This particular woman had participated in government training programs in the past but had yet to have a job outside of a service area such as housekeeping or baby-sitting. She was older than many of the women we interviewed, but more significantly, she seemed to be isolated from information about specific opportunities and access to a machinist job, of which there were many in her community, as it turned out. She also lacked a highly specific sense of her trade and the industrial context because she had only classroom and shop experience and because the quality of the training she got probably wasn't very good.

Another woman who had trained to be an auto mechanic felt she had good skills and got a job immediately, although it was in a small auto shop that paid her only $2.75 an hour. The long hours, her concerns about the needs of her family, and her exhaustion led her to quit the job after a few months.

Well, my health is the main thing. I've never been a super-strong type person but ah—never really sickly either. I was working fifty hours a week and most of the time more. I was working from eight in the morning till six, but most of the time it was like till six-thirty or seven till I got off. So I was trying to come home and take care of the family and I just really got myself run down, plus I was so busy I didn't really have time to eat, so I really got myself in a state of rundownness and the doctor said I had a case of exhaustion. So he told me to take some time off. So I was pretty anxious to quit 'cause my health and my family is more important and I can always look later for another job. I'd like to get back into mechanics, but more or less on a part-time basis rather than full time 'cause then I'd still have time for my family and being home and get involved in, ah, like Bible studies and things like that. It would probably be a small place where I'd work. In fact, my husband keeps trying to talk me into getting my resale license and business license and all that and start a small thing, a little shop maybe, but I don't feel like I'm quite ready for that yet.

This woman didn't really have the strong identification as a working person that is so essential to being a risk taker and putting in the time and energy necessary to make it in a blue-collar job. She was exhausted by the work, but as important, throughout her second-year interview she talked about wanting something she could do part time for a little extra money. That is perfectly legitimate, but for a pioneer it's not enough.

Ann Baker was an example of another kind of woman who had difficulty sticking with her trade. Ann was highly skilled and very bright but she, too, had not yet truly come to terms with working for a living on a full-time basis. In addition, during the period we knew one another she seemed to have developed very little work savvy. Her antagonism toward her co-workers revealed an intolerant attitude toward men and working-class values, and she remained inexperienced in the ways of unionized shops and industrial settings. The following comments suggest this:

I still think the job's a plum and I feel badly about leaving there, except that I feel greatly relieved not to be there anymore. I mean, what it amounted to was it finally reached a point where I was more important than the money I was getting. Let me describe to you what happened. It was real clear to me why I got hired. I mean, there was pressure from the skills center, there's pressure from affirmative action, I was in the right place at the right time, and I'm a nice middle-class girl and I talk a good interview, you know . . . and here I am. A woman at the transit company found out my qualifications, she said, now wait a minute, please back up, you don't have an A.A., I said, hell, no. She said, Wait a minute. . . . I have been royally fucked over. You see she had been trying to get into a trade with no luck and she had qualifications. So she decided to wait till I had completed my ninety-day probationary period . . . and then she put in a grievance, well, anyway, she won her battle and ended up having more seniority than me and I got put on graves. I wasn't getting any training when I started working nights. I hated what I was doing and I was totally isolated and totally pissed! Well, anyway, I just kept having all this conflict with my supervisors. Nobody was doing anything to help me. I was by myself—I was totally by myself. Which I complained about over and over to no avail. And after, after this had gone on for a long time, well, there's more to it. I mean, I complained about it and I also tried to do what I could. I mean, the foreman who was on my shift saw what I was doing and he thought it was fine. I mean, he'd just been made foreman after being a technician there for a long time. He was made foreman when the grave shift was started . . .

which was in June. June or July, I can't remember. . . . So he, I mean, he saw that I was doing fine. But I started to get real bored and real disgusted and I started to feel real invisible. So I, pretty soon I started to think of any excuse I could not to come to work. Although I came to work. And there came a time the supervisor talked to me and said, why are you not coming to work, and I said, well, because I, you know, because I don't like being here. I'm getting no training, I'm getting no attention paid to me, and from what I understood, I mean, it's clear to me that I need help . . . in order to make this job interesting. I can piddle around but to trouble-shoot this complex equipment—I'm supposed to trouble-shoot—I need some help—I need some training. In fact, I'm supposed to get it. And he would kind of shrug his shoulders and say, "What could I do? Put you on days?" and I'd say, "why not" and he would laugh. I tried to get promoted, to get moved, but they'd give it to someone else. I was training guys who get the better jobs I'd been denied! Well, it just all built up real bad and by that time my supervisor wasn't speaking to me at all. I mean, he no longer was even saying good morning. So I wrote this lengthy letter. I told you I was bringing it with me today. I didn't do it. This lengthy letter explaining exactly my perception of what had happened over the past thirteen months. And I sent it to the General and I sent a few copies around. And I quit. I just left there . . . it was just . . . I was, I felt, entirely invisible and I felt lonely, real lonely at that job.

It is very possible that in the ensuing years Ann has found a different blue-collar job in a setting and with a work group more to her liking. It is also possible that with added years and experience she may be more able to live with the apparent inequities and hardships that come with working in large bureaucratic systems dominated by seniority and complex union-management agreements. Jan Spencer, who was the same age as Ann but far more experienced as a worker, saw the very same transit company as an "ideal place" to work.

Over twenty of the women we interviewed in the first year had changed jobs by the second year, but only two had moved back into traditional work. The others had changed skill emphasis or companies in the intervening year. By the third year another half dozen women had dropped out of blue-collar jobs and back into more traditional women's work (although two of those actually moved into better-paying jobs, one in computers and the other in bookkeeping). Lana Miller, a forklift operator who became a reservations agent, described her work as "crummy" but went on to say that she would probably stay with it because it made so few demands on her. Her comments about her current job suggest some reasons why she was not suited to a nontraditional blue-collar job:

What's helped me stay with this job has been . . . for one, a medical leave of absence, let's see, really that was part of it. A medical leave of absence for about a month because I couldn't handle it anymore. The pressure was just too intense. Basically, the fact that we have a union. They can't fire us so easily, number one. Number two, I take a lot of absences. I always use up my sick days. And number three, you know I was unemployed for a little over a year off and on, but basically about a year before I got this job and was just so poor and hungry that, you know, the memories stay, so I'll keep it. Here the money's pretty good. And today there might be something close to a walkout so I'm excited about going to that. So I guess I'd say the money and also the threat of unemployment makes me not seek another job or not quit. And essentially be as close as I can to a so-called good employee, you know, do my work, because of the threat of unemployment. Of course, I've had some problems at this job too. I became really close with this woman at work, lovers with this woman at work, and it was just really difficult, a really difficult situation because I really felt run-down in the relationship. So we were breaking up constantly. This was another reason why it was so hard at work, I had these emotional entanglements and finally, you know, it was very hard to break away from her, and then I became close to this man at work. Believe it or not, really, very difficult. And it was also difficult to relate to a man, period, you know, just all the strange things about that. But strangely enough I have a more equal relationship with him than with her.

This was a delightful interview, and Lana expressed many values suggesting a sensitivity to women's issues and the women's movement, but she had a very casual approach to paid employment. She was afraid of being unemployed, as she lived alone and was self-supporting, but she didn't enjoy work in the way many of the successful blue-collar workers did. She talked a great deal about people and relationships at work. She had been romantically involved with two co-workers after only a few months at work and described her real interests as separate from the workplace. The forklift job hadn't "hooked" her on blue-collar work and by the second interview she seemed unwilling to risk unemployment in an effort to find another blue-collar job. At the time of our third-year telephone interview she was with the same employer as the year before in a similar job.

SUMMARY OF TASK COMPETENCY AND WORK SAVVY

The most critical factor in the success of a pioneer was an acceptable level of competency in understanding the skills, activities, problem-solving strategies, tools, equipment, and resources necessary to do the job. Such a pioneer had to forgo the short-term satisfactions of being liked and accepted by the group *if* it risked learning the job and long-range success. She had to know who could teach her, help her, and sponsor her, regardless of his or her sex or attitudes about women in blue-collar work. Developing competence is easier in some environments than others. Contrary to expectation, our research suggested that successful women workers were more often lone women than in groups, experienced the same amount of harassment from men as did less-successful women, and had no greater access to job-related information and training than did less-successful women. What they did have was an attitude about work that zeroed in on "getting to know how to do the job." They were "active" learners first and foremost. This, combined with a genuine liking for the jobs they were attempting to master and a willingness to put in long, hard hours if necessary, assured success.

"Savvy" is more than knowledge about a particular job or job setting; it means a general sense of the rules of the game in paid employment: how one learns about and finds employment, how to learn a job, a sense of how to build additional opportunities from given work experiences. It's an ability to assess accurately the opportunities and obstacles in the environment, to utilize information and personal networks to one's own work ends, to assess one's own strengths and weaknesses, and to know how to get help. Work savvy is largely a result of lengthy work experience and, in the case of the women pioneers we met, exposure to or experience in blue-collar environments. It is also a result of informal relationships with successful blue-collar workers through family or friends. It embodies a certain familiarity with and sensitivity to the problems and life-style of the community of workers one is a part of: again, in our case, blue-collar men. Most important, it means knowing how to be an "active" learner in the apprentice mode that characterizes training in most industrial settings.

Women who by ignorance, accident, or maliciousness are cut off from learning how to do the job and function in the work setting are at a great disadvantage. Acceptance on the job and friendly, supportive relationships with supervisors and coworkers are not automatically given to a new worker in an industrial setting. He or she must earn them in the first few days and weeks at work. As many of our interviewees pointed out, you can blow it the first day if you make a bad impression. Work savvy involves in large part knowing how to manage first impressions, how to minimize your weaknesses and maximize your strengths in the eyes of a new work group or supervisor. It's knowing how to move from there into good questions, active learning. It's having a willingness, if not the immediate ability, to fine-tune mechanical skills, cultivate mechanical aptitudes, and develop physical strength and agility. Women who make gigantic first efforts and who are quick and active learners will become competent and then find friends and acceptance at work. As the detailed comments of the women themselves point out, and the more statistical material on the women's on-the-job experiences included in the Appendix summarizes, improved task performance results in improved self-confidence and improved relationships at work. But tasks cannot be mastered without certain basic sensitivities and skills from the start.

In summary, for a woman to succeed in a nontraditional job, the individual and the setting must have certain characteristics.

INDIVIDUAL CHARACTERISTICS

A woman likely to succeed in a nontraditional blue-collar job
- identifies herself as a worker from an early age;
- is more task-oriented than interpersonally oriented;
- is preoccupied with puzzles and problem solving;
- gives nonideological interpretations to her own and others' (especially male) behavior;
- has skills resulting from some advanced education;
- knows how to seek out information and opportunities necessary for mastering tasks;
- is in a network of competent, savvy peers;
- receives support from friends and family for risk taking;
- wants good compensation and benefits for her labor;
- is secure about her employment prospects in skilled trades.

SITUATIONAL CHARACTERISTICS

Environments conducive to success
- provide stable jobs;
- provide good compensation and benefits;
- provide effective mechanisms for employee representation;
- provide mechanisms that ensure a minimum level of familiarity with blue-collar work and workers prior to job assignment;
- focus on strategies for helping people become competent at particular jobs rather than striving for acceptance of newcomers in particular jobs;
- spell out job requirements and expectations;
- surround newcomers with competent and savvy men *and* women;
- provide frequent feedback on performance.

What might be done by society, within schools and in general, to foster these individual qualities and institutional supports is the topic of Part Three of this book.

There is still a missing piece in our story, however: such a large and significant piece that it deserves a chapter of its own. That piece is interpersonal relationships and their impact on job execution and commitment. There are relationships at work, at home, and in the community that affect in fundamental ways how a woman does her work, her feelings about her work, and ultimately her success at her work. How these affect women and fit into the range of issues we have been discussing in the last two chapters is the topic of the next chapter.

VI

Relationships at Work

In a very fundamental way, women pioneering in blue-collar jobs were quite isolated. Although many of them used the resources of women's agencies in locating their jobs, only a few were tied into the feminist movement; although many had fathers with blue-collar trades or skilled jobs, few had families rooting for them and helping them make a success of the job; although many described helpful people on the job and even friendly co-workers, virtually none were a part of a tightly knit work group. It's as though the isolation and marginality that characterized the childhood and young adulthood of so many of these women simply carried into their adult work roles and equipped them in some special way to deal with more of the same. In addition to the tenacity, competency, and work savvy described in the previous chapters, it is clear that the capacity to be an "outsider" was a critical factor in succeeding. With the exception of about twenty women who were in classroom situations in which there were frequently three or four women, practically every woman we interviewed in the first year was the lone woman in her immediate work group. Some of the women encountered other skilled women workers in the course of the day or were aware of women in similar jobs in other parts of their organization, but they worked on a regular basis exclusively with men.

When a person is in a skilled blue-collar job the tasks and activities for which the person is responsible for the most part require only one or two people. This is particularly true in the large number of repair and maintenance jobs many of the women were in. Even the less-skilled jobs such as telephone installer, forklift operator, UPS driver, or gardener tend to be jobs where one works alone or in small crews. Thus, apart from the groups of twenty or thirty people in the classroom, the woman developing job skills in blue-collar work must depend for most of her training on small groups or individuals. This is an extremely critical point. The philosophy underlying virtually all training, growth, and advancement opportunities in the blue-collar world is that on-the-job training, on-the-job experience, and on-the-job performance are the best ways to develop *and* evaluate competency. The traditional journeyman-apprentice relationship is still quite strong. The norms governing this relationship place a heavy burden on the apprentice to be an active learner. They also assume that the trainee has great deal of familiarity and even prior experience with mechanical and tooling operations and problem solving. In addition, the fact that women have never been in this "collegial" role before creates problems.

The problems facing the first wave of blue-collar pioneers were truly enormous. Women had to adjust to a philosophy of training that was intimately tied to doing the actual work. They had to adjust to small work groups and trainers who were usually journeymen or supervisors who saw their role as answering questions rather than giving direct instruction. They had to accommodate socially to blue-collar men who had never interacted with women as work peers. All this meant that a woman had to know already, be told prior to job assignment, or figure out pretty quickly on the job what the social reality of the blue-collar setting was. This had to happen in order to ensure that relationships were established whereby actual training and learning could take place. It was possible for a woman to develop friendly relationships at work, even feel liked by her supervisors and co-workers, and not be learning the job. It was possible to be used in an on-the-job situation as an assistant or gofer and not really learn the trade. It was possible to work with people who always tried to do things for her, so that she never had an opportunity to test her own knowledge and ability to identify, assess, and solve technical or mechanical problems. In each of these situations, the woman was not developing competent skills and was eventually "found out" or found out herself and then felt cheated of a fair opportunity to learn.

Given these complications facing trainees in a blue-collar setting, it is important to evaluate relationships at work from a variety of perspectives. First and foremost, we need to identify the kinds of relationships that help or hinder the actual learning of the job and job tasks. Second, we need to identify relationships that help or hinder the new worker in feeling like a legitimate member of the work group and job setting. Third, we need to identify relationships that actually provide support and encouragement. I think it is fair to say before sharing our findings that if a person has relationships that help her learn the job, she is ultimately better off than if she has the other two kinds but not the first. After a woman has demonstrated that she can learn and master a minimum level of tasks, she will then begin to get acceptance and encouragement. What often appears early on as acceptance and encouragement proves to be patronizing or protective behavior on the part of the men.

In this chapter, then, rather than giving a broad picture of the formal and informal relationships at work, we will home in on the three problems a woman bent on success had to deal with— becoming competent, gaining social acceptance, inspiring support and encouragement from fellow workers—and the ways in which relationships at work played themselves out in either hurting or helping this process. We will begin with a discussion of some of the positive learning relationships the women shared with us. By way of contrast, we will then share some of the often harrowing experiences women first confronted when trying to learn the job, and describe how they overcame these. We will address problems of sexual harassment as well as describe the ways in which women were included or excluded in the workplace. Finally, we should get some insight into what the women perceived as the advantages and disadvantages of being a woman in a blue-collar job.

POSITIVE ON-THE-JOB RELATIONSHIPS

I am defining as positive any relationships that helped a woman learn the job requirements and skills so that she eventually mastered them, felt competent, and reported being perceived as competent by her co-workers. This does not mean that the woman functioned without stress or hassles, but rather that, all things being equal, she had a pretty good opportunity within a relatively short time on the job—within the first two months, let us say—to begin learning skills. These women did not have an *easy* time—just a reasonable time in contrast to the experiences of the other women.

It was *normal* for blue-collar men to be reluctant, skeptical, and quizzical about the first woman on the job. It was normal for them to question the sincerity of the woman's interest and commitment to a man's job. It was normal for them to wonder about whether or not the woman was going to get married and take off or get pregnant. It was normal for them to question whether the woman had technical or mechanical competence or the physical strength and agility to do the job. It was normal for them to resent women because they perceived them as taking away a job from one of their own, particularly given the high unemployment rates of recent years.

Encountering all these doubts and reservations was a normal part of each woman's first encounters with a male-dominated blue-collar work group. Such doubts and reservations may be immoral, ignorant, discriminatory, or sexist, but they are real and they had to be dealt with. Even in positive work environments and work group relationships such attitudes and initial questioning occurred. Negative work environments or work group relationships went beyond this kind of "normal" questioning, doubting, joking, or initially cool treatment. They involved actual acts of hostility or sabotage, withholding of opportunities for information and training, persistent sexual innuendos, and open harassment. But first a look at positive relationships.

The persons who fared the best in a new job had related blue-collar work experience or a great deal of familiarity with the company because they had worked there for a long time in another capacity. In other words, people who were less strange were treated with less initial skepticism. There was some basis for "anchoring" such a person, for evaluating her background, skills, interest, and potential for acceptable performance on the job. Jan Spencer, who had extensive training and experience as a mechanic prior to her apprenticeship, was such a person. Molly O'Hara, who had worked as a secretary for her facility nearly ten years before taking on an apprenticeship, was another example. Sandy Harold, who had been tinkering with cars and taking classes at a skills center before signing up for an apprenticeship at a small dealership, also entered a man's job with some feeling for the work and the work context. Each of these people felt they had a great deal to learn about their new jobs, but each had enough familiarity with the job and work setting norms to make a good first impression. Each could call upon employment experiences to which their male co-workers could relate. The ice breaking took less time and had fewer problems. Jan Spencer's very positive feelings about her position with a metropolitan transit company were described in the last chapter. On her relationships with co-workers she said:

I think I've gotten treated the way I expected. I enjoy my job, my shift, and since I've been made a chief mechanic all the people I've had have got whipped into shape. They know what not to say to me and how not to treat me but they were a pretty decent bunch of guys to start off with, you know. I don't have a lot of trouble getting along with men to begin with. Even so, the men here still give me a hard time now and then. Like I was saying before, this job is like a fairy tale for me, but I don't think it's like that for the other women working here. I went through a lot of jobs before I came here and I made a lot of mistakes. But by now I know pretty much how to deal with men, you know. And, face it, I've really got good skills; I've worked long and hard for them. I just can't believe sometimes that it's all finally paying off.

Molly O'Hara, the draftsperson at a military facility, also had very positive relationships on the job. This was attributable to three things. She had worked for many years in a clerical position that provided support to the office in which she was working in a nontraditional job. She was in her early fifties and thought of herself as "motherly" when she embarked on her nontraditional job. Finally, her work interaction was almost exclusively with engineers who, though they were no less "sexist" than many of the blue-collar workers, had had experience in working with female clerical employees. They saw Molly not as a peer but as a skilled support person responsible for translating ideas and concepts into workable designs. In combination, these factors softened the blow of having a woman in this traditionally male job and structured the situation in a way that made it easier for Molly to move into the job.

I'd say there's quite a few people who have been helpful to me. When I first started out, of course, I started out of the same department where everybody knew me. This was a new experience and I was the guinea pig. There's quite a few of the engineers that really were helpful in getting me started. If I had a question I could go to them, and that's why I say that. I wouldn't be where I am today if I didn't have that help from those men. There's really no one who has made it difficult for me. The fact, being a woman, I don't know whether it would have been as easy for a younger woman than at my age. Because, see, I have the motherly image, you know, and they want Mom to make good. In fact, the ones I work with, I'm old enough to be the mother of most of them. My immediate section head is younger than my oldest son. Every once in a while when they come up with "The woman's place is in the home" type thing, and then they just egg me on because they know that I'll take the female part, I'll have to defend womanhood. They call me a women's libber doing a man's job, but it's said in a nice way. They know I know they're teasing. Oh, sometimes I get a little up tight, but most of the time it's on a fun basis. One of our men just likes to egg me on. He's always saying that the women have it so good, you know—how well off they are. Of course, I have to scrape for equal pay, equal work.

Sandy Harold, the well-educated, highly political auto mechanic living in Northern California after the death of her alcoholic father, also had good feelings about her co-workers. Sandy had been taking classes and informally working on cars and hanging around repair shops for about four years before deciding to take the plunge and try to get an apprenticeship in auto mechanics. She was employed by a liberal shop owner in a liberal community, which probably minimized problems. Nonetheless Sandy had to learn to deal with the constant "tits and ass" conversation in her work setting, and she found her open opposition to these kinds of attitudes mellowing over time. Sandy was getting really good training and had very positive relations with her co-workers.

I guess I could say a lot about the people I work with and the various things that go on there. I really like all the people I work with. I think it's an amazing group of people that are somehow magically assembled there. I work with six or seven other mechanics, and there's a woman at the parts counter. She's a first, too. She just got her journeyman papers today as a parts technician. I rely on two people in particular. Steve has a lot of the technical information that I need, and Frank'll come rescue me from freaking out, 'cause he works right beside me. If I start screaming or kicking he'll come and say, Okay, stop, you know, look at this thing or whatever, right, which I also need, 'cause I just get really wrapped up in things and if they don't work out right I can get real frustrated. I don't think anyone's out to get me in particular. A couple of the guys who've been working there the longest both went through a lot of changes to get their skills. They started out at the skill center, right, which is some sort of equivalent to me trying to break in. Only they had this exact opposite attitude . . . if they had to suffer acquiring their skill everybody else did too, and so they were really cool to me for a long time and they weren't into sharing. It took a good six months to break that down, but nobody, you know, has any ax to grind or anything like that.

We asked Sandy about customer reactions to a woman mechanic.

The people there defend me working on cars, you know. If customers or somebody walking by starts getting bent outa shape if their car is being worked on by a woman, almost anybody in the shop would defend me, you know, saying she's a good mechanic, buddy; that's your problem, not hers. You know, you're lucky she's working on your car. I also think I've gotten, in terms of work, I'm a little less militant than I was. I'm not as quick to jump down people's throats when I hear the word "broad" or "chick" or something.

People don't bait me as much and I don't respond to it as much as I used to. And that kind of stuff, I mean, there's this low, like, conversation going on, locker-room-type stuff, that it's, like, impossible to get away from. I mean it just depends. Sometimes there'll be a whole week in the shop when I don't hear anything like that and then sometimes it'll be all day long. I don't know what it is that sets those men off, but I just sorta don't waste my energy on it anymore, you know. I just want to learn to be a good mechanic, get my papers, and have that security. I've been working on cars since 1970, on and off, and I had been supporting myself for almost two years before I got the apprenticeship working on cars exclusively, in kinds of various low-life situations, but that was what I was doing and I was just trying to find the best learning situation and working situation I could. And actually the apprenticeship was sort of the last resort. I tried a lot of different things first and then I wound up with this. It's a pretty good deal, really.

Another person who knew the work environment even though she didn't know the trade was Maggie Patterson, the young electronics mechanic who moved out of a clerical position in data processing into an apprenticeship. She also encountered very little trouble in her relationships. This may have been partly because she had been working at the facility for three years and partly because some of the other apprentices were old friends. By our second interview, she was dating a journeyman and mixing quite comfortably with most of her male co-workers.

Wow, the first day I thought, oh no; in fact I was late, they held me up in data processing for a couple of weeks because they didn't have anybody to take my place. Well, the class didn't start; the people were working but they just had them out in the shops . . . doing Mickey Mouse stuff, but the class was waiting for me, and when it started, the day I came in, I had to process through so when I came up I was about two hours late and I walked in and thought, oh God. And the only place to sit was in the middle so you had to walk through everybody and around, and sit down . . . and then the first break I looked around and there was one guy I went to high school with was in my class, and another guy, when we were like five years old our houses were like back to back, so we grew up together. I hadn't seen him in about five years. . . . So right away I knew some people and it made it a lot easier. Still, you've got to have kind of a thick skin, you have to put up with the kidding and stuff, but I can give it back as well as I can take it, so it's never been any problem, you know. If you let it get to you, it would drive you crazy—at first, especially. . . . One time I got mad and blew up. Well, that was a mistake, you don't ever let them know you're mad because then they'll never get off your back. But I figure they're only kidding and they don't really mean anything. There are a couple of guys that don't think women should be there, but I'm usually not around them or I stay away from them. Most of the guys—99.9 percent of them—are really nice. They're willing to help. I mean, they want you to do your share, they're not going to do extra for you, but they're pretty nice about it.

By our second interview, Maggie was about to make journeyman and we asked her again about her relationships at work.

Sure, I've had my problems, a lot of problems, probably more good-natured harassment than bad harassment. Always, you know, because I was—a lot of places I went, I was the first woman to go into them. But most of the guys have been pretty nice. There's always a few, but you just overlook the ones that . . . most of them don't want to talk to you anyway. But you take a lot of joking and stuff . . . sometimes you feel like you wish they wouldn't but you just got to build up a thick skin, I think. But you know, there's not much of that kind of stuff anymore. A lot has changed. My work environment and my relationship with George . . . I can't really put a finger on anything in general, but I feel that I've changed a lot—just my attitude. I'm out doing more things instead of kind of hiding in the house, you know . . . work, go home, and you know, go to bed, get up, go to work. I'm playing on the softball team and I'm out into more activities, activities at work like the union as well as on the outside.

Another woman who had successfully completed an apprenticeship in production control had moved into her nontraditional job from a clerical position at the same facility. In addition, her husband had gone through the program two years ahead of her and she had friends who were apprentices. She described her first month as absolutely terrible, but after that things smoothed out. She, too, had the advantage of being somewhat familiar with the work and work setting and being known by some people. This helped her manage relationships a bit more easily than someone who might have been a perfect stranger. She described her early on-the-job relationships:

This was strictly a male area. I mean they didn't let any females no way, nowhere, no how, in there and the first woman who came in was pretty masculine and the guys teased her a lot. They also don't feel like she does her job enough, you know. She doesn't do her job the way that it's supposed to be done. They don't feel that way, so she had a lot of trouble adjusting in there, but it made—I think it made it easier for me to come right in. The fact that there was already one woman who had broken the ice. They all seem to really like me and stuff and they think I do a really good job and they don't hesitate to let me know. When I first started, guys were always saying, "May I help you? I'll give you a hand," so that is what I would call a little special treatment. I'd say no way. Then they'd go, "What are you, some type of woman's libber or something?" I'd say, "No I don't need any help—I can do it—this is my job—I don't want people to play favorites or anything else. It's my job—I can handle it." They go, "You must really be a woman's libber"—I'm not a woman's libber—I just kind of let them know it's my job and I didn't want guys hanging around waiting to help me do something. It was important to let them see I could handle the job. Sometimes you wish they would treat you a little more equal and not so helpless sometimes. All in all, people have really been helpful. I think the first week or two, going into a new area, is hard, you know, because there's not hardly any women working out there. That's why . . . just yuckie old men . . . yuckie young men too. Once they get used to you everything's fine. There's usually kind of maybe an adjustment period when you go into a new area. You get a lot of whistles, you know, you have some guys that really are vulgar, really kind of make you feel like you want to turn around and run out the door

. . . but working out there awhile you just kind of get used to it, but some areas are worse than others. But usually, when you get into a new area, then that may happen for the first week or two and then it kind of dies. A lot of them get used to you and then you're just part of the scene.

Finally, Erin Kelly, the chef's apprentice who after our three years of contact had taken a chef's job in a major New York City hotel, had an excellent training experience even though the attitudes of many of the European chefs, cooks, and kitchen workers she met were negative.

I have a very good deal at the place where I work. For some reason I seem to have fallen in with the men in the kitchen very well. I don't have any obvious conflicts with anybody. You know, every now and then we get into fights and stuff. But I think everybody does. But there are some places where cooks are just put in menial positions and left there and if they want to learn anything else they have to go out and do it. That hasn't happened to me, luckily. I'm an apprentice. I'm in my own class. I'm the only woman apprentice there. There's three men. In terms of them, Ron is the most senior apprentice, and I'm the next senior, so I have a pretty good standing there because of all the apprentices, so far I'm turning out the best which helps a lot. The apprentices are really the most qualified workers in the kitchen. Aside from Ron, I'm the only other person who can work all the stations in the kitchen. None of the station cooks can lay claim to that. They work their station and that's it.

André, the head chef, has been just terrific. We work fast together and have a lot of fun. Dan, who was my boss for a long time in the second cook's station, is a very funny man because not a lot of people get along with him. He's an Englishman—and he doesn't approve of women in the kitchen and he's very open about it. He doesn't necessarily think they should be home, you know. He's got a wonderful marriage—he's married to this Englishwoman and she works with a law firm. They don't have any kids and they're very happily married. It's nice—all the men in the second cook's station are happily married and that's nice. He has sort of taken this father image with me. And he protects me like when this guy out in the Dutch kitchen gives me a hard time—Dan is always there to take care of it if I can't. I talk to him an awful lot, like he's involved in the union and I get involved in that with him and he kind of backs me up in the apprenticeship program and stuff.

Most of the people I work with actually are friends and helpful, because a lot of them live around me and they know what's happening anyway. Most of the men in the second cook station are very good friends of mine, and most of them live in a couple-house radius. There's one man in particular that I like to deal with more often than anyone else in the kitchen, and he's the executive sous chef. He's a superb cook but he's kind of a creep as a person. Like, he's a nice person, but he's European and I have a hard time dealing with Europeans. He has terrible attitudes toward women. Even so, there's this one woman cook who's really good and he's really been pushing her in her career. . . . So he doesn't like women but he knows a good worker when he sees one.

Positive relationships at work, then, were relationships which didn't stand in the way of learning the job, which evaluated performance fairly and promoted people when they were deserving regardless of personal feelings about whether or not women belonged in the jobs. Encountering men who were aloof was par for the course for the pioneering blue-collar women. However, that coolness and skepticism, if tempered by at least some sense of fair play on the part of the man and enough work savvy on the part of the woman did not have to inhibit learning and growth on the job. The following comments by a telephone installer summarized the essence of this kind of relationship superbly:

Well, my supervisor surprisingly is one of the most fair supervisors that I've ever seen in any way. He goes completely by the book, you know. He does not single anybody out, you know; if you're doing it by the book that's all he cares about, you know. And it's good to know that at least he won't turn on you, most supervisors will turn on people. He helps me, I mean his help is only in relationship to everybody else which is that I mean everybody else there is so fucked, you know, he looks really good. He helps me in that he is, he's fair and he's not sexist. He is sexist but on the job in working specifically with me he's not sexist. He's made sexist comments around me about women working on the test board and things like that, but when it comes down to showing me how to do things he is not patronizing. He expects from me what he'll expect from a man. And it's really comfortable to finally find somebody like that. Other men that I've worked for I have never really known where I stood. And with him, if he says you're doing a good job, you know, and he'll tell you if you're not.

It also helped a great deal if the woman came with some kind of experience that enabled the men to "anchor" her in a somewhat familiar context. This reduced the strangeness and some of the anxiety. Also, the woman could handle the new situation better because it was not totally unfamiliar. She ran less risk of making bad first impressions or initial mistakes that could turn people against her, undermine her credibility, and thereby make it twice as difficult for her to get the information and training she had to get from her supervisors and co-workers.

Overall, close to half of the women we talked with identified some positive relationships with co-workers and supervisors, and 71 percent described their work environment as generally friendly. This figure does not mean that they had only positive relationships. Many of these same women went on to identify people who had made it quite difficult for them. In the first-year interviews 51 percent identified fellow workers or students as helpful. Only 31 percent identified a supervisor or instructor as helpful. By the second-year interviews this picture had changed somewhat. Co-workers and fellow trainees were perceived as helpful by 77 percent of the women. Forty-five percent of the women had begun to find their supervisors helpful, though only 28 percent went on to say their supervisors were actually friendly; 39 percent reported supervisors were antagonistic. Clearly the work environment was not characterized by warm, friendly, and supportive relationships even among those successful women.

These women were both lucky and smart. The management of on-the-job relationships did not stand in the way of their learning their skills, becoming competent, and ultimately finding acceptance in their blue-collar work group. Other women were unlucky and frequently not very smart when it came to first impressions. Theirs is a story of sabotage and harassment that significantly slowed down or inhibited job performance.

NEGATIVE ON-THE-JOB RELATIONSHIPS

In the first-year interviews close to half of the women described problems with both their supervisors and co-workers. By the second year this figure had been cut in half for co-workers, with about 26 percent talking about negative situations or relationships. And even though problems with supervisors were fewer by the second year, more than a third of the women still had negative situations to deal with. The negative situations related specifically to problems between the supervisor and employee about her competence *as a woman*. By the second year, however, the problems were virtually all attitudinal. There was less overt behavior preventing the woman from learning her job. The following impassioned comments by a welder were the most extreme case of what many women reported:

It's a form of harassment every time I pick up a sledgehammer and that prick laughs at me, you know. It's a form of harassment when a journeyman is supposed to be training me and it's real clear to me that he does not want to give me any information whatsoever. He does not want me to be there at all, and you know, like that happened like my first thirty days. They put me with this one who is a lunatic—I mean, he's really a case and he's the one who drilled the hole in my arm . . . and he did not want to work with me at all. It's a form of harassment to me when the working foreman puts me in a dangerous situation and tells me to do something in an improper way and then tells me, Oh, you can't do that! It's a form of harassment to me when someone takes a tool out of my hand and said, Oh, I'm going to show you . . . I'll show you how to do this, and he grabs the sledgehammer from my hand and he proceeded to try to show me how to do this thing . . . you know, straighten up a post . . . it's nothing to it, you just bang it and it gets straight . . . and he lost the sledgehammer. You know, I mean, and here's someone who falls through holes in the floor. He walked off a ladder once, he walked off a scaffolding, he fell off the roof of a van, you know, and he's the working foreman. It's a form of harassment to me when they call me honey and I have to tell them every day, don't call me that, you know, I have a name printed right on my thing. I stopped talking to them. They don't call me by my name, fuck 'em, I don't talk to them. Ah, you know, it's all a form of harassment to me. It's not right. They don't treat each other that way. They shouldn't treat me that way. It's a form of harassment to me when this one asks me to go out with him all the time. You know, all this kind of stuff. It's terrible.

This particular woman had very little that was positive to say about her work environment, although she loved to weld and had reached a point in her life where she wanted a certified skill so she could be mobile and have employment anywhere. Becoming a journeyman welder would do this for her, and so she was sticking to her job despite her very negative feelings and experiences.

A forklift operator, Holly Glass, also felt she had been subjected to unnecessary testing and harassment by men when she began her job. However, by our third-year contact she was more philosophical and generally satisfied with her job context. She still felt a distance from her male co-workers, but she wasn't angry and bitter. In our first interview Holly described how she had to do extra work and subject herself to unusual physical stress in order to prove herself on the job.

I work all with men. There's only about two other girls on nights besides me. And I stay by myself. I don't sit with nobody. I don't want to be a part of nobody's—guys gossip worse than women do. I don't want to be any part of it. I've been yelled and screamed at before, just by being around somebody. I stay by myself. I take my lunch by myself and everything so I don't know how the groups are. The attitudes are really bad, though, out there. Because the supervisor's attitude is bad. Mostly everybody there has made it difficult at one time or another. Now not so much because they've accepted the fact that I can do it and I'm up there and they can't get rid of me. Well, they used to hide things on me. They used to do things to my fork. The warehouse is big. They used to hide my fork on me and I used to get mad—they were testing me. They told me okay, when I got the job my sister-in-law went in the hospital for brain surgery. I was under a lot of pressure. They gave me two weeks—they were supposed to give me thirty days; I was off a week and I was there for two weeks. It was like training for me because I didn't know anything and they tested me and they didn't tell me. They tested me on a Friday—Thursday and they called me in on a Friday and told me I was too slow. That Monday when I came back to work I had to prove that I could be as fast as the guys. I was really upset. I went back that Monday, and I worked my hardest. See, the reason I didn't work so hard before was because I wanted to get everything down pat—I didn't want to break merchandise, I wanted to do a good job in whatever I did—so that is why I was going slow. I didn't think they were testing me that early. Well, they tested me and called me back in the office and they laughed and said, "Well, I guess we were wrong, you've got the job and you proved it." Okay, they said, but this is what they said, "Are you sure you want to work this hard for your living?" I said, "You know, if I didn't want to work this hard I wouldn't have tried so hard." That was a dumb question to ask me, but they did. They did all kinds of tricks to me—all kinds of things to me. They tried to upset me—tried to discourage and everything. One time before that, when I was still having my thirty-day period to prove myself, they came and got me to stack tires and all the supervisors stood around and looked at me and laughed. They thought it was funny that I had to stack over four hundred tires. Tires are heavy and with the height of me! They weren't just little VW tires, they were the big four-wheel tires—they just laughed. But I did it. I still roll and stack tires, strap 'em, load 'em on the trucks. But you know after I proved myself, after they seen me stack all them tires and they saw all the other things I went through, they respect me now. There are even guys under me now and they respect me.

A woman working as a gas service repairperson the first year described the treatment she experienced trying to learn to use a jackhammer. A very small person, with little prior experience in physical work, she was distressed by the way she had been treated.

Yes, I consider it harassment. They put me on a crew for three weeks and the foreman let me use the jackhammer once for fifteen minutes and then another time, I begged him to let me use it and he let me do it for fifteen or twenty minutes. He apparently made out

a report on me, so the next time I went out to the street department, they put me out on light duty. They had somebody from personnel, which is very unusual 'cause that's downtown and we're out
on the outskirts . . . come talk to me and say, well I hear you had
trouble on the jackhammer, would you like to go into meter reading? And I said I'm not interested in meter reading. And I've only
used the jackhammer twice so I don't think that any judgment can
be made. And one of the supervisors—I guess you might call him a
yard boss, or whatever—called me into his office saying, "Well, I
understand you haven't had much chance to practice on the jackhammer; well, that crew doesn't use the jackhammer much, we'll
put you on a service crew breaking pavement for three or four
hours at a stretch." He said it with a lot of malice. I discovered that
the man they put me out with, they use as kind of a hatchet man.
He has ambition. He'll do their bidding. I went out the first day and
I broke the pavement. I thought, gee whiz, I'm doing great, this is
better than ever. And he said at the end of the day, "Well, I'm
going to have to tell them that you're no good." I said, "Well, I
broke the pavement." And he said, "Well, the pieces were too
small." I said, "You didn't tell me what size pieces you wanted, you
just said, go break the pavement." And he says, "Yeah, you broke
the pavement," and I said, "Well, that's the point, isn't it?"

This woman was eventually transferred into lighter work.

Ardath Hoover, who worked at a similar job with the same
utility company, had a different perspective on this woman's experience based on her own relationships with co-workers and
experiences on the jackhammer.

I'll tell you what was going on. I had to go and tell this one boss
out in the street that "you guys are really wrong, comparing two of
us. She's smaller than I am, she hasn't been dealing with men for
the long period I have, she just doesn't understand." . . . These
guys are big, heavy, burly construction guys, you know, they're
machismos, they're not delicate. Look at my physique. I can do it.
It's not a big male-female thing, it's really just a question of who's
big and heavy and strong. I mean, the beef runs it. You know, if
you've got a female beef they can do it, but there ain't too many of
'em. I rode out, when I first went out in the street department, they
sent me out with the leak crew and the three-man crew, foreman,
some other, and a helper. The foreman they sent me out with was

known as the ax man, he got rid of dead weight for the Gas Department, but he didn't get rid of me. And you know what, he just told the bosses, "Great, she's just like a skinny guy." Which I was. And I am, you know; I can put out the amount of work as one of those smaller gentlemen do. You know. But, I'm smart, and I'm crafty, so I've carried my weight as one of the heavier gentlemen do.

Ardath, who is six feet tall and very strong, was still doing heavy work in the third year and seemed to feel that the other woman she had started out with was better off in a lighter job.

Tam Cullen, whose work experiences have also been described at length, was one of the few women we met who successfully moved from a classroom program into a CETA job and eventually into a permanent position. She became a journeyman pipe fitter at a privately owned shipbuilding company. Her initial experiences on the job were mixed, and in some instances she had to deal with a great deal of overt resistance from journeymen. She described one particular experience where a supervisor simply refused to let her work in his area.

I got transferred to repair and I had wanted to go to repair before because if I get laid off from this company most other shipyards do primarily repair work and they could easily not hire me because of lack of repair experience. And they do not want any women in repair and most of the repair workers are on navy ships and sometimes that's used as an excuse, but actually the conditions are cleaner and nicer. . . . Well, the foreman who was in charge of pipe and repair . . . well, he just said . . . the way he was, he said he was completely prejudiced and perfectly fair, and he spent . . . I got transferred there and what they did was they asked for like seventeen journeymen immediately and so my foreman sent me out there and they thought it was kind of a joke because I would arrive and this guy hates women, he would also assume I was going to be a complete flop, some kind of turkey who was just going to stand around and just watch everything and probably get injured in the process or something. They knew I was going to go in there and kind of drive him nuts, you know, give him a hard time, so I was innocent and I just wanted to go because I figured, oh yeah, let's go. And so he's the sort of guy who says, stands around and says as many nasty things to you as he can think of, and he spent all day like, I'd say three or four days out of a week, you know, just thinking of awful things to say to me and reasons why I wouldn't possibly be there and they wouldn't dispatch me to a ship, they kept me in the shop. And everyone in repair goes to a ship. And then he asked . . . he thought of all these reasons why I didn't want the job. He said, "Well, do you have a car?" And I said no. He says, "Oh well, you can't go to Twenty-second Street because how will you get there?" And I said, "Well, you know, I can take the bus," and then it turned out he was going to send me to Military Island and I said, "Oh well, that's one bus there and I ordinarily take two. It'll be quicker, you know." And then that didn't go, and so he'd go back in his office and try to think of something else and then he'd come out and say, "Do you have children?" And I said no. And then he'd think of all these things, you know, about, "I guess the guys must give you a hard time on the ship." And I'd say, "Well, actually I get along pretty good." And so then he tried just giving me jobs to do and yelling at the top of his lungs and all that kind of thing. But I was doing the job, so all they could do was harass you and so they did that for about a week and a half. After about five days they were finally supposed to send me out on a ship and I was supposed to go out with the shop steward and apparently the shop steward went off on a three-day drunk, because he didn't show. And so what happened was then in the absence of the shop steward they sent me to work in the office doing secretarial work, which I hate to do personally, and which is out of my job classification. But like you can't file a grievance for having done something you didn't do. In other words, if I refused to do it then I could never have filed a grievance, so what you're supposed to do is if they give you work out of your classification you're supposed to do it and then you can file a grievance afterward. So I figured I'd go along and did it, so I did it for a day and I made it real clear to him that I didn't want to do it. They knew I didn't want to do it, you know. And as soon as the shop steward came back I said I don't want to work in the office. I'm a pipe fitter, I fit pipe, and I'm going to a ship or else I'm leaving, you know. And he says I'll go talk to him so he came out and they, you know, dragged me in and said who's your old foreman and then they said you're going back. But you see, I don't know whether they'd violated any rules at all but the shop steward was real worried about it because he figured he'd blown it. Yeah, in his absence, like, these things happened that shouldn't have happened. The job that they assigned me to paid $3.80 an hour and it's a nonunion job, and so, like, they shouldn't have been having me do that work.

Tam's experiences as an apprentice were for the most part less extreme, but her years as an apprentice in shipbuilding were not easy ones. Once she became a journeyman, Tam became very active in her union local and has been on television and in the press as one of the spokespersons for a major strike her local has been waging against the shipbuilding company.

Co-workers and supervisors were not the only people who could make it difficult. The telephone installer who was quoted in the previous section about her positive relationships with supervisors and co-workers had a number of difficulties with clients.

This one woman . . . I'd go in there, and I mean for an installer the guys who go out and install look like shit, you know. They wear T-shirts and some of them look half decent, you know. And I mean I didn't look that bad. I wear nice T-shirts. And so I go into this woman's house to put in a phone. Actually, she was the manager of an apartment building, and so she looks at me and she says, "Look at you, why aren't you at home taking care of your children, what are you doing here, this is a man's job, look at the way you're dressed and you look like a slob." And I turned around, and oh, God, I mean, we're supposed to be nice but I mean this woman was insulting me. So I just said, "Well you don't look so hot yourself. I mean, look, your nylons are sagging." It was so funny. So she got in and started screaming about how, "Oh, you women's libber, I'll bet you're a women's liberationist." And I said, "Damn right I am." And she said, "I knew it, that's all, you just want to do this and that. You don't want to take care of the kids and this," and I was yelling stuff back to her and she was going on, "Anyway you're just a bunch of lesbos and why don't you do this." And I just said—I just said, "Oh, God." So finally I had to leave because I was so upset.

It's clear that the women often had negative on-the-job experiences, primarily not getting information or training. Many felt

they had to work harder than men and were given assignments
—physical and mechanical—for which they were ill prepared. In
addition, a number of women were treated badly by customers. There was another much discussed on-the-job problem
for women moving into nontraditional work and that is sexual
harassment.

SEXUAL HARASSMENT ON THE JOB

Actual sexual harassment—touching, sexual overtures, obscene
language—was mentioned in many of the interviews. Approximately one third of the women at one time or another had to
deal with such conduct directed at them personally. This one
third did *not* include all the women who reported having to
cope with the general "tits and ass" conversation referred to by
Sandy Harold earlier. It pertained only to actions, invitations,
or sexual language directed specifically at the woman worker.
The experiences of women telephone installers, shared by Kay
Mann, were illustrative.

There was an attack on one of our women installers a couple
months ago, right. She was disconnecting telephones and she went in
and the guy told her that it was in the back bedroom. She went in
to take it out and the guy followed her and attacked her. She beat
him off with a telephone. Right, I was really upset to hear that,
needless to say. I have been raped and it's a very touchy issue with
me to start out with. So I was real upset and our supervisor came
and told us that the first thing in the morning, so I'm leaving and
I'm just, oh, my God, you know, what am I doing here and this and
that. My first customer was a Coast City policeman, police officer;
we know people's occupations by our code numbers. So I go in
there and he had just gotten off duty and he was really tired and he
was laying down and I was putting the phone in right next to the
couch where he was laying and he was making small talk. And he
says, "Oh well, I see you girls were on TV the other day," you
know; and I says, "Oh, you mean about the attempted rape on one
of our installers?" And he says, "No, no, she should be so lucky,
you know." I went, I didn't care about that, uh . . . this is a police

officer and they don't say things like that, right. And I said, "Well, what do you mean, one of our installers, there was an attempted rape on her." And he says, "Oh, you know, those installers, they have to get it wherever they can, you know." I almost dropped; I mean I was just—I mean, I went out to the truck and cried, okay. And came back and was able to confront him on it. And I was just really angry and really upset and he apologized for saying that. He says, "Well, you know, I don't really believe that." And I said, "I don't believe that, I think your defenses are down and I think you really do believe that and maybe you're making attempts to change your attitude but it's obvious that it hasn't changed very much, you know." I told everybody I knew and I told one of the supervisors about it and stuff. They were really supportive and it surprised me. Yeah. Then there was a guy who . . . I know one of the women on my crew has been propositioned, you know. There was one guy I put a phone in for that was just about ready to ask me if he could get his head down my pants and I, you know . . . I got out of there, you know. And I've gotten asked out and I basically turn on them. I mean, really, are you serious, you know.

An appliance repairperson commented that her male co-workers became *less* friendly over time, probably because she turned down dates and resisted sexual overtures.

It seemed like a lot of them, they would come on to me sexually and when I turn them down . . . they'd be really nice, ya know, but I guess it was all bullshit 'cause when I'd turn them down, then they would just ignore me completely. Like there's this one guy—I thought we were really close or fairly close and, oh, about the second week on the job he came up and shoved me up against the wall and held me there—said something, he was jealous 'cause I don't know what it was—it was really weird and I just said, "I don't like that," so he wouldn't speak to me for three weeks. So we were getting by that and started to talk more and stuff and he came up behind me and started shaking me one time. I told him I didn't like that, so he's just starting to talk to me again, but I don't ever want to get as close to him. . . . They like to intimidate women. Like rape is only one part of it, but just generally—physically—they intimidate women.

A welder also reported being physically intimidated.

Oh well, you, a lot of these guys, well, like you're propositioned, I mean, in terms of money too . . . you know, it's very blatant. And they're coming up and touching you, trying to touch you. This one guy tried to touch me on the breast . . . one of the first days I worked there. It's mostly verbal things but then once they get used to you, it really gets a lot easier.

Ardath Hoover, who was an extremely assertive and sensual woman, commented only obliquely about sexual incidents.

Well, the foreman is one. He is very aware of people's emotional states but he overkills it. He sees that I'm unhappy and want to get out of the shop and he doesn't let me out of the shop. He likes to look at me so he punishes me and he puts me on the worst shopman's job in the whole shop, he makes me stand in one place for two months. He makes it very difficult for me. The night foreman makes it very difficult for me. He's very stupid. He comes around when I'm new on the job and says, "Oh, what a nasty, ugly job," but yet other guys who are new on the job, they give them a couple of weeks to work into it. Like today he was complaining about three meters that had water in them out of two hundred when I'm doing an outstanding job. There's a couple of guys who make it hard for me on a sexual point of view. The older guys think they're cute and can carry on in a more light manner like I do with some of the younger guys' humors. You know, referrals to male and female differences but they get nasty, obscene, and crude. There's one guy who's fairly bitter who is sometimes the acting shop steward who is black and he's made it difficult for me. He's come on to me too.

A female co-worker provided this perspective on Ardath's problems with sexual overtures at work.

Ardath's attitude about dealing with problems with the men is a lot different. As I said before, I feel that it's not a social club and that I shouldn't have to take care of any kind of problem myself, and she feels that she's the tough lady and she ought to be able to handle things. And I know I'm not tough and I'm probably not going to be able to handle them whether I want to or not, so I might as well not bother. Also I don't feel I should have to. She had a guy grab her tits and she hit him, which I would have done too, but then I would have told the foreman and he would have gotten sent home. But she didn't, she felt that her smacking him a couple of times was enough, which it was, but I just didn't—I'd want people to know that it's not just me they have to deal with, because if I do something like that it's only out of anger—it's not the way I'm dealing with the problem.

UNDERSTANDING HARASSMENT IN THE WORKPLACE

At the beginning of this chapter I suggested that the less strange a woman appeared and felt in the workplace, the less strained her relationships would be. This is because all of the conventional signs and signals which anchor people in the blue-collar work world—that is, provide an indication of common experiences, common concerns, and common norms—are not present when a man encounters a woman with no background or familiarity with blue-collar work. There is no common basis for communication, sharing, and understanding. So people are not only awkward but extremely suspicious of one another. That suspiciousness can translate very quickly into behavior that isolates or intimidates the woman. Something that immediately provides a common base for interaction—such as the fact that the woman has worked at the same place for years, an obvious familiarity with tools and equipment, an ability to talk knowledgeably about previous blue-collar employment—relieves some of that initial tension. In the absence of any such common signs or language it is not surprising that hostility and testing occur, or that sexual harassment occurs. From a sociological point of view, it is not surprising that in the absence of any common signs or anchors, gender and the conventional sexual scripts governing so much male-female interaction become the basis for initial encounters. On the one hand, you can see such behavior as sexist and contemptible. On the other, you can see it as predictable.

It's predictable not solely because men always think of women as sex objects. It's predictable because in the absence of any other common bases for interaction and discourse men fall back on conventional stereotypic approaches to women. This perspective makes on-the-job harassment no less forgivable but certainly more understandable. There is less sexual harassment when people can find a common basis for interacting, some kind of sign or social cue that suggests to a person how to come on to another in a particular situation. Given that most men, and blue-collar men in particular, have had much less opportunity to see and define women in multidimensional or varied roles, women who can define themselves or present themselves in terms that are familiar to the men help take the pressure off. This does not mean the women have to come across as masculine. It does mean that the interests, values, and experiences that provide a common basis for interaction between blue-collar men have to be shared in some way by the new women. In order to cut it, you have to go with the norms of the dominant group. The women who by luck, planning, or hard-lived experience came with these understandings developed good working relationships very quickly. The women who didn't had a tougher time.

Currently there is virtually nothing being done to prepare men or women to work together in the blue-collar workplace. They are just thrown together with little concern for either the skills development needs of the women or the subtle ways in which first impressions on the job and common norms and a common language influence the process of developing competent blue-collar women workers. Before moving into these policy questions, it will be useful to look a little longer at relationships, specifically, at the work relationships of the women who did not succeed in blue-collar employment.

WOMEN WHO DID NOT SUCCEED

A look at one or two of the relationships with co-workers of women who did not succeed in nontraditional blue-collar work is useful because it underscores the earlier point about good relationships at work *not necessarily* resulting in eventual competency, commitment, and employment stability. Many of the women in classroom contexts had more positive experiences than women apprentices on the job. Some employed women also described initially good relationships at work. As often as not, however, these positive relationships were a result of the woman's being protected or patronized, or of her not being perceived as a serious threat to a man's paid job, and not a result of an acceptance of women. It is difficult to understand how the women with *less* satisfying personal relationships in the first year were *more* successful in their jobs than the women with more satisfying relationships unless one has this larger perspective.

Betty Lynn was in a skills center class in auto mechanics when first interviewed. Betty grew up in a working-class family in the South and had always been somewhat interested in cars and tinkering with mechanical things. Married before high school graduation, she was living in California because her husband was in military service. She reported the class as somewhat of a lark while her husband was overseas, but she found nonetheless that she enjoyed what she was learning and the people who were in the class with her. It is important to point out, however, that Betty did not begin the class with a clear intention of seeking full-time employment as an auto mechanic. A religious woman, Betty indicated her family life was very important to her. She felt a job in which she could earn about $4.00 an hour would be ideal. She also commented that she was frequently "emotional at that time of the month." All of these characteristics contrasted rather markedly with the circumstances and personal style of many of the apprentices we interviewed. She described the men in her classes as "fatherly types who looked out for the girls" and as "real friendly." She had also experienced some harassment and sexual advances when she first started but had rebuffed them successfully right away.

By the second-year interview, Betty was unemployed. She had taken a job at the minimum wage in a small auto repair shop that she was referred to by a friend at church shortly after finishing her classes. She reported working long, hard hours and feeling accepted by the men. They were helpful, never swore around her, and treated her like a lady. Nonetheless, she reported being a physical wreck after only four months on the job and had decided auto mechanics was not for her. At this interview, she indicated she would prefer some kind of part-time work that she could combine more easily with her family responsibilities. When we interviewed Betty by phone in our third-year follow-up, she reported that she was taking care of children in her home for about $3.00 an hour. She said she still loved mechanics but it was just too much work and she really preferred working with children for now.

Barrie Burns, while employed as a shipping clerk, was taking classes in plumbing. Barrie's father was a maintenance worker and she reported being a fairly traditional girl while growing up. She had been a secretary for fifteen years after graduating from high school and had taken a job as a shipping clerk while she was learning her skills as a plumber. She had developed an interest in the trade as a result of her increasing involvement with the women's movement and her increasing realization that she had never really "chosen" what she wanted to be when she grew up. Her interest in plumbing came after some courses at a feminist school, but her age (thirty-one) and the attitude of trade unions at that time made it difficult for her to get an apprenticeship or a full-time job with just a couple of courses to recommend her. On the advice of job counselors, she enrolled in a government-funded training program at a community college, hoping that it would eventually lead to employment. Her experiences were extremely disappointing. The quality of the instruction she received was quite poor and she felt that the attitudes of the instructor were negative and demoralizing, not so much because there were women in the class as because the entire class was a "federally funded program for disadvantaged people." She and her fellow students complained to the administration and felt they had gotten results because the quality of materials and instruction did improve after they complained. In contrast to women who were in apprenticeships or in on-the-job training programs, however, Barrie reported very positive relations with co-workers, male and female. She had women friends in the class, said the men and women got along very well, and socialized with some of the students away from school. She felt they helped one another out. But these relationships were not enough to compensate for the poor instruction and the fact that none of them had real jobs to go to once they finished training.

At our second-year interview Barrie was still working as a shipping clerk. She had made some attempts to get a nontraditional job but had no personal connections or employment networks helping her. She was simply submitting applications at a number of places. She was still working on finding a direction for herself and some kind of work she would really enjoy, and she was seeking vocational counseling. By our third-year telephone follow-up, Barrie had a new job as a bookkeeper, earning $600 a month. She was extremely positive about the job and indicated that she had finally found what she really wanted to do. She was taking courses in accounting and auditing and planned to become a CPA.

These two examples underscore how much more important having a real job is, whether an apprenticeship or on-the-job training position, and having opportunities to learn skills than friendly, supportive relations with co-workers. Ideally, a woman should have good training and opportunities to learn as well as friendly and supportive relations at work. But it is clear that good co-workers are not enough to help her succeed as a pioneer. Having a "real" job, even in a hostile milieu, gives one an important edge: first, because there is more security; and second, because one probably has a better chance of gaining a realistic sense of the job requirements and work milieu, which can aid in the actual development of competency and eventual acceptance by co-workers.

We will now consider the different strategies the employed women used to manage the isolation they experienced in the blue-collar workplace and the frequently difficult relationships they encountered—whether in the form of general harassment or sexual harassment.

STRATEGIES FOR MANAGING ON-THE-JOB RELATIONSHIPS

All the women faced some form of negative reaction or initial harassment when they moved into a man's job in a blue-collar environment. The character and extent of the harassment varied. Men differed in the extent of their sense of ease with women. Certainly their age, the employment status of their wives and daughters, and their previous experiences working with women affected their attitudes and behavior. Differences in the characteristics and experiences of the women also affected how they were initially regarded and how they initially reacted to the treatment they received from their male supervisors and co-workers. The more familiar and experienced blue-collar men were with women as workers and the more familiar the women were with blue-collar skills and values, the less likely the probability of harassment and prolonged negative relationships. The more strange each group was to the other, the more likely that stereotypes and harassment would dominate the interpersonal relationships at work. Nonetheless, each woman entering the blue-collar work world had to accommodate the reactions she elicited just by her physical presence. It appears that most women used one or more of four strategies in dealing with the initial negative reactions and as a step toward eventually winning acceptance from male co-workers. These four strategies were (1) overachievement—performing above and beyond the call of duty; (2) accommodation—emphasizing traditional aspects of the female role of mother, wife, daughter, or sex object; (3) conflict—involving direct confrontation with the offending person; (4) intervention—turning to third-party advocates, such as union representatives or grievance counsels. Strategies (1) and (2) were the most frequent strategies and generally successful, most probably because they conformed to male expectations and placed the primary burden on the woman. However, (3) and (4) are not to be underestimated.

The ability to speak up for one's rights and dignity can be an important sign of strength and competency in a blue-collar milieu, and the power of a union or employee organization can be a significant support if things go too far. Personal accommodation and superior effort were important, but could not guarantee success. The power of an organization, the law, or a personal advocate could also be useful. Among the women studied, very few succeeded who were not a part of a larger employee organization, union or otherwise, that could represent them. Most were also employed as a result of equal employment requirements.

In the first year, 67 percent of the women reported some negative consequence to being a woman in a blue-collar job. The most frequently cited problems were active discouragement from supervisors and inequitable treatment in training and access to tools. Women had to exercise cunning and initiative to get at least what the men got. They had to work harder, longer, and at more varied jobs. Examples of such women have been cited in previous sections, e.g., the forklift operator who loaded more tires than her male co-workers; women such as Jan Spencer and Sandy Harold who started as entry-level apprentices despite trade school training and previous employment as mechanics; the gas service repairperson who was expected to run a jackhammer without preparation; the machinist who was given assignments that required her to seek out other tradesmen in the absence of instruction from her supervisor. All these women went the extra mile, passed the extra tests, and eventually proved themselves.

The accommodation strategy was also successful in some cases. Ardath Hoover, despite early experiences, managed to integrate a flirtatious, sensual style with her unusual physical strength in a way that eventually resulted in friendly, hard-drinking, hardworking relationships with her co-workers. Molly O'Hara, entering a trade in her middle forties, a somewhat overweight divorced mother of three grown children, relied on her image as "mother superior" to position herself as the only woman in a work group of young men. Joan Lowery, a successful electrician, epitomized the "wifely" role in the blue-collar context. In addition to being competent in her work, she frequently brought food to work for the men, took phone calls for them, and also demanded that they treat her like a lady, never using foul language in her presence. She pulled all this off because in return for special treatment as a "lady" she did ladylike things such as being a provider of food. Some quotes from our interview with her are illuminating.

I pointedly asked him, "Are you pro- or anti-woman?" and [he] made the statement that "I believe that women should be on a pedestal and I treat them like they're on a pedestal until they prove themselves differently. In other words, as long as they act as a woman and that doesn't mean, I say, being in the kitchen barefooted and pregnant, I don't mean that, I mean that as long as I don't hear a lot of profanities because this is one thing that I hate is profanity in men or women," he says. "But something about women, when I hear them use profanity, it just goes all through me," and he says, "Does that answer your question?" And I said, "Definitely." And so far, he has been our supervisor for about four months, five months, and I can honestly say—five months, that's right—I can honestly say that he has been very true to his word. He's very concerned about us. If we act like we're sick, if we act like we have a headache, if you act like you're having female problems, he's right there: "Go to the rest room and lay down for a while," or "Do you want to go home?" He never throws this up, "Well, you're in a man's job—do a man's work." He never put this up to you. He's very considerate . . . he watches himself when he starts out with a group of fellows and they get to use masculine language. I call profanity masculine language. He'll say, "We have a lady present," and they say, "Get out of the way. . . ." And, I say, "Well, okay." And I'll leave the area so they can say it. And I appreciate them having that type of respect for me. Maybe some other women don't, but I've never—I've always said I love being a female. I love being a girl, an old girl now, yes, but I still love being a girl. And that's just it. I love femininity. I love to dress feminine and I love to act feminine. I just love being feminine, and the very fact that they respect me in that part of life or my part of my job, I appreciate, I really do.

Joan revealed how she felt she had to treat male supervisors.

I don't know whether I could put up or you know, train another supervisor. Yeah. That's really what you have to do to those poor
dears over there, you know. Either stuff them with cakes and
cookies and stuff like that or sweet-talk them or baby-talk them. It's
ridiculous, but that's what you have to do to get along with a lot of
them, you know, so that's what I do.

Such accommodations were successful for a number of the
women we met, although they represent a real affront to the
concepts of equality and integrity in the workplace that most
working women are committed to.

A confrontational personal style was often required by
specific circumstances and did not necessarily result in negative
consequences for the women, particularly if the offense was
one the men as well as the women defined as going beyond
the boundaries of simple "fun and games." Ardath Hoover's
slapping a man who grabbed her breast in front of a number of
co-workers was probably a good strategy under those circumstances. In fact, in the case of sexual harassment, a direct approach nearly always seemed to be the most effective. A candid
rejection of a verbal overture, an angry response to an obscene
innuendo, a slap or physically aggressive reaction to physical
intimidation all resulted in changed behavior according to the
approximately 30 percent of the women who reported sexual
harassment. Such a direct strategy, it should be pointed out, was
in part possible because women in skilled blue-collar jobs were
not as powerless as are many other women subjected to sexual
harassment, particularly secretaries in office situations. In the
skilled blue-collar milieu the woman worked more independently, she was a peer with most of the men, she was a
member of a union that *sometimes* was a resource, and she was
working in an environment which was generally more tolerant
of both verbal and physical aggressiveness. This in part explains
why we found less sexual harassment than some other studies,
which report as much as 80 percent of women interviewed as
having had to cope with some form of sexual harassment. The

down side of the more verbally and physically aggressive character of the blue-collar milieu is the stereotypic assumption that women who "talk dirty" probably are more open to sexual overtures; such women are not put on pedestals. There is probably more actual physical intimidation in blue-collar contexts and more verbal innuendo in white-collar contexts.

Falling back on the union or company grievance procedures was a final step a woman could take. It was taken in 21 percent of the cases reporting harassment and almost always as a way to protest inequitable access to training, tools, and machines or suspected unfair evaluation procedures. In only one case of sexual harassment did a woman go to her committee man, and she had a difficult time gaining his support. Overall, however, these protests usually resulted in improved conditions for the women, most particularly in reassignment to supervisors or journeymen who were more active trainers. In a few cases such protests led to reassignment to work areas that were less physically or technically demanding, but which nonetheless represented legitimate, well-paid blue-collar jobs in the industrial setting. In essence, then, these resources helped the women improve the character of their work situation or resulted in a reassignment that enabled them to continue employment in a nontraditional job. There is no way to measure the extent to which the availabiltiy of these resources created a security that helped women hang in there when the going got rough. Even though the vast majority of the women we interviewed reported feeling that unions did very little for employees, much less women, it is interesting that among the women who were still in nontraditional jobs after three years virtually all belonged to some sort of union or employee organization (by virtue of their employment in a large industry, be it public or private) which could potentially represent their interests.

ADVANTAGES AND DISADVANTAGES
OF BEING A WOMAN

In both the first- and second-year interviews, we asked the women what they felt were the advantages and disadvantages of being a woman. One set of responses related to getting a job, a second to doing the job. Close to half of the women indicated that the present social climate and the pressure on employers with government contracts to hire women improved their chances of getting a well-paid nontraditional job. A majority nonetheless felt, despite recent legislation and the general impression that a woman can get any job she wants, whether she's qualified or not, it was still a disadvantage trying to find employment in the trades as a woman. Comments such as the following were typical of women who felt they had somewhat of an edge in getting a job:

I know I just got this job because they have government contracts so they have to hire a certain percentage of women, but I looked for a job for five weeks, you know, before I got this job, and nobody wanted to hire me. It was pretty clear, like I went into a lot of shops and since they don't have government contracts they can get around not hiring women—they certainly did. Also I was fresh out of welding school, I mean most of them probably wouldn't have hired a young man with, you know, no experience.

A woman in landscape maintenance stated it this way:

Right now, for this specific kinda work, it helps to be a woman, except that . . . on the other hand, I'm not as experienced, I don't have the muscle power, I can't stand out here with a chain saw for, you know, an hour cutting down trees without just getting, I mean falling on my face. But as far as getting into a job and into a gardening job, it helps.

A woman training on the job in the maintenance of electronics instruments for aircraft felt very positive about her abilities and opportunities for other jobs. She stated quite simply:

There are a lot of companies looking for women in the electronics field, so I think I have a good chance for a good career.

The majority were less optimistic about the advantages of being a woman seeking a blue-collar job and made comments much like these of Jackie, a free-lance appliance repairperson:

I've had very bad experiences about this because I figured the American dream or the American way, I could go out and get a training and go out and get a job, make some money at it, and then I would have some experience behind me and then I would make more money, because it's the way most guys do it, but I got a bad taste in my mouth when I went to get a job and I was told no, we don't need anyone, no, are you sure you can do it, how much training have you had, and so forth and so on, and you get the third degree before you even find out if they need anybody and then they say no, we don't need anybody or yes, we need somebody but we're not going to hire you. Something of this nature. Very, very bad taste. I went up to an interview that I knew I had this job before I got there, this woman lined it up and all I needed to do was fill out an application to make it legal and I went out there and filled out the application and they said, "Oh, you're a woman," and that was it, I wasn't hired, and I looked at him and said, "Well, I'm qualified, if I were a man would you have hired me?" and he said yes. . . .

A woman in a relatively secure trade in civil service was not optimistic about her prospects were she to seek another job.

There isn't any more—the blatant thing, you're a woman, we can't hire you—but I'm sure that most of the boards that you go through, the ones that do the interviewing, they're men and I'm sure that in the back of their minds they're thinking—can she handle it, does she have the experience or background that maybe some ex-serviceman might have or would she be able to lift a certain amount of weight, would people take her seriously—that's a big problem and I'm sure that all those things are in the back of people's minds.

Only one or two women felt being a woman helped them get special help or attention at work or equipped them in special ways for blue-collar work. Practically all those interviewed felt their sex created special problems for them. They cited many disadvantages in addition to the negative interpersonal relationships described in the previous section. A number of women reported problems with physical strength and agility, which they attributed to their sex and particularly their non-physical socialization as women. A number also pointed to the difficulties customers and the general public had in accepting them as competent. The following comments by Nannette, the free-lance plumber, captured these issues:

Definitely, being a woman is a problem. If it wasn't for working for myself—I do know one woman that got into the union and I talked to her after we had both been plumbers a year, and for what she knew—she must have had a lot of book learning 'cause she didn't have any practical experience. She had a job of all of two weeks and then during that time I guess she swept shit or something—I don't know what she did. She didn't have any wrenches, she didn't even know what wrenches were, and I said—"Wow, I thought I got burned but now I'm glad I didn't go through a union." She was sorry that she was in the union 'cause they were fucking her around. So I would say it's a problem, and I still get a lot of weird reactions from people—especially if I get a job through my old pal where they'll have talked to him and he'll call me and say "Why don't you handle this." I'll call them up and say, "Hi, I'm coming over," and they'll go, "You're a girl," and I'll go, "Yeah, but I'm a plumber too." Some of them have been a little leery of letting me in. "Well, I wanted Mr. Samson." I say, "Listen, you either take me or, you know, you wait a week for Mr. Samson to be not so busy and can handle you, which do you want." "Well, you might as well look at it," and then when I fix it then they're just smiling and when I charge 'em then I'm smiling. So it really makes a big difference though. I would be much more accepted though if I were a man in my field.

Some of the women also felt at a disadvantage as women because they lacked a mechanical background. The vast majority, however, felt that the biggest disadvantage of being a woman was the skepticism and resistance they had to face daily.

The issue of whether or not being a woman is an advantage in today's blue-collar work world is by no means trivial. Popular attitudes often are that working men don't have a chance anymore, no matter how competent they are, because affirmative action requires that women get all the good jobs regardless of their competency. Further, it is assumed that life at work is a bowl of cherries, with women simply having to bide their time, confident they won't be disqualified no matter how poor their performance. Department of Labor statistics, as well as other figures, contradict these popular assumptions. Women represent under 5 percent in the trades. They are underrepresented in police and fire departments and still participate only marginally in skilled jobs throughout private industry. The qualitative data in this chapter also contradict such assumptions. A few women, after a long hard struggle in the work world, are making it, not because they are women, but because they are competent.

As Caroline Bird pointed out years ago, it takes a supercompetent woman to succeed where only a mediocre man can. The consequences of being female in the blue-collar work world today are precisely those Bird described for the professions.[1] What advantage there is to being female is at the point of hiring, but even there the majority of women are still at a disadvantage, both in finding employment and in getting an apprenticeship. Once a woman has a job or apprenticeship, her sex immediately becomes a disadvantage, in some cases for a short while and in others for a prolonged and often painful period. One of the most important contributions personnel planners, union leaders, and training specialists could make to industry today would be to arrange more effective training experiences and more positive personal experiences for blue-collar women. For now, women are hired in the rush to satisfy government guidelines and simply left at the mercy of a work environment that at best is uninterested and simply resigned to their presence.

In Part Three I will offer a number of observations and recommendations for improving the character of on-the-job experiences of women in blue-collar work. It is clear that something needs to be done to ensure that good training takes place and needless harassment is eliminated. The women we met who are successful are successful for the most part in spite of their relations at work, not because of them. This fact of life for blue-collar pioneers needs to be changed.

PART THREE

SPIN-OFFS

VII

The Meaning of Nontraditional Blue-collar Employment in Women's Lives

Before discussing the policy and training implications of the experiences of these women, we should sum up what has been learned and what it all means in human terms. This brief chapter represents just such an effort. This has been fundamentally a study of work: of how early attitudes and interests develop, of work histories and employment opportunities, of on-the-job experiences and the crystallization of commitments to nontraditional blue-collar jobs. It would have been equally interesting to study the family lives, marital relationships, and parenting roles of women in nontraditional jobs, or the reactions of men—at work, at home, and in the community—to women in nontraditional jobs, or the recruitment, training, and retention strategies of organizations and employers working to move women into nontraditional blue-collar jobs. We picked up bits and pieces of information about each of these areas but had neither the time nor the money needed to follow up these aspects of the story. The real story here is the character of the work experience itself and the special significance of paid employment in the lives of women.

Certain characteristics of women's life experience are com-

mon to all women, regardless of age, education, and background. There are also important differences which derive from
differences in ethnicity, social background, and education.
These similarities and differences play themselves out quite interestingly throughout their childhood, life at work, and family
roles.

NONTRADITIONAL CHILDHOODS

One way of differentiating the experiences of women as children and adolescents is the extent to which their experiences
"break pattern" with traditional expectations. Family contexts,
school environments, community expectations, and unforeseen
circumstances can all affect the opportunities a growing girl has
for independence, experimentation, and the development of interests that have physical and/or mechanical dimensions usually thought of as masculine. An unusually large number of
women we interviewed came from rural and small-town environments where they had freedom to come and go and access
to tools and "outdoor" activities. More significantly, they came
from families that required them at an early age to assume responsibility for at least themselves, and often for some part of
the household, family business, or siblings. These early experiences of being depended on rather than doted on clearly contributed to a potential for autonomy and risk taking as adult
women. In addition, the presence of employed mothers in the
lives of the majority of the women and the experiences many of
them had with fathers or husbands who really couldn't take
care of them made them take paid employment for granted. In
contrast, for most women of their generation, paid employment
was not an essential part of the adult female role.

This is one of the most important factors differentiating
working women from one another. All employed women work
because of a need or desire for money and most want jobs that
are satisfying and interesting. How much of herself a woman is
willing to invest in her paid employment, how many risks she is

willing to take, and how much effort she will make are all tied to this subtle difference. Women who have a basic sense of themselves as working people and whose sense of achievement, fulfillment, and social validity is tied to activities in the work sphere rather than the domestic sphere are going to be the high achievers, whether in blue-collar, white-collar or professional work spheres. Competency is clearly a minimum requirement, but people of equal competency do not succeed equally. Some of that may be attributable to luck, but a good deal of it is attributable to how important success is to the individual and how persistent she is. Of course, women *cannot* succeed if opportunities and access are not there. But in most cases, with opportunity and ability relatively equal, it is the desire for success that differentiates people. If paid employment is seen as tangential, rather than essential, people will not make the same efforts to succeed. This is true for men and women. Historically, however, most males have grown up concerned with doing and achieving in the public sphere of employment whereas women have been channeled into the domestic sphere. Thus, women whose early circumstances or opportunities, intentionally or unintentionally, placed them on a path of commitment to autonomy, action, and achievement outside of their domestic roles were more likely to be the risk takers and achievers.

The existing literature on early childhood socialization and the development of sex role identities has given insufficient attention to which roles girls play that instill a sense of responsibility, autonomy, and need for achievement in them. The experiences women shared with us are examples of events in the lives of girls and young women that set them on paths that ultimately tested traditional expectations. They contrasted vividly with our images of all-American childhoods. Certainly these women did not experience the familial and neighborhood protectiveness toward girls characteristic of many working-class ethnic milieus. Nor did they fit the cultivated, artistic image of the very bright and privileged middle-class girl. Each of these images has its richness and significance. Yet neither is likely to equip a young woman with the skills and dispositions necessary for survival in the paid work force. These women needed something more. That something more was a visceral sense that she the woman was the mistress of her own fate, as well as practice at being in charge and having to come through. This practice does not have to come from harsh social or economic circumstances and personal deprivation, as it did for so many of the women we met. Team sports, individual performance, service to others, shared responsibilities in the home, and working for money or special privileges can all build the sense of responsibility, self-discipline, and mastery that is so crucial in the employment sector. However, most girls are still encouraged to *be* rather than *do*. Pleasantness, prettiness, and compliance are reinforced, rather than astuteness, energy, and critical thinking.

NEED FOR MASTERY

If I were to cite one factor that sums up what differentiates the women in nontraditional blue-collar jobs from other women, it would be their need for mastery. This encompasses all the other traits discussed throughout Parts One and Two: the desire for responsibility and autonomy, the persistence, the willingness to learn, the concern with competency, the understanding of the culture of groups one wishes to be a part of, the need for challenge and recognition, the enjoyment of the work itself, the need to be in control of pacing and output, the desire for a sense of growth and progress. Only the unusual woman has these characteristics. Many who do, especially women from middle- and upper-class backgrounds, often realize them through unpaid volunteer work and personal pursuits. A woman of financial means who has high needs for mastery is still likely to fulfill them in unpaid activities such as volunteer work or crafts, for example. The woman with fewer means will pursue paid employment. Although many believe that America has become one homogeneous consumer-oriented society, these women do not appear ever to have had the discretionary time and money necessary for an elaborate domestic role of home decorating, cooking, special lessons for children, and higher levels of consumption. In addition, they do not participate in a social world of community involvement, volunteerism, book clubs, and social gatherings beyond the family. This is perhaps why many of the women in skilled working-class jobs seemed to be more positive and have fewer conflicts about paid employment than many middle-class and professional women. In addition to the real economic need for the jobs, work (particularly work in many nontraditional fields) provided working-class and low-income women with a challenge, a sense of satisfaction and personal (growth that neither their previous routine paid employment nor their homemaking roles had given them.

Our data suggest that many of the needs satisfied by the more elaborate home management and child-rearing duties and involvements of middle-class women found expression for working-class women through paid employment, particularly employment in some of the traditionally male-dominated fields beginning to open up for women. The "quality of life" concerns characteristic of a middle-class life-style seemed to be articulated and embellished for many working-class women within their work. The importance the women assigned to productivity, creativity, and sociability support this, as does the fact that the women, with a few exceptions, reported minimal associations outside of work and family. Even during periods of nonemployment, this was the case.

FAMILY LIFE

Nontraditional blue-collar women also had a less elaborate sense of what was required to manage a house and relationships with husbands and lovers and children. Numerous commentators have said that the amount of time and effort involved in homemaking never really decreased with modern conveniences and mass marketing because of the new pressures new products created for women to have even cleaner floors, more interesting menus, and new curtains every year.[1] In addition, the surge of interest in child development and the perception of the critical role of mothers to that development paralleled the rise of labor-saving devices in the home.[2] We have managed to preserve an elaborate domestic role for women even though the size of the household is half what it once was, even though most of the arduous work has been mechanized, and even though parents have more time for fewer children and these children have more activities outside the home than ever before. Ironically, the women who have benefited least from these changes are women with less money and fewer household conveniences. They have more children and are less caught up in the current ideologies about the importance of their role in child-rearing. As a consequence, they feel fewer conflicts about the impact of their employment on their families. It is not, as some have argued, that they see employment as a simple extension of their mothering role, but that employment enables them to do more for their kids than what they perceive they could accomplish at home. Most of the women with children indicated they would like more time with their children, but none defined their need for employment as a hardship on children because "what could I do for my kids and husband just sitting around the house all day!" This is not to suggest the women had no problems combining work and family. They clearly did. But they defined their problems differently and solved them differently than middle-class and professional women. In fact, their descriptions of a typical workday showed that most were fully occupied twelve to fourteen hours a day. One shipfitter described her routine in this way:

I start work at seven in the morning and I leave my home at a quarter after six because I live in South Bay and I get here, park the car, and walk in, and I get to the office before we have to hand our time cards in every day, about twenty-five minutes to seven, and my foreman is always there and tells me, "If every man was like you, this place would be running just beautifully." I'm always there too early. I go get my gear, take my gear out, set it out, set up the cable, because the men come so late, the shipfitters, and I have everything set up by the time they came. But I just feel that I have to be early. I don't ever like to go late, it has to be early. Then at the end of the day, you punch out when the clock says three-thirty, but then you quit about three minutes before the whistle. That means you have to unhook all your tools, your cables, shut all the valves, bring all your gear down and, you know, put your big buckets and hang it on your bank, carry it up on the ship wherever you're going, put it in the box, and get ready to punch out. Then walk back that mile. Walking back that mile is really hard, 'cause I get so tired—that I can't go too fast. Going in I walk real fast, coming out I drag a little bit. Then you know, you put another day's work in and you feel good. When I get home I take a shower right away and start into the kitchen. Start making dinner. The kids are home, so I make hot tortillas and make our dinner for our family. Then I put a load in the washing machine, or do the bathrooms or do something in the house, 'cause you never have time to sit down. I sit down about eight-thirty, nine, exhausted, then I take another shower and go to bed. That's what the day is like.

An electronics mechanic apprentice described her day this way:

I get up usually at a quarter to five or five in the morning, take a shower, and wash my hair. My brother works at Military Island, he was riding with me for a while, but he's not riding anymore. So I don't have to pick him up. And I usually get to work about forty-five minutes early and they have a cafeteria right in the building and I usually eat breakfast there so I don't have dirty breakfast dishes to do when I get home. I'll read the paper. Then just regular working, depending on where I'm working, like I said I move every three or four months to a different shop, to different duties. But now I'm out climbing on airplanes and I usually get home about four-thirty or a quarter till five and I pick up my son from my mom's and let the animals in or out or wherever and cook dinner, clean up, and he sits glued to the TV and I yell, "Dinner," and he says, "Oh, no." It's tough—it really gets hard to come home.

You leave the house at six and get home at five—that's eleven hours. And then to have to try to figure out something to eat and then have to do the dishes—it just gets to be a drag. I think that's mainly why I get tired of getting up for work, because of what I know I have to come home to after. Like just—simple things like having to remember to put the trash out for Wednesday and that type of thing. It just makes me so mad—I'm on my way out to work on Wednesday mornings and I think, "Goddamn, I forgot to put the trash out last night," and then I have to go back and take it out. Just little things like that. It's tough, it's hard to do.

Another trainee described her busy pace:

I get up in the morning and I usually start screaming because I've overslept, and I jump in the shower—then I'm out there slamming things around, trying to make some lunches, and cussing at the kids —not swearing, but hollering at them. Try to get them in gear, throw their breakfast together, try to get in my car and leave by six-thirty, and leave to come down to school, drop them off at the baby-sitter's, come down here, and I'm in school for about six hours, then I get in my car and go home, pick up the kids, look at the house, which is a total wreck, and usually fall asleep in the chair for a couple of hours, or start cleaning it up—one or the other, it depends on how tired I am. And I never really sleep because I have a six-year-old and he has to be watched. The ten-year-old, he's pretty independent. Fix supper, which seems to never get fixed until about eight, never get my dishes done, fall asleep on the couch—maybe I'll run through some wash or something like that, and my husband goes to bed and I usually wake up at five in the morning on the couch and then I go into bed, and get up at five-thirty or six. I mean, it's terrible really, but . . .

These brief quotes give you some idea of the busy schedule of women in nontraditional jobs. However, very few of them complained about their situations or their spouses. Most of the married women had husbands who basically supported what they were doing, even encouraged it. Of the 25 percent who were married, close to half were in second marriages and only a few still had children at home (single mothers were a larger group than married mothers), so the household demands were possibly fewer. When asked about the husbands' reactions to their employment, most of the women indicated that the value of their paycheck outweighed the costs of a nontraditional job. The following response was fairly typical:

Oh, he loves it. Especially when he looks at the money I've saved. Sometimes it gets to him because someone will start bugging him,

"Oh, your wife's an auto mechanic," and then the neighbors—the girls—frown on it. The guys don't, but the girls think my place is in the home. I can see their point of view. Every once in a while everybody will get on his case and then he'll snap at me, but that usually doesn't last more than one day. Basically, he enjoys it. He wants me happy. He kind of laughs and makes a remark to the guys, "I don't care what she does—as long as she brings home a paycheck."

The most negative responses from husbands and boyfriends were *not* communicating about the woman's work at all. For example:

I think he's jealous . . . just like all the other men I work with are jealous. They can't take it when a woman—they'll be nice to you until you get the same paycheck that they get and you do the same work they're doing, then they don't like it. They treat you different, they're very mean . . . not my boyfriend—my boyfriend doesn't like me to talk about it—he says, "You leave work at work." He says, "You're the one who wanted to work like that, so it's your fault." 'Cause I used to complain sometimes and say, "Guy, they don't have to be so mean to me."

Clearly, even though the days were busy and some husbands or boyfriends somewhat ambivalent about their jobs, the women didn't feel pressures to change what they're doing to accommodate the family. Husbands did help out at home and with children, particularly when couples worked different shifts. Parents, relatives, and neighbors took care of children and the family was the primary activity for these women away from work. However, the fact that only 25 percent of the women we met were currently married and only about 48 percent had children does say something about who was able to take risks and put in the time and commitment needed to pioneer. When we conducted our interviews (in the mid-1970s), we tapped into the primary areas in which women were working in California, and our group of interviews was fairly representative of the types of women venturing into nontraditional skilled trades. A much smaller percentage of them had children than in the population generally. That may have freed them to be risk takers and achievers in just the way men and women preparing to be doctors and lawyers marry and have children later. With but one or two exceptions, the single heterosexual women we interviewed expected to marry and have children at some point in the future and also intended to keep working afterward.

LIFE AT WORK

Even though there are many things that differentiate the early childhoods and young adulthoods of women, at work their experiences are very similar. With the exception of women who make an early commitment to train for a specific profession such as nursing, teaching, law, or medicine, the employment experiences of women are virtually identical, regardless of education and social class. College graduates are as likely to have secretarial, retail sales, and waitressing jobs after finishing their schooling as are high school graduates. High school dropouts and minority women especially are more likely to be channeled into less lucrative service occupations such as domestic work or unskilled factory work. What is fascinating about the group of women we met, and the occupational data on American women generally, is how similar their limited opportunities are and how low their earning power is. Unless one comes to terms with this fundamental reality of life in America for women, one cannot really grasp why such a wide range of women would find skilled blue-collar jobs attractive. This reality is also important in understanding the appeal of two other little-understood spheres of activity dominated by women: glamour jobs such as modeling, acting, and merchandising and unpaid volunteer work. In light of the limited opportunities for even very talented, well-educated women, it is not surprising that many women pursue glamour jobs. The income, recognition, diversity, and power they can mean is not available elsewhere. Similarly, many of the activities in which volunteers engage provide genuine satisfactions because the quality of the work the women do and the quality of the relationships they have is superior to anything they could realistically expect to find in paid employment. On occasion, women have criticized one another for selling out by working in glamour jobs or unpaid volunteer work. But from the perspective of their limited opportunities, the choice to pursue these avenues is clearly a case of rationally deduced self-interest. Far more women than men are forced to do work in which they have no interest and from which they derive no intrinsic or extrinsic rewards. Skilled blue-collar jobs, glamour jobs, and volunteer work are all ways out of the trap for women to whom secretarial work, teaching, nursing, and social work are not appealing or to whom medicine, law, science, and management have been closed fields until very recently.

It is regrettable that at times women are in conflict with one another over the validity and integrity of their role choices: housewives at loggerheads with employed women; unpaid volunteers in debate with paid workers; women in nontraditional spheres critical of women in traditional or glamour jobs. In fact, our common experience as women with limited opportunities is what leads us to make the choices we do. A commitment to one or another of these sectors is less a *rejection* of the other roles than it is an *affirmation* of a need for meaning, satisfaction, and a sense of worth in one's work. Middle- and working-class women can no longer afford the financial costs of not being engaged in paid employment, so they must seek their fulfillment there. Upper-middle-class and upper-class women still have the luxury of forgoing unsatisfying paid employment for more satisfying unpaid work. But these different choices should not make women opponents. We need a more sophisticated understanding of the economic and social factors that enable women, who begin with similar limited opportunities, to make different choices as adults.

Work experiences as well as opportunities are remarkably similar for women, though strategies for dealing with problems and opportunities differ. So long as a woman remains in traditional women's work, there are no special problems establishing one's competency and achieving acceptance at work. When a woman ventures into an area in which she represents a minority, perhaps even the first on the scene, which was the case with so many of the women in this book, she faces very complex problems establishing her legitimacy and competency and gaining acceptance from co-workers. This is compounded in the blue-collar world by the fact that virtually all the skills are learned on the job. A woman moving into a managerial position in a manufacturing company straight out of an MBA program comes with enough "baggage" so that people can make initial assessments: the quality of the school she attended, the type of courses she took, the grades she got, the internships or special projects she took on. It is a different matter in the blue-collar world. Skills are developed essentially on the job. This is one reason for the importance of familiarity with the work or the workplace in making positive first impressions on the job. The outsider is always viewed with skepticism. If he or she has a few anchor points so that people can place the person or begin conversation, reliance on stereotypic anchors such as sex is less likely. Women who are successful, whether in the managerial or blue-collar world, understand this.

Success is not simply a matter of "networking" and learning the rules of the "boys'" game. It is a matter of establishing genuine common interests in the work, common concerns with competency and productivity, and sympathy with the work group culture. The sooner this can be demonstrated and communicated, the sooner a woman begins to be a part of the on-the-job information and communication links so crucial to survival. Men have no particular interest in facilitating this, so a woman who enters a job with some knowledge of the environment, the product, the tools, or even the people who work there has a head start over a stranger. The ability to talk about sports, military experiences, and other factors that writers in the managerial literature consider so important to success in a man's job may also help break down barriers, but they are not nearly as important as these other factors.

The experiences of women reported in this book suggest competency at the job and skills development *preceded* social acceptance from peers. These women worked in jobs where cooperation from peers was essential to learning the job in the first place. Once these blue-collar women showed they could do the job, often by working longer and harder than the men, they achieved social acceptance, and with this came a certain easing of the pressure to be an overachiever.

In one sense, women have a right to be resentful of all the extra effort they must exert and the special "tests" they must pass to prove their commitment and competence. On the other hand, all outsiders face special problems, not just female outsiders. For the outsider, proving one is committed to the new world one is entering is almost as important as proving one can function effectively in it. This is a dilemma all women working in nontraditional jobs have, and one that Kanter has discussed brilliantly in her book on men and women in organizations.[3] If you are the only O in a group of X's, you're going to stand out. No matter how hard you try, you cannot obliterate your difference from the majority. Being tested by the majority for competence and loyalty is a natural consequence, and until there are almost as many O's as X's in the group, it is unlikely the competence and loyalty of O's will be taken for granted. Women who succeeded seemed to understand this. They were more philosophical, even forgiving, of the bad treatment they received at times. They realized they were perceived as outsiders and as persons not to be trusted until proven trustworthy.

Special problems for women are most visible in the realm of what has come to be known as sexual harassment: the offer of work-related rewards in exchange for sexual favors and the threat of work-related penalties for failing to exchange sexual favors. The world of the casting couch clearly extends far beyond glamour professions. It is by no means a trivial problem and occurs fairly often among the women we studied at some point in most of their work histories. As pointed out in Part Two, the problem of sexual harassment appears to be far more direct and "up front" in the blue-collar environment than in an office environment, where it is often veiled in innuendo and polite suggestions. The blue-collar milieu both encourages and discourages this kind of behavior because it is characterized by rougher language and more physical aggressiveness. Thus a woman who is aggressive and uses obscene language may be seen as an easy target, but she can also use the tolerance for this kind of behavior to her advantage.

As is the case with developing competency and gaining acceptance, sexual harassment appears to be less of a problem for women who are able early to establish relationships at work on the basis of something other than their being women. In other words, they have interests or characteristics that anchor them so that the men do not as easily fall into stereotypical interactions with them. It also appears that blue-collar men are far less persistent in their pursuit and harassment of women than are white-collar and professional men. This has to do with differences in the orientations to sexuality of the two groups (white-collar men probably tend to romanticize relationships more) and, more important, with the greater power differences between men and women in the office, in contrast to the essentially peer-like relationships between the men and women workers we encountered.

Upon reviewing the childhoods, early work experiences, on-the-job experiences, and daily living patterns of women in skilled blue-collar jobs, the worlds they are challenging and the efforts they are making do not seem any more menacing or obstacle-filled than those of other groups of people pioneering in new fields. There are clearly special problems in being a woman that come from the overriding significance gender has traditionally played in our society in assigning expectations, rights, responsibilities, and privileges. But many of those expectations, rights, and responsibilities are beginning to change, although too slowly and too painfully. What looms larger is the problem of being an outsider, "the new kid on the block," the stranger who must both master her new context and be accepted into a new culture. There is much about the experiences of the women we have met that applies to other groups testing the traditional boundaries assigned to them and overcoming the obstacles they face as newcomers. The economic and human needs propelling people beyond traditional boundaries; the factors giving rise to a potential for risk taking; the importance of opportunity to becoming a pioneer; the significance of anchoring traits to early integration in a new context; the importance of competence and commitment to acceptance by the new community; the continued suspicion and need to prove oneself that confronts the outsider; the human capacity to persevere and understand one's situation from the point of view of the insider to whom one's differentness represents a threat: all are elements of the experience of successive generations of ethnic, racial, and now sexual pioneers. There is much to be learned about the general problems and dilemmas of being an outsider from the women pioneering in skilled blue-collar jobs.

VIII

An Agenda for the Future: Research and Policy Implications

This in-depth look at the characteristics and experiences of women moving into skilled blue-collar work raises questions both about the way we have studied and understood work in America and about the way we have formulated social policy and designed training and development programs to deal with the changing character of the work force and the changing requirements of the economy.

RESEARCH IMPLICATIONS

The absence of women from most empirical studies of work, the irrelevance of key economic and sociological concepts to the female experience generally, and the failure to deal in any serious way with the economic role of women in the family or the labor force create serious problems for the general study of work and for the study of women and work. There are essentially two problems with our understanding of work: (1) what kinds of workers are studied; (2) what work-related topics are studied.

WHO IS STUDIED?

The vast majority of research on work has focused on a very small number of occupations. The research on highly educated professional workers is quite diverse, but the research on skilled, semiskilled, and service workers is amazingly limited. Studies of doctors, lawyers, scientists, engineers, college professors, and managers reflect a broader cross section of occupational types, occupational settings, and work-related issues than do studies focusing on the experiences of blue-collar and skilled and semiskilled workers. Some of the classic studies of work such as the early Hawthorne electrical plant study; the study of the printing and typographers' union, *Union Democracy;* Stauffer's *The American Soldier;* and Whyte's studies of restaurant workers have provided valuable insights into the characteristics of skilled and semiskilled workers, their concerns at the workplace, and their values and attitudes.[1] These studies, however, represent isolated examples within a much larger body of literature on blue-collar work dominated by the study of *industrial* workers and workplaces, in particular the automobile assembly line and steel industries.

In his now classic study *Alienation and Freedom,* Robert Blauner criticized this bias in industrial sociology and pointed out the need to recognize the diversity of industrial settings. In Blauner's words:

On the whole this discipline has lacked a systematic, comparative approach to the study of variations within modern industry. It has operated by and large, with an undifferentiated global image of industrial life. The theoretical focus is usually on a "typical" individual form or economic organization or on "industry in general" the whole complex of more or less mechanized production systems.[2]

Through his comparison of four factory industries—printing, textiles, automobiles, and chemicals—Blauner illustrates the diversity of American industrial life. A key message in Blauner's book is that manual work has to be differentiated. In his view, modern industry can be characterized by three

types of work, each of which has different consequences for the
workers' sense of control and satisfaction with the work process. Blauner differentiates among (1) traditional manual skills
associated with craft technology, (2) routine, low-skill manual
operations associated with machine and assembly line technologies, and (3) nonmanual responsibility called forth by continuous-process technology (that is, totally automated production, which the worker monitors). He points out that most
studies of the worker and the workplace focus on (2), assembly
line and machine technologies, even though all the indications
are that jobs such as these are declining whereas jobs characterized by continuous-process technology and craft technology
are on the increase. Blauner asserts that both of these provide workers with controls and satisfactions not characteristically provided by classical industrial assembly line labor.
He argues that "automated manufacturing paradoxically in-
creases traditional craft skill, which is applied, however, to
maintenance problems rather than production work."[3] The very
intricacy of the new machinery and technical processes demands an increased number of workers with high skills necessary to the maintenance and repair of the machinery, whether
the machinery is an electrical typewriter in an office, a sophisticated component of a rapid-transit system, a calibration
instrument for traffic lights, or highly sophisticated printing
presses. These are the types of job in which many of the women
we met were working. It is virtually impossible to compare our
findings with other research because so little has been done on
these jobs, even though they represent millions of workers in
the American labor force.

In addition, as Rosabeth Moss Kanter's work suggests, insufficient attention has been given to the vertical, as opposed to
hierarchical, elaboration of employment options that has taken
place within organizations.[4] Increasingly, "career paths" and
"multiple careers" are supplanting the one job for a lifetime
characteristic of an earlier period. Workers today often find
power, challenge, and satisfaction through a succession of similar yet qualitatively different jobs. For example, a welder who

began in a heavy industry such as shipbuilding may move into a lighter industry such as metal furniture construction and eventually may even open his or her own shop where wrought-iron garden furniture is constructed and sold. Similarly, a keypunch operator may develop elementary computer programming skills, move into data analysis, and eventually supervise an information processing department. Auto mechanics may specialize in electrical parts repair and eventually move into the maintenance and repair of more sophisticated electronics equipment in streetlights or elevators. Jobs such as these involve certain basic skills, but the nature of the tasks to which these skills are applied and the settings in which they are used can be quite diverse. Thus the experiences of the worker may be highly diverse and new, interesting, and challenging. Such diversity has rarely been captured in the study of work.

The problem is compounded by the fact that little attention has been given to major shifts in the overall distribution of occupations. There is a rich body of literature on the "organization man" and the experiences of men and women working in the ever-expanding administrative and managerial white-collar jobs in modern bureaucratic organizations. There is no parallel literature, however, on the increasing numbers of what have come to be known as pink-collar workers, or the less managerial, more skilled white-collar occupations such as office machine repair, computer programming, or secretarial work. Both empirical research and theoretical treatments have failed to include such spheres of work. These spheres are characterized by large numbers of women workers. In fact, with the exception of a few high-visibility women's professional fields such as nursing, the work that women do is virtually absent from both empirical and theoretical discussions. Housework is rarely discussed. Service fields such as waitressing, hairdressing, and food preparation are not treated. Clerical fields, including filing, cashiering, and typing, are rarely explored. Semiskilled fields such as electronics assembly, sewing and stitching, laundering, and dry cleaning are virtually never discussed. As the U. S. Department of Labor statistics for 1975 reported, women represent over 42 percent of the current full-time paid labor force, and yet the work that over 70 percent of these women workers do day in and day out is rarely studied. How certain can we be that the generalizations about work that abound in both the empirical and theoretical literature have much validity when such a major portion of the work force and such diversity of job types and occupational settings have never been seriously investigated?

It is important to note that increasing numbers of male workers also make up these expanding clerical and service occupations. Their experience of work and the workplace has also been invisible. Barbers and waiters, taxi drivers and custodians, retail clerks and door-to-door salesmen, office machine repairmen and telephone installers have all been ignored. To dramatize the size of this problem, it is useful to look at recent employment statistics. Automobile workers and steel workers, on whom there is an extensive body of empirical and theoretical literature, each represented slightly over a million workers in 1975. Secretaries, sales workers, waitresses, cashiers, and sewers and stitchers *each* represented 800,000 female workers. Yet only on rare occasions can one find any of these latter occupations analyzed or referred to in the enormous body of literature dealing with industrial sociology or the sociology of work. It is fair to assume that both the structural and qualitative experiences of a sewer and a stitcher, a secretary or waitress, a sales clerk or barber will differ from those of a steel worker or automobile factory worker. Yet we have tended to rely almost exclusively on the experiences of the latter when generalizing about work in America. The absence of the other work spheres from both the empirical and theoretical literature and from the social analyses of both conservative and radical thinkers raises serious questions about how well or fully we understand the American worker.

One final observation about *who* is studied: although men make up the vast majority of the blue-collar work force, certainly in the more skilled trades and crafts, our lack of any data on the small numbers of women who have also occupied these

positions may have resulted in some critical errors of interpretation. It is important to assess the extent to which the subjective history and characteristics that people bring to their
work—such as those deriving from race or sex—may give rise to
different feelings, attitudes, and evaluations about the work
process or work setting. Does a woman on an assembly line, in
a craft, or in a maintenance job experience the work in the
same way as a man? Or does the woman's different personal
history, different expectations, and different constraints and options result in her experiencing the job differently from a man?
Our research findings suggest that women do, in fact, feel
differently.

Clearly there are some significant gaps in our knowledge of
the American work force: gaps resulting from our failure to
study a sufficient diversity of occupational settings; from our
failure to capture the diversity of job types within organizational settings and even within a general skill; from our failure to give adequate attention to the burgeoning clerical and
service occupations that involve large numbers of women
workers and increasing numbers of male workers; from our
failure to look at the diversity of persons occupying similar occupational positions.

WHAT IS STUDIED?

The issue of what is studied flows quite logically from the issue
of who is studied. Research inevitably reflects the interests of
individual researchers, particularly in terms of the constit-
uencies and life experiences with which the researcher is comfortable and the communities and subjects to whom the researcher has easy access. It is not surprising, for example, that
a great deal of research is conducted with samples of undergraduate students, since they are easily accessible to professors,
or that there are many studies of professionals such as doctors,
lawyers, and school superintendents, since they are approacha-
ble and share many values with college professors and journal-

ists. Similarly, research frequently reflects the interests of the organization or agency subsidizing or benefiting from the findings. It is not surprising to discover that some of the classic studies of organizational settings and workers include such formidable organizations as the United States Army, Western Electric, and the Ford Motor Company.[5]

Who is studied, the contexts in which studies of work have taken place, and the values and experiences of the individual researchers all affect *what* is studied. This is true for both the assumptions the researcher makes in advance and the unexpected issues and insights that may arise in the process of data collection and analysis. Because, however, the settings and individuals that have been researched thus far are not representative of the diversity of workers and workplaces characterizing today's workforce, it is likely that many interesting issues and insights pertinent to our understanding of work have never been raised or investigated. Possibly many generalizations about the work experience might not hold water in a different work context, with a different set of workers. This book, for example, has dealt with work contexts and workers different from those characteristic of the prevailing literature on work. What, if any, new issues or slants on the study of work are suggested by the inclusion of not only working women, but women researchers?

Three main areas of knowledge have suffered from the exclusion of women: (1) our understanding of stratification and, within that, the occupational aspirations and social mobility of women; (2) our understanding of role theory and socialization, especially the occupational socialization and professionalization of employed women; (3) our understanding of the relationship of employment roles to family and community roles. Joan Acker, among others, has been highly critical of the field of stratification theory and research for its failure adequately to take into account the extent to which sex is a basis for social differentiation and one of the most obvious bases of economic, political, and social inequalities.[6]

ASSUMPTIONS ABOUT WOMEN
AND STRATIFICATION

Acker succinctly summarized key assumptions about women and stratification:

In stratification literature, six assumptions are made, sometimes explicitly and sometimes implicitly, about the social position of women. These are most clearly stated by the functionalists but are present also in the work of nonfunctionalists and Marxists. These assumptions are:

1. The family is the unit in the stratification system.
2. The social position of the family is determined by the status of the male head of the household.
3. Females live in families; therefore, their status is determined by that of the males to whom they are attached.
4. The female's status is equal to that of her man, at least in terms of her position in the class structure, because the family is a unit of equivalent evaluation (Watson and Barth, 1964).
5. Women determine their own social status only when they are not attached to a man.
6. Women are unequal to men in many ways, are differentially evaluated on the basis of sex, but this is irrelevant to the structure of stratification systems.

The first assumption, that the family is the unit of stratification, is basic to the other five. Together, these assumptions neatly dispense with the necessity for considering the position of women in studies of social stratification or considering the salience of sex as a dimension of stratification. To put it another way, the fate of the female in the class system is determined by the fate of the male. Therefore, it is only necessary to study males.[7]

These points are critical to the arguments in this book because assumptions about the primacy of the family have important consequences, not only for studies of what constitutes social class, but for a wide body of related literature on occupational aspirations and mobility. If the destiny of a woman is solely determined by the conditions of men, there is no need to study the occupational aspirations of women or their social mobility independent of their relationships to their fathers or their husbands. Acker, however, argues that these assumptions require serious examination. Given that upwards of 12 percent of persons over eighteen are unattached individuals, is it entirely accurate to assume the family is the unit of stratification? Given that research has demonstrated that 40 percent of the households in the United States do not have a fully employed male head, either because women are unmarried, widowed, or divorced, or because husbands are retired, working part-time, or unemployed, is it really accurate to have family status determined by the male's occupation? Given that women increasingly have status resources of their own—education, income, and occupation—is it appropriate simply to assign them the status of their husbands? Given that status has numerous dimensions—income, prestige, and power—which husbands and wives may have in differential proportions, is it fair to assume that the woman's status simply reflects that of the man she lives with? Finally, Acker asks, given that occupation is one of the primary criteria of social status, how do we deal with the fact that there is no occupational status ranking given to the occupation of housewife, even though half the women in this country are housewives?[8]

Because of these deficiencies in our understanding of stratification, until very recently there was relatively little written on the development of vocational interests, status aspirations, and social mobility that included female samples or the female experience. Most were studies of white males.[9] What little there was on aspirations and achievement also tended to be disproportionately based on studies of predominantly white college students or professional women. In some instances, such as the early work on achievement motivation, women students were not even included in the studies. In other studies of college student aspirations and occupational values, the apparent low aspirations of women were explained away by the assumed primacy of the marriage and family role. The lower aspirations were not seriously examined. More critical, however, is the nearly total absence of data on the aspirations and expectations of non-college youth and particularly non-college girls (outside of the traditional vocational testing field, which until recently standardized tests for girls on the basis of female occupations and for boys on the basis of male occupations). Finally, studies of social mobility end up mapping male mobility by comparing father and son and female mobility by comparing the status of the father with the status of the husband. In each of these instances, it has been assumed that occupational choice, status aspirations, and mobility were tangential issues for women and were indirectly resolved through seeking and finding a mate. We have thus failed to examine seriously the processes whereby women develop and test vocational interests, the extent to which women feel they need to meet their economic and status needs through their own activity rather than through attachment to a male, and the extent to which marriage is the locus of identity for women.

A second problem with the study of work is that much of what we know about career training and on-the-job socialization reflects the concerns of occupations such as medicine, management, and law. This presents a picture of career development as a logical process that includes the development of interests, formal education, and finally socialization to the workplace, thus suggesting that occupational socialization is both *linear* and *intentional*. For persons pursuing highly professional careers requiring many years of preparation, it is not surprising that there appears to be a logical sequence of clarifying values and interests, selecting a college major expressive of those values and interests, pursuing professional school training in a relevant skill area, and finally breaking into the profession and learning the formal and informal rules of the game. What is problematic about the research on the professions is that it sometimes leads us to assume that all occupations involve a similar linear and intentional path.

For large numbers of people, the sequence might be quite

different, particularly for people from backgrounds that provide them with less time and fewer resources to explore and test interests. For many people, employment may be the first step and the primary context in which values and interests become solidified. It may take a number of jobs before it is clear what the person enjoys most. He or she might discover a whole world of unanticipated interests and abilities on the job which then become the impetus for training or education at a later phase in life. Some people may have three or four different careers in a lifetime. The extent to which economic and social circumstances affect the process of vocational interest development, to which employment experiences themselves can be the locus of value and interest development, and to which people may pursue many careers in a lifetime and the processes by which they make those shifts is almost never addressed in the literature on occupational socialization. This is in part due to our failure to study the work experience of women.

There also has been a tendency to interpret the employment decisions of skilled and semiskilled workers as purely a matter of available options and economic incentives. More complex values tied to the intrinsic nature of the work and more subtle aspects of the vocational interest development process are ignored by many. All too often, we patronizingly assume that only well-educated people have complex feelings about their work and that they require more challenge and gratification from their work than do blue-collar workers. Thus, in addition to the gap in understanding created by the failure of the stratification literature to take sex into account, there is another gap in understanding resulting from the failure of the literature on occupational socialization to give sufficient attention to the process whereby interests and commitments to jobs develop in nonprofessional fields.

Finally, until the recent advent of interest in women and work, the study of work has paid scant attention to the nature of the relationship between employment roles and family and community roles. Such a relationship plays itself out in a number of important ways. The most obvious is the extent to which considerations about employment opportunities affect decisions about family and community roles *or* the extent to which considerations about family and community roles affect occupational choices. We have always *assumed* that men adjust everything to accommodate their work roles and that women do just the opposite, adjusting everything in life to accommodate their domestic roles. Regrettably, very little work has been done to explore the validity of these assumptions. Clearly, they need to be revised. Many men make work decisions that enable them to relate to spouses or children in more flexible ways. Many men are required by circumstances or early marriage or parenthood to adjust their career plans. Increasing numbers of women, in turn, are resolving work-related questions before making marriage and family commitments.

Increasing numbers of men and women are facing a future in which the necessity of paid employment for both husband and wife has to be integrated with traditional desires for children and family life. The problems of household management, child care, and conserving emotional resources in such an environment are just beginning to be addressed. (Only the problems of "professional" couples have been extensively looked at.) Similarly, in spite of the changing technological and economic realities of twentieth-century life, it is only recently that attention has been given to the costs and benefits of significant alterations in the actual structure of jobs. The possible consequences of part-time work, shared jobs, and flexible work hours have received serious public attention in only the last few years and this may be largely because of the failure to give sufficient attention to the ways in which *people,* not just women, try to integrate work, family, and community roles. In addition, millions of people today work afternoon and evening shifts, all night, and on weekends. The impact, if any, this has on relationships and activities outside the workplace has barely been discussed.

Finally, as noted previously, there has been insufficient discussion of the consequences of the decline of traditional industrial production and the increase in maintenance, service, and highly technically skilled occupations. Serious research and writing on the actual content of these new jobs, the work experiences and relationships to which they give rise, and how these affect people's feelings about work and its significance in their lives is essential. Many of these service and maintenance jobs provide the worker with flexible hours, control over the pacing of the work, and variety in the work setting. As such, they represent interesting alternatives to the images we have of employment. Popular stereotypes and academic discussions of what is involved in combining employment with family and community roles derive from an overly narrow image of the types of work people do and a traditional attitude about what comes first in the lives of men and what comes first in the lives of women. Many "new" jobs and dozens of traditional ones that we have never bothered to study may allow for a kind of discretion and control which means that they can potentially be combined with family roles in ways we have never really thought about. An example might be a small-appliance repairperson who can work out of her home, out of a truck, or in the field a few hours a week as easily as she could as a serviceperson for Sears. A plumber, like a doctor, can potentially limit the number of calls she makes in a week, have time for personal or family pursuits, and still earn an income superior to that in most traditional women's jobs. These fields and options have not been looked at seriously. Clearly they must be if we are to understand how family and employment combine in the lives of working people.

THE LIMITS OF CURRENT RESEARCH SUMMARIZED

The gaps and limitations characterizing the study of work, particularly women and work, suggest the need for studies of new populations of women workers and of more diverse jobs. New questions must be raised and new research techniques used. The inclusion of women respondents and women's jobs and the use of methodologies that allow for the incorporation of subjective definitions and comparative studies should greatly enhance our general understanding of work. They should also provide a new perspective on that 40 percent of the work force which has been virtually invisible: women workers.

The prevailing attitude remains that the traditional male world of work constitutes *the* world of work. This has some important consequences. The first is that theory and research often proceed on the basis of inaccurate or poor assumptions. These, in turn, give rise to large numbers of "deviant cases" or anomalies that cannot be accounted for. Thus research findings cannot be used to generalize or predict. In addition, the exclusion of women is ahistorical. Even those analysts who use historical events as their data base have often failed to recognize and incorporate important sociosexual shifts relevant to economic and occupational life. As important, the personal biography individuals bring to their given situations needs to be incorporated into explanations of their behavior. As noted earlier, women's experience of the same tasks and workplace may differ significantly from men's because of the comparisons they make between what they are doing with what they used to do (i.e., housework) or what is available to most women (i.e., low-paying jobs). Finally, the myopia that results from the image of the world of work as a man's world is potentially repressive at all levels of society. Just as female industrial workers have been limited to dull and low-paying jobs because they have been defined as temporary workers whose primary gratifications come from the family, so the wives and colleagues of white-collar men have been curtailed by work norms and formal policies that have failed to deal with the significant questions of home and child care. All people, men and women, need meaningful work.

A truly comprehensive and useful understanding of work in American society has to include the experiences of *all* kinds of working people. It must present a truly comprehensive picture of the occupational structure, including those invisible jobs in which most women work. And it must include the female experience of traditionally male-dominated work spheres. This book represents a modest step in that direction. Because it has provided some brief glimpses into the lives of rarely discussed working women, of women in invisible occupations such as cosmetology as well as women moving into male fields such as auto mechanics, it may begin to fill some of the gaps in our understanding of work.

POLICY IMPLICATIONS

In addition to raising questions about the way we think about work and workers, this research raises some important questions about the strategies employers and policy makers might use in recruiting, training, and retaining women in nontraditional jobs. Much attention has been given to the "burden of regulation" that public and private institutions have to live with because of policies such as affirmative action. Institutions find themselves faced with the dual problem of *finding* and *qualifying* new categories of workers for jobs traditionally dominated by white males. In all traditional male fields, whether chemistry or mechanics, engineering or drafting, financial management or office machine repair, there seem to be two common assumptions working against the entry of women: (1) special basic skills and aptitudes are required to succeed in the field, and (2) people who are acceptable to work in this field should have demonstrated prior interest and involvement in it. Because women do not appear to have the skills and aptitudes and because they have not attempted to enter the field until recently, it is assumed they are unlikely to be successful at it. The experience of the women we talked to suggests that under certain conditions women *do* develop skills and aptitudes. In addition, it demonstrates vividly that, at least in skilled blue-collar work, interest in a job is a result of opportunity and access to on-the-job experiences. These experiences can then develop into real competencies *and* commitment to skilled work. Each of these findings has important policy implications.

DEVELOPING BASIC SKILLS AND APTITUDES

Among those women who reported some aptitude for technical or mechanical problems and some interest in doing technical or mechanical tasks before their actual employment, early access to tools and equipment and hands-on experience were crucial. Early opportunities to participate in nontraditional activities such as building a house, repairing a car, or even chopping firewood helped to demystify male activities for many women and also helped cultivate basic skills. In addition, encouragement of or opportunity to engage in physical activities as a child—such as sports or outdoor work in the country—contributed to the desire to have an active job and to use one's body in one's work. Such experiences were in the backgrounds of the women we met who were successful in blue-collar work. Their lack of attachment to narrow definitions of femininity also contributed to their ability to try new roles. How can the potential for developing such traits be encouraged in young girls? Our findings reinforce the proposals of many feminist groups, as well as those of other researchers.

Opportunities in the home, at play, and at school have to be opened up to girls so they can have experiences on the basis of which they can evaluate their level of interest and potential for competency in physical, mechanical, and technical activities. This means opening up vocational education in skilled areas to girls as well as boys. It means expanding opportunities for participation in team sports to girls as well as boys—from elementary school age on. In addition, images of girls and women in storybooks and school texts, as well as in the media, have to include girls in nontraditional roles as well as traditional ones. Even though recommendations of this nature have been made in the past, it is important to state them again and again. This research provides further data on the significance of early-childhood and young-adulthood opportunities to the development of interests and predispositions that will be acted on when concrete opportunities develop later.

DEVELOPING COMPETENCY AND COMMITMENT

If one accepts (1) that access to opportunity is the first step in the development of job interest and (2) that an active, apprenticelike relationship is the best way to develop competence in a skilled job, then certain strategies to facilitate job entry and success among women become obvious. Clearly, additional opportunities need to be opened up. This means that more information about a greater variety of jobs needs to be disseminated. The information must reach a larger and more diverse group of women. Using the media can help reach the general population, but it is imperative that companies use the services set up to identify women for nontraditional jobs. These services work to the extent that they link people in search of new alternatives with employers ready to take on women in nontraditional jobs. However, employers are remiss if they feel they can find women only through some sort of special agency. We encountered enough secretaries and keypunch operators who were recruited from their traditional jobs into nontraditional ones with the same employer to convince us that current women employees are very good prospects, not just because they are there and easy to recruit, but because they have a better chance of success since they know something about the work context and would be less like strangers to the new work group. Based on our findings, other characteristics of likely succeeders in nontraditional blue-collar jobs would be women who have prior work experience, are money-oriented, like autonomy in their work, enjoy physical activity, and are able to communicate some understanding of the blue-collar work milieu. Any indicators from their pasts suggesting the ability to take charge and to handle difficult situations on their own could also identify a woman with high potential. Did she work in her parents' business? Was she in the military? Did she play sports of any kind? Is she a mountain climber or a hot-rod hobbyist? Many women are. Is she good at math? Does she have hobbies such as building radios or dollhouses? Most important, does she appear to have a serious and lifelong commitment to paid employment? Any one of these questions can help identify promising prospects.

In addition to opening opportunities and probing for indicators of work potential, an employer must offer a *real* job. The most successful women in our sample were women in apprenticeship programs. Their success was largely because the training period was long enough so that trial-and-error learning could take place. Also, the pay was good and the prospect of paid employment secure enough that the women could put up with a great deal of grief for it. School training and special government training which is time-limited and has no assurance of employment is less successful. Other recent research is bearing this out.[10] We met a few women who had been successful after starting out in CETA programs, but in these instances the training situations led directly to permanent employment.

Once a person embarks on her training, an important concern should be how well she understands the way in which she will have to go about getting the information and help she needs. Some sort of preassignment orientation is therefore desirable. This should give the woman an overview of what her job will be and the various competencies she will have to develop. This sort of preassignment orientation could be as short as a day. It could be covered in a notebook or workbook given to the employee. The orientation should be specific, not superficial. Concepts, vocabulary, tools, and equipment that are a routine part of the job should be introduced so that the woman (1) feels a little more confident her first days on the job; (2) makes a good first impression on the men, since she needs them to teach her; (3) can be a more active learner, asking better questions and taking some initiative. A woman who enters a nontraditional job with some self-confidence, a little familiarity with the job, tools, and culture, and an ability to ask good questions is going to have a much better chance. Certainly the women we met had an advantage because they possessed these traits. A counselor, a personnel officer, or a good supervisor can help a new woman employee by taking the time to give her a proper orientation to the job and the workplace.

Once a woman begins her job in earnest, the tasks that have to be done and the skills required to do them must be spelled out and the woman must have sufficient opportunity to do hands-on work. Only in this way will she become truly competent and accepted as a work peer. There are many ways to systematize this process—through regular oral communication, workbooks suggesting tasks to be learned, or evaluations based on the employee's progress. What is critical is that expectations be clear and opportunities to learn be continuous. Women who end up being used as assistants or gofers are not successes. An employer has to ask what systems are in place to ensure that this does not happen.

Parallel research on women in skilled jobs has resulted in findings similar to these. Sylvia Navari, in her 1979 monograph *Women in Skilled Labor: Problems and Issues* (based on a sample of over two hundred workers), summarized her findings as follows:

Overall, women who have already entered skilled labor occupations have done so with a minimal amount of training. This, in itself, contradicts the conventional notion that women need specialized training programs before they can enter nontraditional jobs. Strong motivation and desire, more than anything else, seem to be the key ingredients necessary for women wanting to enter skilled labor occupations. This is not to say that training programs are unnecessary, but rather, that they are not the prime requisite. Furthermore, training programs will only be useful if they contain each of the following four elements: 1) training program planners must know exactly what skills are required for specific occupations—and the training program must be designed for specific occupations, 2) the equipment necessary for hands-on experience should be readily accessible to the training program, 3) the training program must have access to real jobs, and 4) the training program must be adequately financed.

While training programs are useful, quality training programs are few, and these quality programs exist predominantly in the private sector—sponsored either by unions or private employers. Private sector training programs spend up to 10 times more per trainee than the average government training program; and, more importantly, have ready access to real jobs and the knowledge and resources necessary to provide quality training. Government training programs (CETA, WIN, etc.) have not had a significant impact upon the number of women entering skilled labor. Nor have school counselors or vocational education courses contributed significantly to an increase in the number of women in skilled labor.[11]

To summarize, it is at the minimum essential to open opportunities to women and provide some assurances of a permanent job if the woman demonstrates competence. Once these two conditions are present, the employer must develop systems to help women enter and succeed in nontraditional blue-collar jobs. These systems must include: (1) recruitment strategies, (2) preassignment orientation, and (3) competency-based training and evaluation.

SYSTEMS NEEDED TO FACILITATE SUCCESS

SYSTEM	ELEMENTS NEEDED
Recruitment Strategies	–Identify high-probability sources (inside industry/outside agencies)
	–Develop a "pitch" package
	• Describe industry/trades/craft
	• Long-range outcomes, both financial and other
	• Apprenticeship process
	• How to begin
Preassignment Orientation	–Physical facilities and tools
	–Tasks related to specific hands-on trade/craft
	–Formal work norms
	–Informal work norms
Competency-based Training and Evaluation	–Lists of tasks/performances/ behavior by area for supervisor, journeyman, and apprentice

–Task-based evaluation forms for
each phase of the job
–Regular intervals for assessing
overall progress
–Extension of probationary
period to allow time to learn

This schematic checklist emphasizes the need to systematize
on-the-job training in a way that is not done currently in most
skilled-work sites across the country. Traditional approaches to
training skilled workers, especially for industrial jobs, have
changed very little over the years. Industry flourished for years
by recruiting skilled blue-collar workers from rural areas and
family farms, from military veterans and sons of skilled
workers. When these men began training they came with a set
of expectations, understandings, and basic skills that equipped
them to be active learners and useful helpers. Their operating
mode was to watch carefully and ask good questions. A journeyman or trainer, in turn, could assume a minimum level of
knowledge and understanding in his apprentices or trainees and
worried very little about formalized approaches to training. In
the past, this training philosophy worked. In the last decade,
however, the characteristics of workers entering blue-collar
industries have changed radically. It is not only the appearance
of women and minorities that is responsible for this change.
There are fewer burly, mechanical boys just off the farm, fewer
highly skilled military veterans, and fewer sons of blue-collar
tradesmen and craftsmen following in their fathers' footsteps.
Vocational programs in high schools have been increasingly de-
emphasized. As society has become more affluent and mass education has spread, the interest in and familiarity with blue-
collar work and work settings has diminished.

Today apprentices and trainees—male and female, white,
black, and brown—are all in need of a better orientation and
training experiences in the workplace than the traditional, informal journeyman/apprentice relationship provides. Traditional
methods for training and evaluating apprentices no longer en-

sure that they become competent. This is not just a problem for women. For the most part, training methods consist of simply rotating apprentices from job to job with no explicit statements about what has to be learned and what skills have to be mastered within given areas and time periods. In many settings, becoming a skilled worker is simply a matter of putting in your hours rather than demonstrating skills attainment. There is little structure to the journeyman/apprentice relationship to ensure that teaching and learning take place. The on-the-job responsibilities of the journeyman or trainer can easily interfere with teaching and training. A carpenter, electrician, or mechanic may be skilled at his job but not at communicating how to do it. Evaluations of trainees are often based on indirect traits (e.g., good work habits) and are conducted by untrained people. With the insecurity and lack of familiarity many trainees bring to their new jobs, it is not surprising that people often end up being rotated through job areas without mastering skills.

Such an ambiguous milieu is not a positive one for training people. It is also difficult to disqualify incompetent people. Myths and prejudices about women and minorities getting by "without having to do anything" persist in such environments, and claims of discrimination are easily supported in the absence of clear measures and indicators of performance. Competency-based training and evaluation makes the environment less ambiguous. It does so by spelling out learning objectives and by comprehensively listing concepts, skills, and abilities that must be developed and mastered over specified time periods. (Note: This argument has been made elsewhere by the author.)[12] The experiences of the successful women in skilled blue-collar jobs confirm again and again the importance of a context or a person that makes expectations clear and helps the woman master the necessary skills. More needs to be done if women are going to succeed in large numbers and become bona fide co-workers of blue-collar men.

CONCLUDING SUMMARY

Much has been made throughout this book of the special characteristics and pattern-breaking experiences of the women pioneering in skilled blue-collar jobs. This chapter has emphasized the research and policy questions that must be addressed if large numbers of women, rather than just a few superwomen, are to enter and succeed in nontraditional work. We have learned a great deal from the experiences of these very special breakthrough women, but it would be a mistake to model our notions of who should make it and how they can make it too closely on their experiences. First of all, there are not enough of them. Many overcame tragic circumstances. Each has a kind of hearty individualism that is atypical for men and women today. They are pioneers, the first wave of new job entrants, and the qualities it takes to be a pioneer are different than those it takes to be a good worker or journeyperson. We must not forget that.

In addition, we must not forget the ever-changing history and sociology of women's roles. Women's motivations and abilities have been framed by the economic and social times in which they have lived. Ours is a different era, and we must of necessity change some of the economic and social arrangements limiting women's roles if large numbers of women are to have improved employment. It is not simply a matter of individual women changing themselves. Employers and policy makers have an obligation to continue examining the wide range of issues affecting women and employment. The lives of the women you've met on these pages raise provocative questions. They deserve to be answered.

Appendix

RESEARCH METHODS

FIRST-YEAR INTERVIEWS

The women interviewed in this study were selected with a number of criteria in mind. They had to be beginning some sort of training or on-the-job program in a skilled or semiskilled occupation as of the fall of 1975. This was because I wanted the opportunity to follow people through the early stages of career development and observe the kinds of experiences, supports, and obstacles that influence the development of job skills, as well as interest and commitment. By interviewing entry-level women, I was able to follow this process quite effectively.

Another important consideration was to have a cross section of training or employment settings so that I could examine some of the differences in experiences tied to differences in such things as the counseling and training provided the employee, the nature of the formal group relationships encountered by new employees, and the attitudes of instructors, co-workers, and supervisors toward women moving into nontraditional jobs. It was important to include a variety of programs or settings.

In addition, although the main subject of this study was women in nontraditional jobs, I wanted to have a representation (of somewhere between 25 and 33 percent) of women moving into traditional occupations. This was to be sure that the experiences I uncovered were not simply those encountered by *any* person moving into a *new* skilled or semiskilled job, but rather something unique to nontraditional work. The women in traditional employment provided a kind of control group for discussions of the sources of interest, career paths, and employment experiences of nontraditional women. As important, however, women in traditional jobs in the skilled and semiskilled world are interesting. They are so rarely studied that it became clear early on that it was important to talk to a large enough number of such women to assure a good portrait of their employment concerns and interests.

Finally, the dictates of time and money, in addition to the existence in 1975 of small numbers of women in nontraditional jobs throughout the state, suggested the wisdom of recruiting respondents through employers or training programs rather than through some sampling technique based on locating individuals. My extensive involvement with employment issues gave me a familiarity with a number of training and employment settings that were involving increasing numbers of women in nontraditional jobs. Therefore, rather than doing some form of random sampling, putting advertisements in papers soliciting respondents, or using a "snowball" technique whereby one person gives you the name of a friend who in turn gives you more names, my decision was to recruit respondents through agencies, schools, and employers which I knew were providing training and employment satisfying the three criteria outlined above.

Thus I initially contacted key individuals within agencies or industries and tried to interest them in the study. These key individuals then made lists of female employees available, with names and addresses, so that the research staff could recruit them directly. With these lists, which totaled 175 names, we then sent a brief introductory letter to each of the women informing her of the research and indicating that someone from the staff would be calling her in the next few days to set up an interview at her convenience. Each respondent was offered ten dollars for her time. Interviews were scheduled at locations close to the respondents' place of work, using YWCA centers, schools, and downtown hotels as interview sites.

In all, we interviewed 117 women, 34 of whom came from the San Francisco Bay Area, 70 from the San Diego metropolitan area, and 13 from Los Angeles.

Each of the 117 women we interviewed in the first year spent from two to three hours in a private interview with one of our five interviewers. The entire open-ended interview was tape-recorded. (All respondents agreed to have their interviews taped.) In addition, each respondent filled out a six-page paper-and-pencil questionnaire and provided in the course of the interview pictorial representations of her work setting and of her concept of the social class structure in this country. In addition, the interviewers filled out lengthy observation sheets at the completion of each interview. These provided information on the respondents' race, attire, body language, and general presentation. They also provided information on the interviewer's own feelings about the respondent—whether she liked or disliked her, and how she assessed the respondent's feelings during the interview. In this manner we hoped to record some of the more subtle qualities of respondent and interviewer interaction that could not be picked up solely by word-for-word transcription of tapes.

Although we conducted full interviews with 117 women in the fall of 1976 and the spring of 1977, we have only 108 fully transcribed tapes. Nine of the tapes, because of sound problems or mechanical failure, could not be fully transcribed. Of those, 4 were partially transcribed and summarized in the interviewer's own words. The other 5 tapes were totally unusable. Questionnaire, interviewer observations, and other standardized data were available for these 9 respondents, however. Also, 4 of these 9 respondents were successfully interviewed in the second year, so I have been able to reconstruct much of what was lost in the faulty tapes from year one. The following tables summarize the essential characteristics of the women interviewed in the first year.

TABLE I
Sources of Respondents

San Diego

WOMEN'S CENTER JOB PROGRAM	COMMUNITY COLLEGE SKILLS PROGRAM	MAJOR MILITARY INDUSTRY	COUNTYWIDE SCHOOL OF COSMETOLOGY
12	25	16	17

Total = 70

San Francisco

CALIFORNIA APPRENTICESHIP BOARD	BAY AREA-WIDE WOMEN'S COUNSELING JOB REFERRAL PROGRAM
4	30

Total = 34

Los Angeles

CITYWIDE WOMEN'S	ON-THE-JOB
COUNSELING/JOB	PROGRAM REFERRALS
REFERRAL PROGRAM	
8	5

Total = 13
Grand total = 117

TABLE II
Work/Training Settings of Respondents

	No.
Government industry (OJT)*	26
School (with applied experience)	41
Private industry (OJT)	27
Retail/service (OJT)	15
Union (apprenticeship)	4
Self-employed	2
Unknown	2
Total	117

*OJT = On-the-job Training

TABLE III
Racial Distribution of Respondents

RACE	TRADITIONAL		NONTRADITIONAL		TOTAL SAMPLE	
	N	%	N	%	N	%
White	17	55	64	74	81	69
Black	3	10	12	14	15	13
Asian	2	6	2	2	4	3
Latina	9	29	5	6	14	12
No information	—	—	3	4	3	3
Total	31	100%	86	100%	117	100%

TABLE IV
Age Distribution of Respondents

AGE	TRADITIONAL		NONTRADITIONAL		TOTAL SAMPLE	
	N	%	N	%	N	%
18–21	6	19	4	5	10	8
22–30	13	42	62	72	75	64
31–40	8	26	9	10	17	15

41+	4	13	9	10	13	11
No information	—	—	2	3	2	2
Total	31	100%	86	100%	117	100%

TABLE V
Educational Attainment of Respondents

EDUCATION	TRADITIONAL		NONTRADITIONAL		TOTAL SAMPLE	
	N	%	N	%	N	%
0–8 years	1	2.5	1	1	2	2
9–11 years	8	27	6	7	14	12
High school graduate	9	30	14	16	23	20
Some college (includes required courses in training)	10	33	42	49	52	44
College graduate	1	2.5	16	19	17	15
Advanced work	1	2.5	5	6	6	5
No information	1	2.5	2	2	3	2
Total	31	100%	86	100%	117	100%

TABLE VI
Marital Status

MARITAL STATUS	TRADITIONAL		NONTRADITIONAL		TOTAL SAMPLE	
	N	%	N	%	N	%
Married	18	56	21	24	39	33
Ever married	6	19	23	27	29	25
Never married	7	25	42	49	49	42
Total	31	100%	86	100%	117	100%

TABLE VII
Number of Children at Home

NUMBER OF CHILDREN	TRADITIONAL		NONTRADITIONAL		TOTAL SAMPLE	
	N	%	N	%	N	%
0	12	39	54	63	66	56
1	0	0	13	15	13	11
2	5	16	9	10	14	12

NUMBER OF CHILDREN	TRADITIONAL		NONTRADITIONAL		TOTAL	SAMPLE
3	1	3	2	2	3	3
4 or more	5	16	1	1	6	5
No information	8	26	7	9	15	13
Total	31	100%	86	100%	117	100%

SECOND-YEAR INTERVIEWS

In the fall of 1976 and into the winter and spring of 1977, the second-year follow-up interviews were conducted. We attempted to contact all 117 women we had interviewed in the previous year and eventually reinterviewed 61 of them. The other 56 were not reinterviewed, primarily because of difficulty in either locating them or in reaching them. Twenty-five of the women had changed home addresses, and we were unable to find a new address or phone number. Nine of the previous-year respondents declined a second-year interview because they didn't feel they wanted to give the time. Four of the women broke their appointments with us, and we were unable to reach them or to set up new appointments. Three of the women had moved out of state to Hawaii, New York, and Denver. They each wrote us, indicating they were still employed in nontraditional fields and were looking forward to any publications we could share with them. The remaining 15 women were simply impossible to contact, we assume because of a lack of interest. We had addresses and phone numbers and contacted them on numerous occasions, leaving messages, but never received return calls. Selected characteristics pertinent to the second-year interviews are summarized below.

TABLE VIII
Reasons for No Second Interview

REASON	TRADITIONAL		NONTRADITIONAL		TOTAL	SAMPLE
	N	%	N	%	N	%
Unlocatable	11	52	14	40	25	45
Moved out of California	0	0	3	9	3	5
Locatable but unreachable	9	43	6	17	15	27

Declined						
interview	1	5	8	23	9	16
Broke						
appointment	0	0	4	11	4	7
Total	21	100%	35	100%	56	100%

NOTE: Although overall we were able to reinterview 52 percent of the first-year respondents, the nontraditional group made up a much larger share of that group than did the traditional. We retained approximately 60 percent of the nontraditional respondents in contrast to only 33 percent of the traditional. This differential rate of respondent turnover is fascinating. Although traditionals represented 26 percent of the original sample, they represented 38 percent of the lost cases, thus reducing their second-year representation to 16 percent.

TABLE IX
Employment Status of
Second-Year Reinterviews

WORK ROLE	TRADITIONAL		NONTRADITIONAL		TOTAL SAMPLE	
(SECOND YEAR)	N	%	N	%	N	%
Stable	5	50	39	75	44	72
Changed	1	10	5	10	6	10
Unemployed	4	40	4	8	8	13
Undetermined	0	0	3	7	3	5
Total	10	100%	51	100%	61	100%

NOTE: Seventy-two percent of the women we reinterviewed in 1976–77 were still in their same jobs. Of this group, nontraditional women actually fared a bit better than the traditional; 75 percent of them, compared with 50 percent of the traditional, were in the *same* jobs.

TABLE X
Employment Status in Year II
of Not Interviewed
but Located by Phone

WORK ROLE	NONTRADITIONAL (NOT REINTERVIEWED)	
(SECOND YEAR)	N	%
Stable	16	46

292   APPENDIX

	NONTRADITIONAL	
WORK ROLE	(NOT REINTERVIEWED).	
(SECOND YEAR)	N	%
Changed	10*	29
Unemployed	1	2
Undetermined	8	23
Total	35	100%

* 4 into other nontraditional; 6 into traditional

NOTE: More than half of the women we did not reinterview continued to work in nontraditional fields, and most of those in the same
jobs they had been employed in when we first interviewed them.
The greatest sample loss—and employment turnover as well, was
among less educated, white and minority women in traditional jobs.

TABLE XI
Selected Characteristics
Differentiating Year I and II Respondents

CHARACTERISTICS	YEAR I		YEAR II		% DIFFERENCE
	N	%	N	%	
	(117)		(61)		
Race					
White	81	69	46	77	+8
Black	15	13	5	8	−5
Asian	4	3	2	3	0
Latina	14	12	7	11	−1
No information	3	3	1	1	−2
Age					
Less than 21	10	9	3	5	−4
21–30	75	64	40	66	+2
31–40	17	15	8	13	−2
41+	13	11	10	16	+5
No information	2	1	—	—	−1
Education					
Less than high school	16	14	3	5	−9
High school	23	20	14	23	+3
Some college	52	44	27	44	0

B.A.	17	15	14	23	+8
Advanced	6	5	3	5	0
No information	3	2	—	—	−2

Marital Status

Married currently	39	33	17	28	−5
Ever	29	25	13	21	−4
Never	49	42	23	38	−4
No information	—	—	8	13	+13

Family Income

Less than $3,000	14	12	8	13	+1
Less than $5,000	15	13	7	11	−2
Less than $10,000	19	16	14	23	+7
Less than $15,000	21	18	14	23	+5
$15,000 or more	25	21	12	20	−1
No information	23	20	6	10	−10

TABLE XII
*The Impact of Education and
Race on Sample Turnover*

Year I

Education

	TRAD.	NONTRAD.	TOTAL
Less than high school	9	7	16
High school graduate	9	14	23
Some college	10	42	52
College graduate	1	16	17

Race

Black	3	12	15
White	17	64	81
Latina	9	5	14
Asian	2	2	4

Year II

Education

	TRAD.	NONTRAD.	TOTAL	% RETAINED
Less than high school	1	2	3	19
High school graduate	6	8	14	61

	TRAD.	NONTRAD.	TOTAL	% RETAINED
Some college	3	24	27	64
College graduate	0	14	14	82
Race				
Black	1	4	5	33
White	6	40	46	57
Latina	3	4	7	50
Asian	0	2	2	50

NOTE: The low racial retention rate is more truly a function of lower educational attainment.

THIRD-YEAR TELEPHONE FOLLOW-UPS

The general trends in sample characteristics in year two were borne out by the third-year telephone follow-ups done in the spring of 1978. Once again, a general pattern of employment stability among the nontraditional women emerged, as the data below demonstrate.

TABLE XIII
*Employment Status as
of Third-year Contact*

EMPLOYMENT STATUS	NONTRADITIONALS	
	N	%
Stable	34	40
Changed (into other nontraditional;	7	8
into traditional)	7	8
Unemployed	6	7
No information	32	37
Total	86	100%

Notes

INTRODUCTION

1. See especially Helen Z. Lopata, *Occupation Housewife* (New York: Oxford University Press, 1968); Cynthia Fuchs Epstein, *Woman's Place* (Berkeley: University of California Press, 1970); Athena Theodore, *The Professional Woman* (Cambridge, Mass.: Schenkman Publishing Co., 1971); Alice Rossi, *Academic Women on the Move* (Glencoe: The Free Press, 1974); James W. Grimm, "Women in Female-Dominated Professions," in Ann H. Stromberg and Shirley Harkess, eds., *Women Working* (Palo Alto: Mayfield Publishing Company, 1978); Michele Patterson and Laurie Engelberg, "Women in Male-Dominated Professions," in Stromberg and Harkess, eds., *Women Working;* Margaret Hennig and Ann Jardim, *The Managerial Woman* (Garden City, N.Y.: Anchor Press/Doubleday, 1978).
2. Francine Blau, "The Data on Women Workers, Past, Present and Future," in Stromberg and Harkess, *Women Working,* p. 43.
3. Janice Hedges, et al., "Sex Stereotyping: Its Decline in Skilled Trades," *Monthly Labor Review* (May 1974).
4. U. S. Department of Labor, *1975 Handbook on Women Workers* (1975), pp. 92–93.
5. Robert Dubin, *Handbook of Work Organization and Society* (Chicago: Rand McNally, 1976); Harry Braverman, *Labor and Monopoly Capitol* (Boston: Beacon Press, 1974); Stromberg and Harkess, *Women Working;* Myra M. Ferree, "Working-Class Jobs: Housework and Paid Work as Sources of Satisfaction," *Social Problems* (Apr. 1976), pp. 431–41; Virginia L. Olesen, "Urban Nomads: Women in Temporary Clerical Services," in Stromberg and Harkess, *Women Working.*

6. See especially Blau, "The Data on Women Workers . . . ," in Stromberg and Harkess, *Women Working,* pp. 30–40; Joan Acker, "Issues in the Sociological Study of Women's Work," in Stromberg and Harkess, *Women Working,* pp. 142–47.
7. Linda L. Holmstrom, *The Two Career Family* (Cambridge, Mass.: Schenkman Publishing Company, 1972); Jessie Bernard, *Academic Women* (New York: Meridian Books, 1966); Felice N. Schwartz, et al., *How to Go to Work When Your Husband Is Against It, Your Children Aren't Old Enough and There's Nothing You Can Do Anyhow* (New York: Simon & Schuster, 1972).

CHAPTER I

1. Muriel Lederer, *Blue Collar Jobs for Women* (New York: E. P. Dutton, 1979), p. 80.
2. U. S. Department of Labor, *1975 Handbook on Women Workers,* p. 92.

CHAPTER II

1. Lilian Rubin, *Worlds of Pain* (New York: Basic Books, 1978); Joseph L. Howell, *Hard Living on Clay Street* (Garden City, N.Y.: Anchor Press/Doubleday, 1973); Jacqueline Wiseman, *Stations of the Lost: Treatment of Skid Row Alcoholics* (Englewood Cliffs, N.J.: Prentice-Hall Publishers, 1970).

CHAPTER IV

1. James Davis, *Great Expectations* (Chicago: Aldine Publishing Company, 1964), and *Undergraduate Career Decisions* (Chicago: Aldine Publishing, 1965); Helen Astin, *Women: A Bibliography on Their Education and Careers* (Washington, D.C.: Human Service Press, 1971); Athena Theodore, *The Professional Woman.*
2. James Davis, *Undergraduate Career Decisions.*
3. Everett C. Hughes, *The Sociological Eye* (Chicago: Aldine Publishing, 1971).

NOTES 297

4. Mirra Komarovsky, *Blue Collar Marriage* (New York: Vintage Books, 1962), p. 68.
5. Ibid., pp. 62–69.

CHAPTER V

1. U. S. Department of Labor, *1975 Handbook on Women Workers*, p. 73.

CHAPTER VI

1. Caroline Bird, *Born Female* (New York: Pocket Books, 1969), p. 109.

CHAPTER VII

1. Joann Vanek, "Housewives as Workers," in Stromberg and Harkess, *Women Working.*
2. Alice Rossi, "The Equality of Women: An Immodest Proposal," in *Daedalus* (Spring 1964), pp. 607–752; Philip Slater, *The Pursuit of Loneliness* (Boston: Beacon Press, 1976).
3. Rosabeth Moss Kanter, *Men and Women of the Corporation* (New York: Basic Books, 1978).

CHAPTER VIII

1. F. J. Roegheisberger and William J. Dickson, *Management and the Worker* (Cambridge: Harvard University Press, 1939); Seymour Martin Lipset, Martin A. Trow, and James S. Coleman, *Union Democracy* (Garden City, N.Y.: Anchor Books/ Doubleday, 1956); Samuel A. Stauffer, *The American Soldier: Adjustment During Army Life* (Princeton: Princeton University Press, 1949).
2. Robert Blauner, *Alienation and Freedom* (Chicago: University of Chicago Press, 1964), p. 186.
3. Ibid., p. 356.
4. Kanter, *Men and Women of the Corporation.*
5. Irving Louis Horowitz, *The Use and Abuse of Social Science:*

298 NOTES

Behavioral Research and Policy Making, 2nd ed. (New Brunswick, N.J.: Transaction Books, 1975).

6. Joan Acker, "Women and Social Stratification: A Case of Intellectual Sexism," in *American Journal of Sociology* 78 (1973), p. 936.
7. Ibid., p. 937.
8. Ibid., pp. 938–39.
9. Peter Blau and Otis Dudley Duncan, *The American Occupational Structure* (New York: John Wiley, 1967).
10. Sylvia Navari, *Women in Skilled Labor: Problems and Issues* (Sacramento: Institute for Human Service Management, 1979).
11. Ibid., pp. 54–55.
12. Mary L. Walshok, "Some Innovations in Industrial Apprenticeship at General Motors: Locally Developed Competency-Based Training as a Tool for Affirmative Action," in Felician Foltman, ed., *Apprenticeship Training: Emerging Research and Trends for the 1980's* (Cornell University, Institute for Industrial and Labor Relations, 1981).

Index

About the Author

Mary Lindenstein Walshok is an Associate Adjunct Professor in the Department of Sociology and Dean of the Extension Program at the University of California, San Diego. She has been a consultant in the field of women and work to such organizations as General Motors, Navy Public Works, and the San Diego police and fire departments.